Legal Liability
&
the Nursing Process

by

MARY PHILPOTT B.A.,B.Sc.N.,L.L.B.

W.B. SAUNDERS COMPANY CANADA LIMITED
One Goldthorne Avenue, Toronto, Ontario   M8Z 5T9

W. B. Saunders   1 Goldthorne Avenue
                      Toronto, Ontario M8Z 5T9, Canada

                      1 St Anne's Road
                      Eastbourne, East Sussex BN21 3UN, England

                      West Washington Square
                      Philadelphia, PA 19105, USA

                      Apartado 26370—Cedro 512
                      Mexico 4, D.F., Mexico

                      Rua Evaristo da Veiga 55, 20° andar
                      Rio de Janeiro—RJ, Brazil

                      9 Waltham St. Artarmon, NSW 2064

                      Ichibancho Central Building
                      22-1 Ichibancho, Chiyoda-ku, Tokyo 102, Japan

                      94 Granville Rd., Tsim Sha Tsui East
                      Kowloon, Hong Kong

Legal Liability and The Nursing Process
ISBN 0-7216-1321-7

Last digit is the print number: 9 8 7 6 5 4 3 2

Canadian Cataloguing in Publication Data

Philpott, Mary, 1937-
   Legal liability and the nursing process

Bibliography: p.
Includes index.
ISBN 0-7216-1321-7

1. Nursing — Law and legislation — Canada.
2. Liability (Law) — Canada. I. Title.

KE2714.N8P48 1985   344.71'0414   C84-099485-0

Disclaimer
The material contained within this text is believed to be current and accurate. However, because changes in the law are frequent and laws vary from province to province, the reader should not rely upon this text to solve personal legal problems.

To
Emily Neville and Thelma Pelley
in appreciation

Acknowledgements

Many friends and colleagues in the fields of law and health, and other disciplines, contributed materially to this work. For their support and advice I am sincerely grateful:

—Walter Bailey, who, as President of W.B. Saunders Company Limited, and dear friend, invited and encouraged the writing of this book;

—Katherine Daley, Director of my alma mater, St. Clare's Mercy Hospital School of Nursing, and faculty, and the many students and registered nurses in Newfoundland, Nova Scotia and Ontario who raised the issues and concerns from which this book evolved;

—Mary Barry, Associate Professor, Department of English, Memorial University of Newfoundland, for her editorial contributions and friendship;

—Jean O'Leavey, Chairman of Programs, Health Sciences Division, Conestoga College of Applied Arts and Technology, Kitchener, Ontario, and her able associate, Patricia Legault, for their detailed and helpful analyses of this book at the manuscript stage, and Thelma Pelley, colleague and dear friend for her review and suggestions;

—Friends and colleagues in the Association of Registered Nurses of Newfoundland for the opportunity to be involved in the design of "Report on Nursing Practice Standards: A Critical Path".

—Friends and colleagues on the Board of Trustees of the Newfoundland Hospital Association, the St. John's Hospital Council, and the Waterford Hospital;

—Leo Barry, the firm of Halley, Roberts, Barry, sincere thanks to them, and to Cynthia Tucker who typed the final draft of the manuscript;

—Susanne Duke and Katherine Penney of the Newfoundland Law Society's library, and Mona Pierce, librarian with Newfoundland Justice Department, for their assistance in tracing elusive case material;

—Norma Jean Richards, Legislative Librarian, Province of Newfoundland;

—Trevor Jones and Gerry Mungham of W.B. Saunders Company Canada Limited for their assistance during the publication phase;

—Students, faculty and members of Perth-Huron Regional School of Nursing, and affiliating hospitals in Perth and Huron Counties, Ontario, whom I remember with affection and gratitude;

—Finally, my family: my mother, and brothers, Myles, Larry, and Vincent and their families, and personal friends, Derek Hammond, Harry Watts, Connie and Robert Butt for their tea, and sympathy and support throughout the fourteen months of writing this book.

Mary F. Philpott, B.A., BSc.N., LL.B.,
Health Care Consultants
and Management Limited,
St. John's, Newfoundland
September, 1984

Table of Contents

Page

Preface

"LEGAL LIABILITY AND THE NURS-ING PROCESS" is written for nurses, about their nursing process, from a per-spective of legal and professional account-ability for the quality of their practice. The text is not a comprehensive treatise of the law impacting on nursing practice in a par-ticular province or territory. The focus is, in the main, on a selection of Canadian law, using a case analysis approach. Certain cases and statutes are examined in detail. The purpose of this approach is to focus on standards of practice as they have been pub-lished by the nursing profession, or as they have been defined and applied by Canada's courts and tribunals. The overall goal of the text is to promote the design of reasoned and reasonable nursing policies, and practi-ces, to reduce foreseeable patient risks.

This book is intended as a teaching tool to promote the intelligent use of the nursing process. It is designed for use by students of nursing at the undergraduate and graduate levels, by nurses providing direct patient care, and by nurse educators and nursing managers at the senior level.

"LEGAL LIABILITY AND THE NURS-ING PROCESS" draws mainly from Canadian case and statute law. However, the approach to the concepts of the nursing process, standards of practice, and individ-ual accountability, makes the book suitable as a comparative reference, for nurses prac-tising in the United States, Great Britain and other jurisdictions.

Chapter Outlines

Chapter Three:

Tort of Battery and Consent to the Nursing Process

Chapter Five:

Nursing Records, Evidence, Access and Confidentiality

Chapter Six:

Regulation of Nursing Practice in Canada:

I.   Concept Objectives

II. Introduction

III. Mandatory and Permissive Legislation

IV. Conduct Subject to Discipline:
1. *Professional Misconduct*
2. *Incompetence*
3. *Incapacity*

V.   The Disciplinary Process and the Rules of Natural Justice:
1. *Limits Set by the Rules of Natural Justice*
    (a) Audi Alteram Partem Rule
    (b) Nemo Judex in Causa Sua Rule
2. *Limits Set by Statute and by the Charter of Human Rights and Freedoms*

VI. Disciplinary Proceedings:
1. *Laying the Complaint*
2. *Right to Notice*
3. *Right to Legal Counsel*

VII. Procedure at a Disciplinary Hearing:
1. *Preliminary Matters*
2. *Presentation of Evidence*
3. *Arriving at a Decision*
4. *Invoking a Penalty*

VIII. Remedies:
1. *Appeals*
2. *Application for Prerogative Writs, and, or Damages:*
    (a) Writ of Prohibition
    (b) Writ of Certiorari
    (c) Writ of Mandamus
    (d) Declaratory Judgment
    (e) Injunction
    (f) Damages

IX. Ethical Standards: The Professional Code of Nursing Ethics:

X.   Endnotes

Table of Cases

Chapter One:

Introduction: Concepts of Law and Accountability for Nursing Practice:

I. Concept Objectives:

The intent in this chapter is to:
— define such concepts as law, rights, standards, responsibilities and accountabilities
— identify the sources and nature of laws affecting nursing practice in Canada and the structures empowered to create law
— examine the Charter of Human Rights and Freedoms in limiting the exercise of power
— define the nursing process and describe the legal dimensions of such functions as independent, dependent, interdependent and advocacy functions involved in nursing practice
— promote the use of the nursing process as a nursing tool to prevent harm to patients; and to protect health care workers and agencies from liability for patient injury.

II. Introduction:

In a distant and simpler past, health care was delivered, in the main, by two categories of workers—physicians, who had a curing role, and nurses, who had a caring role under the direction of physicians. In this hierarchical structure, nursing was commonly perceived as being totally dependent on the authority of physicians for the legitimacy of its nursing roles and for the delegation of its functions. Not so, today. Contemporary health care delivery requires a wide range of health care professions, each with unique and sometimes independent roles and functions. When functioning at their best, these groups do not follow a hierarchical, dependent pattern with a doctor at the top of a pyramidal structure, but instead, operate as interdependent groups of professional peers, all working to a common end—the delivery of safe, effective and humane health care. In today's structure, the place of the nurse demands a strong base of technical knowledge and skill, and also a firm base of professional, ethical and legal values. In this far more complex health care environment, there also exists a clear need for efficient, effective systems of communication among the various disciplines involved, as well as

the skill and the will to communicate positively and accurately. The very nature and numbers of complex services, equipment, and professional groupings create potential for conflict, and it is in light of this reality that members of the various health care professions need well honed skills in conflict prevention and resolution.

There is a historic difference in the perspective of health care workers and the orientation of law. The former are oriented to meet perceived health needs while the latter is directed to the protection of those interests which qualify as legal rights. In the complex sociological and technological environment of contemporary hospitals, patients' interests may not always be in tandem with the policies and practices of the institution, or with the particular interest of the employer, the union, a valued professional peer, or with those of the nurse herself. Situations will arise which call for the reconciliation of differing rights, needs, and duties, and that also demand acceptance of consequences for the particular choices made.

Legal remedies or sanctions imposed after the fact of injury or insult are not real solutions. The toll is often needless hardship for the patient, and loss of trust in the care providers and health care institutions concerned. The situation will not be redeemed in any meaningful way through: the payment of damages, imposing of sanctions following criminal convictions, or suspension of the institution's licence to operate or accreditation certificate, or through removal of the health care worker's certificate or licence to practice. Real solutions lie, as does effective health care management generally, in the prevention of unsafe, illegal or unethical practice. When the values and skills necessary for this prevention are acquired as a result of, and not in spite of, an educational philosophy and curriculum, the individual practitioner will likely be better skilled in conflict resolution.

It is with the foregoing in mind that this text examines the concept of law, certain legal rights and duties and the concept of accountability in law for one's nursing practice. The text is restricted to the examination of legal aspects of nursing practice but recognizes that many of the legal principles governing nursing practice are also applicable to the scope and limit of practice of many other health disciplines. (The reader recognizes, of course, that there is no precisely defined body of knowledge that is "nursing law". Rather, there are many rules and principles of statutory and case law origin which suggest the required standard as well as the scope and limit of professional practice.) In this text that which the registered nurse offers the patient (a nursing process) is examined from the perspective of the torts of negligence and battery, using a case approach. Also examined are the structures, functions, powers, and duties of tribunals regulating nursing practice and enforcing standards. A review of nursing records as evidence of compliance and non-compliance with required legal standards is also included.

There are, however, many areas of law, which are not, for a number of reasons, addressed in this text. These include such areas as the registered nurse as an independent contractor, labour law and the professional health care worker, criminal law and nursing practice, legal aspects of caring for the patient with mental illness, and the legal dimensions of caring for the dying patient. Hopefully this text will serve as a point of departure for a study of these important concerns at a later time.

III. History and Source of Canada's Laws:

From its earliest history as a federation, Canada has had two distinct systems of law; one, originating from early Roman times, has become the civil law system in effect in Quebec. The other system, which is in place in the remainder of Canada, is the common law system from early Britain.

1. The Civil Law System:

The civil law system of Quebec is the older of the two systems, having its origins in the Twelve Tables of Rome of 450 B.C. These Tables were codified by the Corpus Juris Civilis of Justinian and were adopted by France in 1804 as the Napoleonic Code.

By 1859 this (Napoleonic) Code became the legal system for Quebec. When Great Britain conquered Quebec, the province was permitted to retain the system for resolution of such private law disputes as contractual disputes, and Quebec's equivalent to the common law tort. This system of law differs significantly from the common law system. Its courts apply the Code rather than judge made law to disputes. The Code, amended from time to time, is the creation of Quebec's National Assembly.

2. The Common Law System:

The common law system evolved from the so called "common laws" of early Britain. It was a tradition which began with the invasion of Saxon Britain by William of Normandy and establishment of Norman rule with the Battle of Hastings in 1066. By 1154 King Henry II, a descendant of William, had brought the court system under his royal control. These royal courts actually had the king sit in judgment of the particular dispute and impose the appropriate penalty for breach of the king's peace, or provide a remedy for private disputes. This royal court system was considered to be more fair and impartial than its predecessor, the feudal court system in which feudal lords judged disputes involving the peasants who occupied the lands of the particular feudal lord. This impartial royal court system was widely available by the end of the reign of Henry II (1188) when a uniform system of laws was established. Jury trials were now used, in which the judge would instruct on the law and twelve people from the community would determine the verdict after examination of the particular facts.

In the thirteenth century, the control of the king (the Crown) was separated from the judicial system when King John of Gaunt was forced, by the English barons, to sign the Magna Carta. This constitutional enactment was signed by the King at Runnymede. It stipulated that royal subjects could no longer be deprived of their rights to life, liberty and property except by judgments in accord with the law of the land. This historic document regulated the administration of justice and effectively created a legal authority higher than the King and to which authority the King could be made accountable. The charter effectively entrenched the principle that no man is above the law.

3. Sources of Legal Authority:

Stare decisis
Legislative authority

(a) Stare decisis:

From the twelfth century written reports of various disputes and the judgments of the court were permanently recorded in law reports so that reference could be made to them by parties in subsequent and similar disputes. The custom evolved that the earlier cases would serve as precedents for the deciding of later cases having similar facts and legal issues. This custom of deciding like cases alike (*stare decisis*) was intended to ensure a measure of predictability in the legal outcome. Thus, a body of common law principles emerged forming the so-called Common Law. Each report would commonly contain two categories of material: the *ratio decidendi*₁ was the portion giving the reasons or the point in each case which determined the particular judgment, while the *obiter dicti* was the name given to other statements which were not considered the point determining the particular judgment, but which could well be cited and applied in later cases. This common law, shaped by the decisions of judges, and expressed in the ratio of the case, would remain the law on a particular point until reversed by a higher court, and would be binding on all inferior courts within the jurisdiction.

In reality, however, there are never two perfectly identical fact situations before the court such that the *ratio* from the first case must necessarily apply to the second dispute. The courts often "distinguish" the current case and refuse to apply the particular precedent if the case at bar is sufficiently different. It is also possible that a particular court decision will be "overruled" in a later decision rendered by the same court or by a superior court in the same system. This occurs when the later judgment upon the same question of law is directly opposite to

that which was rendered previously, thereby depriving the earlier opinion of all authority as a precedent.

In Canada there is a hierarchy of courts including the trial court or court of first instance, the appeal court of the particular province and the Supreme Court of Canada. The civil or criminal dispute is initially heard before the court of first instance. Oral and documentary evidence is presented on behalf of each of the parties, arguments are made by counsel for each of the parties and a judgment is rendered by the court. The court's decision is the law unless and until it is successfully appealed to the next level of court. Such appeals must be taken within a particular time limit. The appeal court reviews the trial transcript and hears legal argument from counsel. The appeal court will either agree with the judgment of the trial court and dismiss the appeal, or overturn or vary the initial decision. The judgment of the appeal court is binding on the parties to the dispute. The decision is also good authority for subsequent disputes heard by the lower courts in the same jurisdiction. The decision is *not* binding, however, on lower courts, in other provinces but may well be of persuasive value. Access to the Supreme Court of Canada for further appeal of the judgment may, depending on the significance of the legal issues, be granted. Prior to 1976 there was an automatic right of appeal to the Supreme Court of Canada for any suit involving ten thousand dollars or more. Following this date, Parliament limited access to Canada's highest court to those cases of national or public importance, and to cases in which there had been conflicting points of law created by two or more provincial appeal courts. The Supreme Court of Canada consists of nine judges with five judges constituting a quorum of the Court.

(b) Legislative Authority:

The Canadian Parliament and the provincial legislatures are a second source of Canadian law. These legislative bodies are empowered to create, amend and repeal laws which take the form of statutes, and in some instances, regulations pursuant to the particular statute. For example, the federal

Parliament exercised its power to create legislation known as the Narcotic Control Act of Canada. From time to time Parliament has amended this act and repealed certain sections of it. The statute has regulations which are intended to direct persons dispensing and administering drugs controlled by this Act. Health care workers are required to comply with the regulations and the Act so as not to be "in possession of" drugs contrary to the criminal law. Similarly, provincial legislatures have created and amended and repealed a number of statutes which impact on the services offered by such health care agencies as hospitals. Each province, for example, has a form of public hospitals act. Such a statute stipulates certain duties and delegates certain powers to the hospital authority which it would not otherwise have.

4. Division of Power:

The federal Parliament and provincial legislatures do not, however, have unlimited power to create law. The source of each of their authority is the British North America Act. This nineteenth century imperial statute (statute of British Parliament) empowered its colony, Canada, to govern itself within the limits set out in the statute. Until that time, 1867, Canada did not have the necessary power to create law by statute. The British North America Act created the federation that is Canada today. The act united Upper and Lower Canada (Ontario and Quebec), Nova Scotia and New Brunswick into a federal union. The statute also provided that other provinces could be admitted in the future. Subsequently Manitoba joined Canada in 1870, British Columbia in 1871, Prince Edward Island in 1873, Saskatchewan and Alberta in 1905 and Newfoundland was admitted to the federation in 1949.

The British North America Act, however, did not give Canada independence from Britain. Under it Canada remained subordinate to the British Parliament with the latter retaining the power to enact laws governing Canada and to invalidate laws made in Canada and the provinces. It wasn't until 1931 that the British Parliament enacted the Statute of Westminister. It provided that Canada could create laws independent of Britain as long as such laws were not in conflict with the powers allocated to the federal Parliament and provincial legislatures pursuant to the British North America Act. Canada did not receive final legal independence until 1982 with the proclamation of the Constitution Act[2] by her Majesty, Queen Elizabeth II. Canada now has the authority to amend the British North America Act, should it so desire, in accordance with an amending formula set out in the Constitution.

Under the British North America Act[3], Canada's federal Parliament was given the power to make laws for the peace, order and good government of Canada in matters not expressly assigned to the provinces under the Act. Specifically, there were twenty-nine grants of power given to the federal Parliament including power to raise money by taxation, to direct Canada's postal service and to legislate with respect to marriage, divorce and criminal law. The provinces were assigned sixteen grants of power including power to make laws relating to the establishment and management of public hospitals, education, property and civil rights in the province and matters of local or private nature.

Although the provinces were given exclusive jurisdiction over health services under the British North America Act, federal Parliament has impacted on the field through the latter's fiscal powers. For example, in 1957 federal Parliament enacted the Hospital Insurance and Diagnostic Services Act, and in 1966, the Medical Care Act. These statutes set out the conditions under which the provinces would be eligible for federal grants, and later, for block funding of health care costs incurred by the provinces. The philosophy of the federal legislation was to "insure" the public against personal economic loss due to illness. In the interim, some of the provinces, pursuant to their power to direct health services, implemented user fees, and some physicians initiated extra billing in addition to physician fees incurred by patients and payable through the medicare insurance system.

The balance of the fee set by the medical profession in the particular province, was charged directly to the patient concerned.

On April 17, 1984 the federal Parliament of Canada restructured the funding of the country's health care system by means of the controversial Bill C-3, 1983-84, entitled *The Canada Health Act*. On that date the bill received royal assent and was deemed in force from April 1, 1984.

This federal legislation reaffirmed and strengthened the federal government's power to control cash contributions to the provinces for services being provided under provincial health care insurance plans. One of the purposes of the Act is to promote access to provincial health services without direct, out of pocket costs to any individual using the system. The legislation requires that certain conditions be met by each province in order for it to receive full payment of its health costs from the federal government. The most controversial of the conditions is the elimination of user charges by hospitals, and extra-billing by physicians.

The stated intent of the new federal legislation is "to protect, promote and restore the physical and mental wellbeing of Canadians." In furtherance of this intent the new legislation does not limit funding to hospital based service, but now insures "extended health service." The latter is defined in the legislation to include nursing home intermediate care, adult residential care, home care and ambulatory care. The expansion of federal funding is intended to promote more appropriate access to preventive and rehabilitative services, in balance with curative aspects.

This new legislation is also significant in that it permits insurance of services offered by "health care practitioners." The latter category is defined as "persons lawfully entitled under the law of the province to provide health service." Consequently provincial governments are now free to authorize insurance of services by a variety of health care professionals, in addition to the services of physicians. This legislative innovation will encourage provincial governments to examine the present roles of various health care professionals in relation to

economical community and home based service, as an adjunct and alternative to the more costly accute hospital, and physician directed services.

Nurses are, by far, the largest group of health care professionals in this country, constituting approximately two-thirds of the total number of such workers. (In 1982 there were 138,000 nurses registered in Canada). In light of the increasing need to redistribute the limited health care funding in the most cost effective manner, it is probable that governments will endorse, in time, the movement of nursing into a larger and more independent health care role in the community. Nursing role expansion, and independent nursing practice within the community, will require increased nursing competencies, clear statements of standards, and the legislated means and will to monitor and enforce reasonable and safe standards of care.

There are however limits to what federal Parliament and provincial legislatures may legislate pursuant to the British North America Act. These limits have from time to time been challenged by resort to the courts. Since Canada is a federal state, its courts may, on application, interpret federal and provincial powers. If either legislative group exceeds its powers in the creation of a particular statute, the courts will declare the act or the offending section of the act to be *ultra vires,* that is, beyond the scope of the body's authority and therefore of no legal validity.

5. *Legislative Structures:*

Within the federal and provincial levels of the federation, the exercise of power is also checked and balanced by the very nature of the government structure. Federally and provincially there are three distinct bodies: judicial, executive, and legislative, each with its unique role and function.

The judicial body, the courts, is independent of the other two branches of government. Judges are appointed for a term of office extending to retirement. Their tenure of office is not limited or reviewable, except for cause due to serious conduct in conflict with the judicial position. Application to the courts may be made to review the exercise of power by the other two branches of government.

The executive body, at the federal level, includes the Prime Minister and his cabinet, and at the provincial level, includes the Premier of the province and his cabinet. This executive committee of government constitutes the Lieutenant-Governor in Council, and has power to create law in the form of *orders in council*. These are orders given on the advice of cabinet, without the specific consent of Parliament or the legislature. The purpose of such orders is to authorize the carrying out of certain administrative acts of a government department or body.

The legislative body, (federal Parliament and provincial legislatures) has power to create statutes. Federal Parliament is made up of two houses and her Majesty the Queen acting through her Canadian representative the Governor General of Canada. The two houses consist of the Upper House which is the Senate composed of senators appointed by the Prime Minister of Canada, and the Lower House which is the House of Commons, made up of elected members. The party with the majority of votes in a federal election is called upon by the Governor General to form the government. The party with the next largest number of votes forms the official opposition. Provincial legislatures, in contrast, consist of one house: the legislature. The party obtaining the largest number of votes in a provincial election, is called on by the Lieutenant-Governor of the province (The Queen's representative), to form the government, and the party with the next largest number of votes forms the official opposition.

6. The Legislative Process:

It is within the Parliament or the legislature that statutes are brought into law in accordance with a protocol which varies somewhat depending on whether the proposed bill is a private one governing rights of particular individuals or groups, or is a proposed public act governing the public interests of society.

Initially the proposed act is researched and drafted in the form of a bill. This preliminary document contains a formal title setting out the name of the bill and a short title by which it is cited in the statute books. It contains a series of clauses to carry the intent of the bill into effect. The bill is subject to three readings, and usually each reading occurs on separate days of Parliament. The first reading involves the introduction of the bill in the House of Commons (or the legislature as the case may be). The bill may be introduced by a private member or by a member of cabinet and is limited to setting out the general purpose of the bill. A date is then set for the second reading at which stage the principles and objectives of the bill are debated by the members of the house. Suggested modifications may be successfully passed and the objectives are then confirmed, and an order is made to send the bill to committee. This third stage provides for the bill to be examined by either a select committee struck to study the particular bill, or by a standing committee which exists to study all and any bills assigned to it, or a committee of the whole house. At the committee stage, the bill is examined in detail and a report is made back to the house where further amendments if any, are made. At the report stage, the bill goes forward for third reading and voting. If passed it is proclaimed into law on a definite future date, or will be left to be proclaimed, or will become law on the date it receives royal assent.

IV. New Limits on Power: The Constitution Act (1982):

" The Constitution of Canada is the supreme law of Canada, and any law that is inconsistent with the provisions of the Constitution, is, to the extent of the inconsistency, of no force or effect. "[4]

In November 1981, the federal and provincial governments, with the exception of Quebec, reached agreement on a formula for repatriating (returning) the Constitution to Canada. In December of that year, a resolution was adopted by the House of Commons, and approved by the Senate, requesting the Queen to bring before

British Parliament, the necessary bill for repatriation. British Parliament subsequently enacted a statute of the United Kingdom. It was entitled *the Canada Act (1982)*, U.K., C-11. Schedule B of this statute contained *the Constitution Act (1982)*. The latter was proclaimed in force, by Queen Elizabeth II, in a historic ceremony, in Ottawa, on April 17, 1982.

Entrenched in the Constitution is a *Canadian Charter of Human Rights and Freedoms*. This Charter guarantees such protections as: *Fundamental Freedoms, Democratic Rights, Mobility Rights,* and *Equality Rights*. These rights and freedoms are not absolute, but section 1 of the Constitution guarantees that they are "subject only to those reasonable limits prescribed by law as can be demonstrably justified in a free and democratic society."

—**Fundamental Freedoms:**
Include protections of freedom of conscience and religion, of thought, belief, opinion and expression, including freedom of the press and other media of communication, freedom of peaceful assembly, and freedom of association.

—**Democratic Rights:**
Protect the right to vote.

—**Mobility Rights:**
Protect the right to move to and take up residence in any province, and to pursue the gaining of a livelihood in any province.

—**Legal Rights:**
Include the right to life, liberty and security of a person, and the right not to be deprived thereof except in accordance with the principles of fundamental justice. (sec. 7). This section has already been raised in challenges to ministerial decisions, and challenges to the Criminal Code of Canada with respect to abortions. It is likely that the future will also bring challenges with respect to use of life support systems, euthanasia, sterilization, and surrogate pregnancies.
—The right to be secure against unreasonable search and seizure is protected in section 8. Challenges to the admissibility of evidence of contents of body fluids, seized by police, have been heard by the courts

pursuant to this section. Cases involving hospital personnel are referred to later in this chapter.
—Section 10 of the Charter provides that everyone has the right on arrest or detention, to be informed promptly of the reasons therefor; to retain and instruct counsel without delay and to be informed of that right; and to have the validity of detention determined by way of habeas corpus, and to be released if the detention is not lawful. Historically, habeas corpus has been a traditional right granted to all subjects of the Sovereign. The Charter enshrines the right. A writ of habeas corpus will issue when it is shown that there is reason to believe the applicant is unlawfully held in custody. It allows the court to inquire into the cause of his imprisonment, and if appropriate, to order the applicant's release. The availability of such a writ to patients committed involuntarily to psychiatric hospitals pursuant to section 10 of the Mental Health Act R.S.P.E.I. 1974, c.M-9, is discussed in *Reference Re. Procedures And The Mental Health Act*[5], later in this chapter.
—Section 11 of the Charter protects the right to a trial within a reasonable time, the right not to be compelled to be a witness against oneself, and to be presumed innocent until proven guilty. The section also protects the right to a fair and public hearing by an independent and partial tribunal.
—Section 12 contains the right not to be subjected to any "cruel and unusual punishment, or treatment". This section has already been used to challenge the legality of certain medical therapies.

—**Equality Rights:**
This section of the Charter is to be proclaimed in 1985. The purpose of the delay is to allow time for the provinces and the federal Parliament to amend any legislation which is presently in apparent conflict with the Charter. This section of the Charter provides that every individual is to be equal before and under the law, and is to have the right to equal protection and equal benefit of the law without discrimination. The section is intended to protect individuals against discrimination based on race,

national or ethnic origin, colour, religion, sex, age, mental or physical disability. In the previously mentioned *Reference Re. Procedures and the Mental Health Act*, the court made brief reference to whether involuntary commitment under mental health legislation constituted a denial of equality on the basis of mental disability. The court did not give a definite answer but choose to resolve the question by reconciling the Mental Health Act with section 1 of the Charter.

Persons whose rights or freedoms, as defined in the Charter, are allegedly breached, may apply to a court of competent jurisdiction for any remedy the court considers appropriate and just in the circumstances. The applicant must establish, through evidence and argument, that the facts of which he complains constitute a breach of the Charter. The opposing party then has the burden of demonstrating that the right was not denied but merely limited, and that the limit imposed was reasonable within the meaning of section 1 of the Charter, i.e. that it is within "... those reasonable limits prescribed by law as can be demonstrably justified in a free and democratic society".

In 1984, the Lieutenant Governor in Council brought the above mentioned reference before the Prince Edward Island Supreme Court. In a reference, the court gives its opinion on specific written questions presented to it. The opinions would then be followed if the same questions arise in subsequent contested cases.

The *Reference Re. Procedures and the Mental Health Act*, arose because of an earlier court decision on a habeas corpus application by a patient who had been committed involuntarily to a psychiatric hospital. The committal was pursuant to section 10 of the *Mental Health Act, R.S.P.E.I. 1974, c M-3*. Interested groups and persons, represented by counsel at the reference, included the provincial medical society, involuntary patients at psychiatric facilities, the hospital to which the patient had been committed, and the psychiatrist who had completed the certificate required for committal under Section 10 of the Act. Certain questions concerned the legality of the section in terms of the

Charter. The court rendered the opinion that the restrictions imposed on persons suffering from mental disorder, by section 10 of the Act, were reasonable limits within the meaning of section 1 of the Charter. The court also rendered the opinion that habeas corpus, as guaranteed by section 10 of the Charter, was available to patients committed under section 10 of the Mental Health Act. Such a hearing, however, is restricted to examination of the psychiatrist's certificate. If the certificate complies with the requirements of the Act, the judge may not go behind it.

Section 32 applies the Charter to Parliament, legislatures and governments. The section alters the doctrine of Parliamentary supremacy. It gives the courts a mandate to examine government action, and the social basis of otherwise valid legislation. The courts now have the constitutional power to strike down any federal or provincial statutory sections conflicting with Canada's new supreme law. For example, on July 15, 1983, the Canadian Government decided to permit the Government of the United States to test air-launched cruise missiles in Canada. In *Operation Dismantle Inc. et al v. the Queen°*, a coalition of peace groups challenged this decision. They claimed that the testing was a violation of their right to life, liberty and security of person within the meaning of section 7 of the Charter. Counsel for the Government of Canada applied to strike out the plaintiff's statement of claim on the ground that it disclosed no reasonable cause of action. The Government's application failed at first instance, but succeeded on appeal to the Federal Court of Appeal. Leave to appeal to the Supreme Court of Canada was granted on December 20, 1983. When the Court rules on this case it will likely clarify the roles of government and court in such social policy matters. (The lower court stated that the Charter applies to Parliament and as such erodes its supremacy to the extent that the political body cannot breach the rights and freedoms guaranteed by the Charter). The Supreme Court of Canada has the interesting task of determining to what extent, if any, will the court be permitted to review the decisions which politicians were elected to make.

Since the proclamation of the Constitution in 1982 several thousand challenges have been taken before the courts pursuant to the Charter. A small number of these applications involved issues of concern to persons working in, or receiving care in hospitals. In *Re. Davis*[7] for example, the Alberta Court heard a challenge based on the Charter right to religious freedom, as to whether the *Child Welfare Act*, in authorizing the welfare authority to take custody of "neglected children" and consent to the administration of blood transfusions to the child of Jehovah's Witness parents, was in conflict with the Charter. The parents applied to strike down the Act because of its alleged conflict with the entrenched freedom of religion. However, the court held that the particular section of the Act did not relate to religion, but to child welfare and public health. The court stated that the state's right to safeguard the health and welfare of children prevailed over parental rights to practice religion.

The applicant in *Borowski v. the Attorney General of Canada and the Minister of Finance (1984)*[8], sought a declaration that section 251 of the Criminal Code of Canada breached section 7 of the Charter (the right to life, liberty, and security of person, and the right not to be deprived thereof, except in accordance with the principles of fundamental justice). The applicant alleged that section 251, which authorized abortion committees in hospitals to decide on therapeutic abortions, denied the right to life, and the right of the unborn not to be deprived of life, except in accordance with principles of fundamental justice, as guaranteed by section 7. The Saskatchewan Court of Queen's Bench held that such rights were not violated by the process, because "everyone" referred to in the Charter, did not include a "foetus". The applicant was also unsuccessful in his argument that the Criminal Code breached the newborn's right not to be subjected to cruel and unusual treatment, within the meaning of section 12 of the Charter.

Some court challenges pursuant to section 8 of the Charter, (right to be secure against unreasonable search and seizure), have involved issues of concern to health care institutions. A number of applications have been made challenging the admissibility of evidence obtained from persons while they were in hospital for treatment. The applicants alleged that the evidence was obtained without consent, and for evidentiary rather than medical use, and without authority to obtain the evidence concerned. Such arguments were made in *R v. Carter*[9], *R v. L.A.R.*, *R v. Decoste* and *R v. Sante*.[10] In *R v. Carter (1982)*, the accused had been taken to hospital following a motor vehicle accident. Hospital personnel removed a sample of blood from the accused for medical purposes. The sample was later seized by police, pursuant to a search warrant, and for evidentiary purposes. The hospital personnel were subpoenaed to give evidence, concerning the blood test, at the criminal trial of the accused. Counsel for the accused objected to the admission into evidence, of the blood sample, (the report of its alcohol content.) Counsel argued that the evidence had been obtained as a result of an unreasonable search and seizure within the meaning of section 8 of the Charter. It thereby constituted a denial of the accused's right to fundamental justice pursuant to section 7 of the Charter. The trial judge accepted the argument and refused to admit the report of the blood test. The court stated that the blood sample had been taken for medical purposes and subsequent seizure, under warrant, violated the accused's rights. The Crown appealed successfully. The appeal court held that seizure of the blood sample, which had been drawn for medical purposes, but seized by the police pursuant to a warrant, did not violate the Charter. The report of the blood sample was therefore admissible as evidence.

In *R v. L.A.R.* the courts resolved the conflict in favour of the Crown; In *R v. Decoste*, the accused succeeded. Both cases turned on the application of section 24(2) of the Charter. In *R v. L.A.R.*, the Manitoba Court of Queen's Bench ordered a new trial following acquittal of the accused by the trial judge.

The accused juvenile had been charged with impaired driving. The trial judge had refused to admit evidence obtained from the accused while he was a patient in a hospital immediately following an accident. A police officer had instructed a nurse to remove a urine sample from a urinary drainage bag. The sample was seized, without a warrant, for analysis of its alcohol content. The accused claimed that he had given consent to provision of the sample to assist in his medical treatment; that the consent did not extend to the police to remove samples for evidentiary reasons; and that therefore the seizure constituted theft. At trial, the court held the seizure to be unreasonable because it was made without a warrant. On appeal, the court concluded the seizure was not an unreasonable one, despite the absence of a consent or warrant. It also stated that if the seizure was unreasonable it did not qualify for exclusion on the basis of section 24(2) of the Charter. In *R v. Decoste* (1983), counsel for the accused was successful in his application to the Nova Scotia Supreme Court for exclusion of evidence of blood alcohol content, (the report of the sample.) Application was made pursuant to sections 8 and 24 of the Charter. The facts of this case are distinguishable from those in *R v. Carter*. In *R v. Decoste*, the accused was assaulted in order to obtain evidence. He had been taken to hospital shortly after being involved in a motor vehicle accident. The police officer instructed the attending physician to remove a blood sample from the unconscious patient. Expressed consent was absent. The evidence was subsequently seized with a warrant. The court held that assaulting of the accused in the particular circumstances, caused the seizure to be an unreasonable one; that to admit the evidence obtained from the unreasonable search and seizure would bring the administration of justice into disrepute; and that therefore section 24(2) was triggered and the court refused to admit the report into evidence. The trial judge said:

" I believe that members of the public consider a hospital as a place where the sick and injured are treated and not a place where

a doctor would take blood from an unconscious or semiconscious person for the sole purpose of satisfying the unlawful demand or request of a police officer. "

" Had there been some legislative provision permitting a taking of the blood sample then the taking would be lawful and not an infringement of a person's rights or freedoms. Had the sample been taken for a medical procedure in relation to the patient's treatment or well-being or where her consent would be implied, then probably other principles would apply. "

Similarly, a Saskatchewan provincial court, in *R v. Santa (1983)*, granted the accused's application to exclude the report of a blood alcohol sample. The sample had been removed by a physician, from the accused patient when he was in shock, in hospital. The vials of blood were subsequently seized by the police.

Evidence obtained by a process that infringes Charter rights will not automatically result in exclusion of the tainted evidence at trial. Section 24(2) provides for mandatory exclusion of evidence where there has been an infringement, *and* where the admission of evidence obtained by that infringement would bring the administration of justice into disrepute. The court looks at the circumstances of the particular case, and determines, on balance, whether the evidence so obtained, would, if admitted against the accused, bring the justice system into disrepute. The court, in *R v. Therens* (1983)[11] excluded a breath analysis certificate from the evidence, because the accused had not been told of his right to counsel. The Saskatchewan Court of Appeal affirmed the trial court decision. The Crown has appealed the ruling to the Supreme Court of Canada. Such factors as failure to inform a person, on arrest or detention, of the right to legal counsel, and to be informed promptly of the reasons for the arrest may very well trigger 24(2) in favour of the accused. The presence or absence of a warrant, and the presence of a legally effective consent to the touching of the accused in the collection of evidence, may activate section 24 of the Charter.

The extent to which the Charter will protect entrenched rights and freedoms remains uncertain. This uncertainty will continue until a sufficient body of law, on the many sections of the Charter, has been accumulated, and basic Charter principles have been confirmed by the Supreme Court of Canada. It will likely take a decade of court challenges before the impact, if any, is felt. Much will depend on how the courts choose to interpret the particular sections of the Charter. If the courts take a liberal rather than a narrow, legalistic approach, it will bring an interesting and new era for Canadians.

V. Concept of Accountability and Nursing Practice:

1. Law (Defined):

The study of law engages one in a process of analyzing rights of various parties in relation to each other and to the community, and identifying the legal standards of conduct required for orderly community living.

"Law" refers to rules which govern one's conduct in private and public relationships. Rules which qualify as "law" are *expressed* (usually in writing) by a body which has authority to express the rule. To qualify as "law" the rule must have a means of being consistently enforced, and by an authority empowered to do so. It involves the imposition of sanctions if a public law is breached, and imposing a remedy for breach of private law (such as contract or tort law). Law enforcement requires courts and court like tribunals to resolve disputes arising from breach of the law, (an accounting system). The nature of the tribunal or authority differs depending on whether the dispute is one involving the criminal law, an employer-employee dispute, discipline by one's professional body, or a dispute involving a patient pursuant to a contractual or a tort duty.

All persons living in the community are limited by law in what they can do, and must meet certain legal standards in the performance of particular acts. For exam-ple, a member of the community does not have the right to have the care and control of an automobile on a highway without first qualifying for and obtaining the necessary driver's licence. Once he has the legal right to drive a car, he has a duty to operate the vehicle within the limits set down by highway traffic legislation, and a duty not to demonstrate wanton disregard for human safety within the meaning of the Criminal Code of Canada. There is also a separate and private duty of care owed to other drivers and pedestrians recognized in the tort of negligence.

Persons working within or receiving care within the hospital community are limited by certain laws in what they can do, and a certain standard of care is required of them in the performance of their activities and functions. There are definite duties owed by the corporate authority (represented by the board of trustees), independent contractors granted admitting privileges to the hospital, and by employees to patients to whom health services are offered. For example, a person is not permitted to carry out activities that constitute the practice of medicine unless he is credentialled in accordance with the appropriate provincial legislation. A licensed physician has a duty not to breach the Criminal Code of Canada in the process of medical practice, and has a separate duty of care to his patient which may be recognized in contract or in such torts as negligence or battery. The physician also has the obligation to comply with the standards of competency and professional conduct expressed in the medical act of the particular province in which he practises.

The registered nurse is frequently an employee of the hospital corporation, operating under a contract of employment (or under a collective agreement, if she is a member of a nursing union certified to represent the nursing group in the particular hospital). There are certain enforceable legal rights and duties operating in an employment contract, or alternatively in the collective agreement and its superimposed labour legislation. The nurse may be employed in the position of director of nursing, nursing supervisor, head nurse or unit manager, nursing teacher or staff nurse. Each of these positions has unique responsibilities requiring varying levels of technical, teaching, management and inter-personal skills. The particular job description may be expressed in writing setting out the responsibilities, the job requirements and the lines of authority. To practice nursing at the registered nurse level, a current certificate or licence is required and is available to qualified persons pursuant to the nursing act of the particular province. The nursing statute prohibits incompetence and unprofessional behavior on the part of its members. Apart from employment responsibilities and professional responsibilities, the registered nurse owes a personal duty of care to the patients to whom she is assigned. This duty is recognized in tort law. The registered nurse also has a duty not to breach the Criminal Code of Canada in the process of nursing practice. In addition to the foregoing relationships there are rights and duties which exist between the nurse and the union in which she holds membership.

2. Contractual Accountability:

Re. Mount Sinai Hospital and the Ontario Nurses Union[12] (1978) contrasts employer-employee rights and responsibilities and the responsibilities which arise pursuant to membership in the nursing profession. The case also points up the relationship between *responsibilities* and *accountability*. The events in this case occurred on February 26, 1976. A medical resident notified the nursing staff in the hospital's intensive care unit that he wished to admit a patient suffering from a coronary problem, to the unit. The nurses refused to admit and provide nursing care for the patient. Following their refusal members of the medical staff provided the care which the nursing staff would ordinarily provide. The employer disciplined the nurses by suspending them for three extended tours of duty. The disciplined nurses, exercising their rights under the collective agreement, grieved the employer's action alleging that such was unfair discipline. The employer took the position that the disciplinary action was fair because the nurses' wilful refusal to

provide nursing care constituted insubordination. Therefore if wilful refusal occurred, such constituted a challenge to the employer's authority to order and direct the work place, a power which he had retained under the collective agreement. If wilful refusal was proven to have existed the employer was entitled to discipline. The grievance was heard by an arbitration board with the union and the employer represented by counsel. Two defences were submitted to the allegation of insubordination. Neither of the defences succeeded.

The nurses' first line of defence was that it was never communicated clearly to them that they were expected to provide nursing care to the particular patient, and they were under a sincere, though mistaken belief that the physician had willingly agreed to provide the necessary care. The arbitration board rejected the defence stating that in the labour relations context, the medical staff have no supervisory authority over nurses. Rather the employment relationship which carries such authority is between the hospital as the employer and the nurses. The board determined that nursing office, in the person of the nursing supervisor directs nurses in what they do; that a direction had been given by the nursing supervisor, as the employer representative, which direction had not been carried out. (Insubordination could only arise where nurses refused to respond to a direction given by the employer representative.)

The nurses second line of defence was that of *justification* to refuse the direction because the condition of the patients already in the unit were such that to admit another patient could place their care in jeopardy. Counsel for the nurses argued that potential liability to civil suits, and to disciplinary action by the College of Nurses of Ontario (the nursing registering body), made it unfair to discipline the nurses in the circumstances. Counsel argued that the circumstances were such that the nurse was caught between conflicting demands of her employer, legal liability, disciplinary action and her own professional conscience. The arguments did not succeed.

The arbitration board made a finding of

fact that the nurses as a group were not in a position to make an informed judgment as to the capacity of the unit to accept the patient; that they lacked the information necessary to make such a judgment. Although each nurse had knowledge about the condition of the patient for whom she was caring, her knowledge of the condition of the other patients was insufficient. At no time did the nurses conduct an organized review of the patient load in an attempt to devise a plan of reassignment nor was any request made of any of the physicians for a reassessment of the conditions of the patients in the unit:

" . . . no conclusions can be reached solely on the basis of numbers since there is no necessary connection between the workload and the number of patients in the unit. A unit containing six seriously ill ventilator patients may present a greater workload than one with twelve cardiac patients whose condition can be relatively easily monitored by the nurses' station. " [13]

It appears the arbitration board found that the necessary assessment of the overall nursing care needs in the unit was not done and therefore one could not determine whether the admission of another patient would jeopardize the welfare of the patients already in the unit. It is accepted within the nursing profession that the responsibility of the nurse in charge of the unit is to complete a timely nursing assessment of the care needs of the patients in the unit, and to communicate the data to the person in charge of nursing and staffing of the particular units, with requests for increased staffing where necessary.

With respect to the second aspect of the defence, that potential civil liability, discipline pursuant to the nursing legislation, and the nurse's individual conscience, made it, in the circumstances, unfair to discipline, the arbitration board disregarded the argument. They stated that for such a defence to succeed, it would at least be necessary to establish that the dilemma of choosing between these masters was present in the minds of the nurses at the time of the conflict; the board determined that such was not present.

The board referred to the "obey and grieve" rule in labour matters wherein the employee is required to carry out the work order or direction given by the employer and use the mechanisms provided under the collective agreement to grieve the direction at a later date. They noted that in Ontario there were two exceptions to this rule in which the employee may refuse to obey a direction:
— When the employee is directed to carry out a task which is unsafe or reasonably believed to be unsafe, or
— When the employee is directed to carry out an illegal act. (The board determined that neither of these exceptions applied to the particular dispute.)

When a person contracts to render certain services for remuneration he may do so as either an independent contractor, (one who practices an independent business and retains control over the means by which he accomplishes the end results), or as an employee. Under employment contracts the employee becomes the "servant" of the employer and the employee is subject to the control of the employer. In such a contractual relationship the employer retains all of the powers he does not specifically delegate to the employee. Commonly the employer has the right to determine how, when and where the needed services are to be rendered. In terms of responsibility to one's employer the nursing expert, in Re. Mount Sinai Hospital and the Ontario Nurses Union made the valid point that:

" It is difficult to separate the responsibility to an employer from her responsibility as a professional because I believe that my first responsibility to my employer is for me to behave as a competent, professional nurse if my employer has hired me as a professional nurse. " [14]

As to the responsibility of the nurse who is requested or ordered to assume the care of a patient when, in her professional judgment, the patient she already has would be at risk, the same witness identified the reality in such a conflict. The obligation is to communicate her concern to her immediate supervisor. If no assistance is then provided the nurse must then make a professional judgment call as to how much, if any, care she is to provide and be accountable for that judgment to her employer, the professional registering body and to the nurse's own conscience.

" As professionals they are accountable for their behavior rather than accountable to someone in a hierarchy and as persons who are accountable for their professional behavior they must make judgments about the appropriateness of their nursing actions and if at any time they believe that an order is questionable those nurses are obliged by the ethical code governing nursing and by the contents of and the regulations under the Health Disciplines Act of Ontario to refuse to carry out questionable orders until they satisfy themselves that the carrying out of the orders would not be in conflict with their professional ethics and with their commitment to excellence in the practice of their profession... " [15]

(See Table of Cases for further reference to this case).

An employment contract consists of legally enforceable promises: the promise of the employee to perform activities and carry out the responsibilities in the particular job description and to bring to the job the knowledge, and skill he is holding himself out as possessing. The employer promises to pay a certain salary to the employee and provide certain fringe benefits. The contract may be written or oral. Certain terms may be expressed and others may be implied. If either party breaches a term of the contract such breach gives rise to certain rights, for example a right of the employer to discipline or to terminate depending on whether the term breached is a major or minor term of the contract. Likewise, the employee who is wrongfully dismissed may have a right to a remedy. In *Charlesworth v. Morris Hospital District No. 25*[16] (1982) a decision of the Manitoba Queen's Bench, the court ruled in favour of the plaintiff registered nurse in an action for wrongful dismissal. The nurse had been employed for seven years, six of them as director of nursing in charge of two hospitals and two personal care homes with responsibility for the direction of a sixty

member nursing department. The nurse was allegedly dismissed without notice, following a management survey report in which the allegations against her were unfair employee treatment and lack of communication. Evidence at trial indicated serious problems in the hospital district in all aspects other than nursing and good nursing management by the plaintiff despite difficult circumstances. Evidence did not substantiate the survey report. The court ruled the plaintiff was entitled to ten months notice.

3. Accountability in Tort:

In terms of sources of duties and legal liability in nursing practice, there is, in addition to contractual and professional duties, a personal duty of care owed by the professional to the patient. Historically, the common law has assigned a duty of care to professional persons who hold themselves out as having particular knowledge and skill on which a party relies. The duty of care owed by the registered nurse to the patient to whom she is assigned, is to exercise the knowledge, skill and care at the reasonable and prudent nurse standard. If the job responsibilities are carried out in such a way as to effectively result in a breach of that duty of care and a patient injury, the patient may well have a remedy pursuant to the tort of negligence. If the patient considers that he has been treated without a legally effective consent he may pursue a remedy in battery. (These particular torts are described in more detail in chapters two, three and four of this text.)

4. Accountability Under Criminal Law:

It is uncommon for health care workers to be charged with criminal offences resulting from criminal activity within their job activity. Nevertheless there have been instances where courts of criminal jurisdiction have concluded that certain omissions or acts by health care workers constituted breaches of the Criminal Code of Canada.

Crimes are breaches of a public right or a public duty and if such breaches are successfully prosecuted by the state (the Crown) in a criminal proceeding, one of a number of sanctions may result.

The Crown has the burden of proving the presence of the *acteus reus*, and the *mens reus* in order to obtain a criminal conviction of a person charged with a criminal offence. The *acteus reus* is the physical act or omission committed against the victim, property or the state itself; or it is the failure to perform a duty required under the criminal law. The *mens reus* is the presence of a guilty mind or a criminal intent. Offences may be summary conviction offences, and are considered to be of a less serious nature in the scale of criminal offences, sometimes referred to as misdemeanors. Other acts may constitute indictable offences which on conviction carry penalties ranging from two years to life imprisonment. In certain offences the Crown has the discretion of whether to proceed by way of summary conviction or indictment.

The Criminal Code of Canada sets out in specific sections, certain offences such as manslaughter, infanticide, criminal negligence, criminal assault and theft. No one has the authority to commit a criminal offence with protection from possible prosecution if the offence comes to the notice of the Crown.

The Canadian approach to criminal (and civil) trials is adversarial: the court attempts to arrive at the truth in a dispute by permitting each of the parties to the dispute to place his evidence before the court and to attempt, within the limits of the rules, to refute the evidence of the opposing party in the hope of ultimately defeating the opponent's case through proof and argument. Parties to a dispute vary. In a criminal trial one party is the *accused* and the opponent is the *crown*. He who accuses must prove and it is the Crown who carries the burden of bringing evidence of guilt before the court. The Crown must prove *beyond reasonable doubt* that the accused committed the *offence* with which he has been charged. If it fails to bring such proof the accused is *acquitted*. If the burden of proof is discharged a *conviction* will be registered (usually), and certain criminal sanctions will be imposed for the breach of the peace. Sanctions may include one or more of a fine, prison term, suspended sentence, conditional or unconditional discharge. In contrast a civil dispute takes place between parties known (usually) as the *plaintiff* and the *defendant*, (and depending on the situation *third parties* may be joined.) For example, if the hospital corporation is being sued in negligence and the investigation shows that any liability of the defendant would be due to the negligence of a nurse employee the latter may be joined as a third party by application of the defendant. The plaintiff in a civil dispute, such as a negligence action, has the burden of proving his case but the burden is not as heavy as it is in a criminal trial. The civil burden is on *a balance of probabilities* so that the plaintiff has to bring a little more evidence to bear than his opponent. If the plaintiff is successful, *damages* (money to compensate for the loss) will be awarded or such other remedy as the court deems appropriate.

A knowledge of criminal law principles and practices is important for intelligent health care. Registered nurses more than occasionally have assigned to them care of patients who are under investigation by the criminal justice system, and who may have been arrested, charged or convicted of a specific crime (such as impaired driving, criminal negligence, criminal assault, including instances of sexual assault). Or a nurse —employee may be the first contact for a victim of crime on admission of the victim to hospital. There are considerable evidentiary and reporting considerations involved and such considerations vary if the patient is a victim of assault, negligence, or specifically sexual assault (such as is involved in child abuse or rape). Regardless of the criminal and evidentiary aspects, the "authority" in the health care facility needs to ensure that clearly articulated policies are, in fact, in place, and are current for use by the health personnel operating in emergency and out-patient (and other) departments. They are dependent on certain policy directions as they offer services on behalf of the agency to patients who are either accused, convicted, or victims of crime.

5. Union Accountability:

In 1980 there were approximately

155,178 registered nurses practicing in Canada. Sixty-five percent of these nurses were employed on a full time basis in that year. In the past twenty years large numbers of such nurses have felt the need to organize in order to benefit from the collective process in negotiating for improved terms of employment. This added dimension of union membership rights and responsibilities requires today's nursing practitioner to have a current knowledge of labour law principles, practices, responsibilities and accountabilities. As a unionist the nurse has the right and the responsibility to attend union meetings, to know the issues and to exercise the right to vote on the issues. The philosophic base of unionism is brotherhood, sisterhood and strength in unity. In order to carry out its mandate the union requires the intelligent support of its membership.

There may be occasions of potential conflict between rights and duties operating by virtue of union membership and the previously described professional responsibilities and accountabilities. Such conflicts, however, are usually reconcilable by exercising appropriate knowledge and reasonable judgment in the particular situation. The strike event can create such conflict. For example, when a nurses' union has the right to strike and serves notice of its intention to strike, the shop stewart then proceeds to notify its members of its strike plan and time of the pending strike. Nurses on duty at the time retain certain professional responsibilities to assigned patients. It would not be appropriate for the individual to abandon assigned patients in the process of proceeding to strike. Such could foreseeably place patients at risk. The nurse concerned would have a professional responsibility to notify the person in charge of the nursing department of her intended departure. The purpose of such notification is to arrange to pass over care and control of the unit or assigned patient load to the nursing management representative. The nurse who exercises contractual or union rights and in the process places patients at risk will not be immune from possible discipline by the professional association. Neither will she be immune from a suit by the patient who suffers injury from the lack of reasonable and safe nursing care on the part of the striking nurse.

The foregoing sources of potential liability direct attention to the concepts of responsibility and of accountability.[17] *Responsibilities* refer to that which should be done—the expected or necessary action. They are obligations requiring the performance of particular activities and functions delegated to persons by virtue of the particular position they hold, for their control and management. The particular activities and functions are expected to be performed at a certain level or standard acceptable to the authority concerned. Responsibilities may vary somewhat depending on the legal source of the duty(s), such as statutory, contractual or tort, and the duties also differ in nature and scope depending on the position. For example, in the employment context, duties vary within the organizational hierarchy. The board of trustees has the responsibility to set the goals and policies of the institution; the chief executive officer, or administrator, is responsible for the day-to-day operation of the institution, and is accountable to the corporate authority for such. The director of nursing is usually accountable to the administrator directly for the management of the nursing department. Her job responsibilities differ from those of the supervisors, head nurses and staff nurses within the department. Such duties are usually defined within written job descriptions.

Accountability concerns itself with an examination of the manner in which certain duties or responsibilities are carried out. It is a process of examining what in fact was done in a particular instance, in comparison with the responsibilities which had been delegated. Accountability infers that some authority has the power to enquire into the matter in dispute for the purpose of determining whether the required standard had been met. If there is a finding that the standard has been breached, the authority may impose a sanction, or provide a remedy or compensation, depending on whether the authority concerned, is a labour tribunal, a disciplinary body, or a court of criminal or civil jurisdiction. Subject to appeal, the person against whom the sanction has been invoked will have no choice but accept the consequences for the sanctioned action. Accountability for what one does or fails to do is real and is a process over which an individual may have no control after the fact. It is also a reality that on rare occasions a single incident may give rise to an accounting to a number of authorities with differing mandates. For example, in 1980, in Canada, a laboratory technician was convicted of criminal negligence under the Criminal Code of Canada for her failure to group and cross-match blood. The failure resulted in the death of a patient during cardiac surgery because of an allergic reaction to the mismatched blood.[18] Subsequently, the convicted technician was terminated from her employment, her certification in her professional association was revoked and the family of the deceased sued the hospital for the negligence of its employee.

VI. Nursing Functions:

One Canadian author,[19] in addressing the topic of professional accountability, lists three broad functions in nursing practice:
— Independent Nursing Functions
— Dependent Nursing Functions
— Interdependent Nursing Functions.
Other authors have included advocacy functions as well, as part of legitimate practice. Following is a brief examination under the four functional categories as a means of identifying that which the nurse offers under the umbrella of nursing service. (In subsequent chapters with a case analysis approach, the dependent and independent nursing functions are examined to highlight the court's evaluation of the duty owed by nurses in carrying out these two particular functions.)

1. Independent Nursing Functions:

Include those functions which are strictly within the jurisdiction of the nursing team rather than the physician team and jurisdiction is based on the premise that nurses are the ultimate authority on basic nursing care. Such functions do not authorize the nurse to carry out medical diagnosis of disease, or to order and implement medical and surgical treatments clearly within the jurisdiction of those holding licences and credentials to practice medicine.

Independent nursing functions concern the *overall management* of the nursing care needs of all patients within the nursing unit. These functions involve the *supervision* of various levels of nursing personnel and *delegation* to them of certain aspects of nursing care within the scope of their knowledge and experience. These functions also include *teaching* of patients and nursing staff, periodic performance *evaluation* of nursing staff, all for the purpose of ensuring a safe and reasonable *nursing process* for each of the patients requiring nursing care. The design, implementation and assessment of the nursing process that will meet the needs of individual patients is the central or core independent nursing function.

In this text the term "nursing process" is used merely as an abstract way of looking at and giving structure to the practice of nursing just as the "medical process" is a term used by the writer to encompass those activities which come within the jurisdiction of the physician and constitute the practice of medicine.

What is the "nursing process"? The profession would likely agree that it is not a haphazard approach to nursing care; it is not a trial and error method. Rather it is a systematic approach to identifying the presenting or probable nursing care problems of a particular patient. It is the deliberate selection of certain nursing actions for the purpose of eliminating, minimizing, preventing or controlling problems interfering with the health and survival of the patient.

The nursing process includes a series of interrelated stages that are closely related in time and characterized by the fact that the quality and timeliness of one phase dictates the success and safety of the next stage of nursing care. The quality and timeliness of the nursing process ultimately determines whether the patient improves because of the nursing care, or in spite of the nursing care, or is injured because of it.

The nursing process is commonly described in four stages which parallel the stages involved in the physicians care of the patient. These stages include:
1. Assessment
2. Design of a written plan of care
3. Implementation of the plan of care
4. Evaluation of the patient's response to the care and modification of the care as needed.

In the chapter dealing with the Tort of Negligence and the Nursing Process a comparative study of the nursing and medical process is made and the duties of care owed by the nurse within the nursing process are outlined.

2. Dependent Nursing Functions:

These depend upon the presence of a legitimate medical order which order flows from the medical assessment and the resultant medical diagnosis. Dependent nursing functions may also flow directly from the presence of a hospital policy and from the job description. In the main, however, dependent functions refer to those which flow directly from the presence of the medical order, and without which order, the nurse has no jurisdiction to perform the activity concerned. Such functions are distinct from the independent nursing functions. The latter are totally within the jurisdiction of nursing and flow from the presence of a written and reasonable nursing order.

Should the nurse carry out certain health care functions without the presence of a legitimate medical order, such activity could constitute the practice of medicine without a licence. For example, if the nurse determined that the patient to whom she is assigned requires medication for pain, and proceeds to prepare an injection of demerol 100 mgs and administers it to the patient she is "prescribing" medications; this has traditionally been within the practice of medicine. In contrast, if the nurse, in her assessment of the patient identified one of the problems to be the patient's ineffective sleep patterns, the nurse would carry out a number of nursing measures to encourage

sleep without the physician "ordering" her to do so. If, in addition to the nursing measures, the patient required sedation, the latter would require a clear and reasonable order prior to the nurse administering the sedation to the patient.

There are two prerequisites to the carrying out of dependent nursing functions:
— That the nurse have a clear understanding of the nature of the medical order (or the hospital policy) and the intended purpose and goal of the order, and
— That the nurse exercise reasonable judgment and skill in the carrying out of such order.

The 1981 case, *Meyer v. Gordon*,[20] (see Table of Cases for further reference to this and other cases throughout the text), is of interest as well in terms of the dependent nursing functions, the overlapping responsibilities of the physician and the nurse in the matter of medical orders and the carrying out of the medical order. In the particular case a negligence action was brought against the obstetrician and the hospital following the birth of an infant. The infant suffered severe brain damage during the birth and the parents alleged the damage was caused by the negligence of the physician and the nurses in the obstetrical unit. One of the nurses gave evidence that she telephoned the obstetrician and reported on the patient's progress in labour. The physician ordered 50 mg of demerol and gravol "stat" to alleviate the pain. The nurse who took the telephone order then directed another nurse to administer the medication. The latter did administer the medication without completing a current nursing assessment prior to administering the drugs. One of the allegations of the plaintiff was that there was a failure to assess the mother's labour by the physician and by the nurses. The court concluded that the hospital staff and the physician ought to have initiated a vaginal examination prior to the administration of the demerol and the gravol. The court apportioned liability for the omissions twenty-five percent against the physician and seventy-five percent against the hospital for the omission of its nursing staff.

3. Interdependent Functions:

These collaborative functions are founded in consensus through the active participation of nurses with their colleagues from other health care professions for the improvement of health care. Included under this umbrella of functions is the so called transfer of functions process. Each province has a mechanism in place whereby certain functions which traditionally fell within the jurisdiction of the practice of medicine, could, under certain controlled circumstances, be performed by nurses. The historical development of medicine and nursing reveals that at one time, such procedures as the taking of the patient's temperature, the determination of the patient's blood pressure and the administration of injections constituted the practice of medicine. As the function became common practice in health care "transfer" occurred and it became appropriate nursing function as well as appropriate medical function.

Each province now has in place a liaison committee with representation from the registered nurses association of the province, the medical association, (and the hospital association representing the employer, in certain of the jurisdictions). The purpose of this committee is to review requests for the transfer of certain functions to nursing, to approve appropriate procedures, designate the special education required beyond the basic nursing education, and to set out obligations to be met by the particular health care institution in certifying certain personnel permitted to carry out the function.

Some of the functions which have been published in current "Guidelines for Medical Nursing Procedures"[21] include:
— Initiation of intravenous therapy;
— Administration of certain medications into intravenous tubing;
— Administration of certain vaccinations and gamma globulin;
— Initiating and maintaining inhalation therapy;
— Performing electrocardiography;
— Performing cardiac resuscitation including cardiac massage and countershock

therapy, i.e. cardioversion and defibrillation, in an emergency situation;
Continuing injections, after the initial injection by the physician of epidural anesthesia for obstetrical patients in the labour process.

In Ontario in 1978 there was a coroner's inquest into the death of a mother and infant during an epidural anesthesia. In the incident, the epidural catheter, which was placed in the epidural space by the physician in initiating the anesthesia, slipped from the epidural to the subdural space causing shutdown of the patient's vital functions.[22] The "Topping up" has been approved, in some provinces, for registered nurses who meet the prerequisites for performing the procedure and have been certified to do so in the particular institution. The foregoing occurrence of such a complication points out the critical importance of controlling the transfer of functions, ensuring that the educational base and certification is well in place, and that the individual nurse has the required knowledge and skill.

The nurse is deemed to know what procedures have been approved in the province in which she is working, and which of the approved procedures are permitted by the institution in which she is employed. She is obligated to ensure that she has the necessary knowledge, and skills to perform the function concerned. The fact that it is an approved function does not permit the particular nurse to perform the function with less than the necessary knowledge and skill. Should the patient be injured, a nurse using defective knowledge, skill and care may well find herself accountable in law for the injury. In this sense, interdependent functions have legal significance.

Sample Policy: Transfer of Functions[23]

The following statement is a modified version of how one health care facility balanced the need for transfer of certain functions from medicine to nursing practice, and the potential risks involved. The policy and practice in a particular facility should be researched and expressed in light of current statutory and case law applicable in the par-

Sample Policy

_____HOSPITAL

TOWN (CITY):_____

PROVINCE:_____

Authorized By: Board of Directors

Effective Date: May 19, 1980 No. L-3 Page 1 of 1

Revision Dates: February 21, 1982; June 30, 1983

Departments Primarily Affected: Medical Staff, Nursing Departments, Administration

Subject: Transfer of Functions: Medical and Nursing Practice

Policy: In the delegation of medical acts to the registered nurse the criteria as approved by the provincial association of registered nurses and by the board of directors of the _____ Hospital shall constitute medical-nursing procedures, and shall be transferrable on the recommendation of the director of nursing in accordance with the procedure set out herein.

Policy Purposes:
1. To promote the safety of the patient by providing the necessary training and certification of the particular member of the nursing department;
2. To protect the registered nurse by restricting nursing practice in the hospital to those procedures that are within the role of the registered nurse.

Procedure:
1. Each procedure to be delegated to the registered nurse shall be approved by the director of nursing, the medical advisory committee of the hospital and its board of directors.
2. The educational preparation shall be planned by the nursing department at the in-service level, and approved by the medical advisory committee.
3. Each registered nurse, having successfully completed the preparation through an in-service programme, and certified to perform the procedure shall be issued a certificate signed by the director of nursing, the chairman of the medical advisory committee and the administrator of the hospital.
4. The medical staff shall be notified in writing of the nurses certified to carry out the particular procedure.
5. Certificates and curriculum outlines relative to the approved procedure(s) shall be filed in the office of the director of nursing, the chief of the medical staff, and the administrator.
6. A current list of the procedures as approved by the association of registered nurses for the province shall be filed with the chief of the medical staff and hospital administrator together with a current list of registered nurses on staff approved for the performance of the particular procedures, at yearly intervals; and a list of the approved procedures in effect in the hospital shall be forwarded to the association of registered nurses on an annual basis.

Approval: _____ Board Chairman:
                                    Signature   Title
Date:

---

ticular province or territory, the philosophy and goals of the agency, the type of patient population being serviced by the facility, the probability of risks involved in the procedure considered for transfer, the availability of an effective educational program and availability of a monitoring certification and recertification system to ensure safety for the patient.

4. Advocacy Functions:

An advocate is one who assists his client with advice, and who defends him and pleads for him. An advocacy function is not a "legal" function for nursing in the sense that neither case law nor statute has expressly mandated the registered nurse as a patient advocate. It has, nevertheless, been expressed in official statements by provincial nursing associations.[24]

Advocacy focuses on the support and protection of a particular patient's need for privacy and dignity, and his need for accurate and current information about his plan of care. These needs require that the nurse utilize appropriate channels of communication. Within the context of advocacy, patient needs (for safety, as an example) may require the nurse to question certain medical orders or institutional policy if they pose a threat to the patient's safety. This challenge, in turn, will require careful and appropriate documentation and reporting, together with possible refusal to carry out the order or policy concerned.

An advocacy function is based in the unique character of nursing, in its caring role in which the nurse acts as the mouthpiece for the patient who is unable to speak for himself. In one hospital advocacy is recognized as part of the responsibilities of the clinical nurse specialist for example, in the unit where lung transplants are performed. In addition to working with the patient, his family and nursing staff in providing the necessary psychological supports, the particular nurse would also play a role in representing the patient's interests in privacy and rest, in what is ordinarily, a very busy environment.

The formal recognition of advocacy func-

tions in nursing practice within health care facilities could assist in the prevention and resolution of problems and conflicts in health care delivery.

In summary, the concept of law and accountability for nursing practice concerns itself with standards of practice. A standard is a measure or model to which other similar things should conform. This text focuses on standards of practice within the context of negligence law, law of assault and battery, and in the regulation of nursing by the various professional bodies. A standard basically describes the behavior below which it is unacceptable to practice. Assuming that the standards adopted are reasonable, enunciated clearly and published for the consideration of the community of workers concerned, their ultimate success is still determined by consistent enforcement. Their intent is to prevent or reduce the possibility of risks to clients receiving care.

The various health care professions have the necessary expertise to identify and articulate reasonable standards. The 1970s saw the beginnings of interdisciplinary consultation and collaboration in designing standards as part of quality assurance programs in health care. It is fair to say that the Canadian Nurses Association and its provincial and territorial counterparts have led the way in this exercise. It is appropriate that the nursing profession take an active role in standard setting—of all the health care professions they have the largest interest. It is the individual nurse who has the largest communication challenge in the implementation of care plans in which a variety of other professional groups have had input. These other professionals depend on the nurse to understand their intent, to assess the patient's response to the multidiscipline care plan, and to communicate findings on a timely basis for safe modification of the care plan to prevent harm to the patient.

In the final analysis consistent enforcement of appropriate standards of practice and of care, will likely decrease the need for courts to enforce standards after the fact through imposition of remedies, or penalties as a consequence of injurious practice.

The registered nurse should be familiar with the statements of standards published by the federal professional association and its provincial or territorial counterpart where she is practising. (See the references set out in chapter four: The Tort of Negligence and the Nursing Process.) The nurse should also be familiar with the Standards For Accreditation of Canadian Health Care Facilities, published by the Canadian Council on Hospital Accreditation in January of 1983. Such statements are but two of the sources to which tribunals may turn to identify the standard of care required of a particular professional and or a health care agency in the event of a dispute.

VII. Endnotes:

1. Black H.C. *Black's Law Dictionary* (St. Paul, Minn, West Pub. 1979) p. 1135
2. Constitutional Act, 1981. S.C. 1982 c. 11
3. British North America Act, 1867, 30 & 31 Vict., c. 3
4. Supra n. 2 sec. 52(1)
5. Reference Re. Procedures and the Mental Health Act (1984) 5 D.L.R. (4th) 577 (P.E.I.S.C.)
6. The Queen et al v. Operation Dismantle Inc. et al. (1983) 3 D.L.R. (4th) 193, 49 N.R. 363, (Fed. C. A. reversed (1983) 1 P.Q. 429 T.D.) Leave to appeal to the Supreme Court of Canada granted on December 20, 1983
7. Re. Davis, Can. Charter of Rights Annotated, June 1983, p. 9
8. Borowski v. Attorney Gen. of Canada et al [1984] 1 W.W.R. 15, (1984) 4 D.L.R. (4th) 112, (Sask Q.B.)
9. R v. Carter (1982) 2 C.C. (3d) 412, 144 D.L.R. (3d) 301, 39 O.R. (2d) 439;
10. R v. L.A.R. (1983) 4 D.L.R. (4th) 720 (Man. Q.B.); R v. Decoste (1983) 60 N.S.R. (2d) 170 (N.S.S.C.T.D.); R v. Santa (1983) 23 M.V.R. 300 (Sask. Prov. Ct.)
11. R v. Therens, 33 C.R. (3d) 204 (Sask. C.A.)
12. Re. Mount Sinai Hospital and the Ontario Nurses Association (1978) 17 L.A.C. (2d) 242
13. Supra n. 12 at 251
14. Supra n. 12 at 267
15. Supra n. 12 at 266
16. Charlesworth v. Morris Hospital Dist No. 25 (1982) 16 Man. R. (2d) 333 (Man. Q.B.)
17. See Kron T., *The Management of Patient Care: Putting Leadership Skills to Work* (Philadelphia, W.B. Saunders Company 1981) at page 12
18. R v. Lockyer (1978) unreported (Nfld S.C.T.D.)
19. See Flaherty D.J., "Accountability In The Nursing Profession". *Health Management Forum*, Toronto, Extendi Care Ltd. 1980) p. 23
20. Meyer v. Gordon (1981) 17 C.C.L.T. 1
21. See, for example, "Guidelines Medical Nursing Procedures" published by the Registered Nurses Association of Nova Scotia, the Provincial Medical Board and the Nova Scotia Association of Health Organizations, (Revised January 1980)
22. Globe and Mail, March 1, 1978 at page 9. A report on an Ontario coroner's inquest in the death of a woman and her unborn child, during labour.
23. Modification of a policy from Sir. Thomas Roddick Hospital, Stephenville, Nfld.
24. For treatment of advocacy functions see the Association of Registered Nurses of Newfoundland: Quality of Nursing Care Standards, (1984)

Chapter Two:

The Tort of Negligence: An Overview

I. Concept Objectives:

The law of negligence governs the majority of legal actions taken against hospitals in Canada for alleged breach of the duty of care owed by its health care workers. The intent in this chapter is to:

— distinguish the characteristics or critical elements of actionable negligence and contrast it with the concept of negligence as it is known in ordinary, non-legal usage

— examine the content of the duty of care owed by professional health care workers, and the standard required to be exercised in nursing practice

— examine the defences of nursing custom, error in judgment and nursing misadventures

— contrast the corporate authorities direct duty of care with the personal duty owed by servants of the corporate authority

— set the basis for application of tort principles in the chapter concerning the tort of negligence and the nursing process.

II. Introduction:

Examination of the concept of "negligence" reveals that it has at least two meanings: the first is based in ordinary usage of language; the second is defined by Canada's courts in a way that determines whether or not a plaintiff may obtain a remedy against the person he considers to be negligent.

In its ordinary usage, negligence is characterized as careless conduct or trial and error behavior, such as careless driving on public highways, smoking in restricted or highly dangerous areas, use of dangerous equipment or drugs, or performing nursing care without the required knowledge, care or skill. Persons may demonstrate such negligent conduct or behavior as a matter of course but such does not guarantee a legal remedy to a person offended by the behavior.

For negligence to be actionable at law (i.e. to provide grounds for legal action) much more is needed. To be successful in court the offended party, the plaintiff, must not only commence legal action within a certain time limit as determined by the applicable statute of limitations, but he must also meet the burden of proving certain "critical elements" of the negligence alleged against the party or parties named as "defendants" in the action. Only if such critical elements are proven to be present will the offending party (defendant) be found liable in negligence and be required to remedy the situation by payment of "damages". (i.e. compensation in money for the loss.)

III. Negligence (defined):

As early as 1856 the English courts defined negligence as:

" ....the omission to do something which a reasonable man, guided upon those considerations which ordinarily regulate the conduct of human affairs, would do, or doing something which a prudent and reasonable man would not do...."[1]

At that early time it was determined that negligence could be due to the failure to do that which a reasonable man would do, or the doing of that which a reasonable man would not do, i.e. omissions or commissions. But again, negligence in legal terms incorporates much more. Professor Fleming set out five elements required for a successful action in negligence, four of which must be present to prove liability and one of which, if present, may not defeat the case entirely but will decrease the amount of damage otherwise due to the offended plaintiff:[2]

1. The presence of a duty of care by the defendant to the plaintiff.

2. The defendant's conduct must constitute a breach of that duty of care, i.e. must have failed to comply with the required standard of care.

3. The plaintiff must have suffered a material injury.

4. The negligent conduct must have been the proximate cause of the injury.

5. There must not have been contributory negligence on the part of the plaintiff and he must not have voluntarily assumed the risk.

It is within this artificial construct that the critical elements at play in the determination of the presence or absence of nursing negligence will be set out.

IV. Critical Elements Constituting Actionable Negligence:

1. *Critical Element # One: Duty of Care:*

A first prerequisite to be met if the plaintiff is to obtain a remedy in negligence, is to establish that the particular defendant owed a duty of care to the plaintiff—one does not owe a duty of care to the whole world. The courts decide as a matter of public policy whether or not a duty of care existed between the parties at the time of the incident or accident:

" ... there is such a duty only where the circumstances of time, place and person would create in the mind of a reasonable man in those circumstances such a probability of harm resulting to other persons as to require him to take care to avert that probable result. " [3]

The concept of "duty" is a device used by the courts to limit the kinds of relationships which would give rise to a duty of care. In determining whether a relationship exists creating a duty, the courts have looked at such factors as:
— Foreseeability of the risk
— The presence of an undertaking by the defendant and the presence of reliance by the plaintiff on the undertaking.

(a) Foreseeability of the Risk:

" The existence of a legal duty of care by a defendant depends upon whether the hypothetical reasonable man would foresee the risk of harm to a person in the situation of the plaintiff vis-a-vis himself and his activities. " [4]

Where an omission or commission would constitute an unreasonable risk to others, the reasonable man would not create such a risk by his action. This foreseeability test was first pronounced in 1932 in England:

" You must take reasonable care to avoid acts or omissions which you can reasonably foresee would be likely to injure your neighbour. Who, then, in law, is my neighbour? The answer seems to be—persons who are so closely and directly affected by my act that I ought reasonably to have them in contemplation as being so affected when I am directing my mind to the acts or omissions which are called in question. " [5]

This concept of duty arising in circumstances of foreseeable risk will be examined in the nursing negligence case *Dowey v. Dr. W.O. Rothwell and Associates*[6] (1974). The case points out not only the matter of foreseeability but also the other two factors in creation of the duty, that of "undertaking" and "reliance". The above case is analyzed in terms of these two latter concepts.

(b) Undertaking and Reliance:

"To undertake" is defined to mean "to accept responsibility for the care of, or to engage to look after".[7] A physician, licensed to practice medicine in a particular province or territory, once he initiates the physician-patient relationship, effectively "undertakes" to treat the patient. The physician commonly is free to contract directly with the patient and can choose whether or not he will initiate a relationship. Once that relationship is initiated, he is deemed to have undertaken certain responsibilities vis-a-vis the patient. In contrast, the registered nurse is not commonly an independent contractor but an employee and she does not have the same choices open to the independent contracting physician. The reality of the work place is such that the nurse is not free to say: "I will nurse Mr. Jones but will refuse to provide care to Mrs. Brown." As a member of the nursing team she is commonly assigned particular patients and such gives rise to a nurse-patient relationship in which the nurse undertakes certain responsibilities vis-a-vis the patient. As early as 1925 the English courts set out the matter of undertakings giving rise to a duty of care:

" If a person *holds himself out* as possessing special skill and knowledge, and he is consulted as possessing such special skill and knowledge by or on behalf of a patient, he owes a duty to the patient to use due *caution* in undertaking the treatment. If he accepts the responsibility and undertakes the treatment and the patient submits to his direction and treatments accordingly, he owes a duty to the patient to use *diligence, care, knowledge, skill and caution* in administering the treatment. No contractual relationship is necessary or that the service be rendered for reward... " [8]

There is a variation in the content or

nature of "undertaking", depending on whether the registered nurse is a director of nursing, supervisor, head nurse, team leader, or a member of the nursing team assigned to particular patients.

"Reliance" is synonymous with "trust" and "confidence". Physicians and nurses carry with them all the trappings of authority and special skills: thermometers, stethoscopes, injections, medications, white uniforms and black bands. The reality is that the patient tends to pass over care and control to those persons he perceives having special skill and knowledge. The patient relies on the perceived superior knowledge, skills and professional opinions. He does so in the expectation that the professional person knows what is best for him, and that he will be caused no harm in the application of that special knowledge and skills:

> " The public profession of an art is a representation and undertaking to all the world that the professor possesses the requisite skill and ability. " [9]

The foregoing factors creating a duty of care are evidenced in the previously mentioned *Dowey v. W.O. Rothwell and Associates*[10] which involved a negligence action against the employers of a registered nurse. The thirty-five year old plaintiff suffered a severe arm injury when she fell from the examining table in the defendant's office.

The plaintiff had been treated for epilepsy by one of the physicians in the defendant partnership for the previous ten years. She had been taking phenobarbital to control the frequency and severity of grand mal epileptic seizures. Just prior to the incident the plaintiff had stopped taking the prescribed medication because of her association with persons of the Christian Science religion.

On June 5, 1972, the plaintiff felt "an aura" (warning of an impending epileptic seizure). She went to the office of the defendant at approximately 9:15 a.m. and told the receptionist she was an epileptic, that she had not been taking her pills and she felt she was about to have a seizure. Mrs. D was the only qualified nurse on the premises. Evidence at trial indicated that

she had graduated from a hospital school of nursing forty years before and had been working for the physicians for twenty-two years. At the time of the incident she wore a nurse's uniform with a nurse's cap, a black band, and a pin indicating her qualification.

Mrs. D attended on the plaintiff and escorted her to an examining room. She then assisted the plaintiff onto an examining table that measured approximately six feet long by two feet wide. The evidence indicated she stayed with the patient for half an hour. She then left the patient and went to the file cabinet to remove the plaintiff's file. At that moment the plaintiff experienced a grand mal seizure, fell from the examining table to the tiled floor, causing a severe comminuted fracture at the wrist end of the radius with separation at the joint. The seizure continued for ten to fifteen minutes.

As a consequence of the injury, the plaintiff required hospitalization for five days and an arm cast for approximately thirteen weeks. When the cast was removed it was discovered that bone was protruding which required further hospitalization and surgery. The repaired arm left an appearance of deformity, a possibility of arthritis but no functional impairment.

At trial the court asked:

> " What did the patient have a right to expect when she entered the office of the general practitioners who had been treating her over an extended period and to whose staff she made a full disclosure of her situation at the particular time bearing in mind that a nurse is a professional person with special training and special skill and knowledge? " [11]

The court then noted the standard of care as set out in the 1925 case of *Rex v. Bateman*, and as cited in this chapter:

> " If a person holds himself out as possessing special skill and knowledge... he owes a duty to the patient to use due caution in undertaking the treatment... " [12]

The court notes that the foregoing principle embraces all public professions[13].

Every profession has its own standards to which all its members must conform. To determine the standard of care inherent in the duty owed by the nurse to the plaintiff, an expert nursing witness gave opinion evidence. She stated that the public has a right to expect from a person with nursing qualifications, a reasonable standard of care under all circumstances. In the instance of an adult patient who states she is an epileptic and that she feels she is about to have a seizure, the nurse should believe this, and should place the patient in a safe place, usually on the floor, and remove furniture beyond the patient's arm and leg length, and stay with the patient. If the nurse is told that the patient has not taken the prescribed anti-epileptic drugs, the nurse should expect "a dandy, a grand mal seizure". The expert went on to say that the presence of the nurse in the situation was important because she could prevent injury or minimize the possibility of injury.

One of the publications entered into evidence was the St. John's Ambulance Manual of First Aid. This reference sets out the emergency care of a person anticipating and experiencing a seizure. The reference also describes the common signs, symptoms and possible complications and the need for continuous supervision and a safe environment.

The court evaluated the evidence given by the registered nurse Mrs. D:

" Strangely, Mrs. D indicated that she cannot remember having had any training with regard to epilepsy and in her time as a nurse she has only seen one epileptic seizure. It is significant that since the time of her graduation Mrs. D has taken no refresher course whatsoever nor has she made any effort to update her training. In the year immediately following her graduation she had taken the St. John's Ambulance First Aid qualification and was familiar with the manual St. John's Ambulance First Aid to the Injured. "[14]

The court held the employer vicariously liable for the negligence of its nurse employee:

" ... She went to their offices where she made a full and complete disclosure to the persons in attendance there and placed herself completely in the care of Nurse D. In breach of what would be regarded as a min-

imal standard of care Nurse D left the patient in a position where she could do harm to herself for a period of time in which such harm could occur, and that which was reasonably foreseeable happened... "[15]

Could a nurse be expected to have foreseen the particular risk of harm? If the answer is "yes" then the nurse has a duty to refrain from the particular dangerous activity.

In summary: the existence of a duty is a question of law for the courts to determine. They do so by examining the presence of undertaking and reliance and/or the presence of foreseeability. In the Dowey case there was an undertaking by the nurse, and reliance by the particular patient and "that which was reasonably foreseeable happened". The nurse has a duty to take reasonable care to avoid acts which she could reasonably foresee would be likely to injure the patient. The nurse is expected to take precautions commensurate with the danger inherent in the activity and circumstances and when the *potential risk is high*, or the *potential damage or injury is great*, it may be that the creation of the risk of occurrence may create liability. One author suggested that the precautions reasonably to be taken would be determined by:

— The social object of the activity.
— The magnitude of the risk involved and likelihood of injury being caused.
— The cost of eliminating the risk.[16]

The patient is, in law, the nurse's neighbour, i.e. a person who is so closely and directly affected by the nursing act or omission that the nurse ought reasonably to have that patient in mind when she is directing her mind to the act:

" The rule that you are to love your neighbour becomes in law you must not injure your neighbour... "[17]

This foreseeability test which was first pronounced in 1932, applies to the nurse-patient relationship:

" You must take reasonable care to avoid acts or omissions which you can reasonably foresee would be likely to injure your neighbour. Who, then, in law, is my neighbour? The answer seems to be persons who are so closely and directly affected by my act that I ought reasonably to have them in contemplation as being so affected when I am directing my mind to the acts or omissions which are called in question. " [18]

In the context of the health care delivery system, it is not difficult to prove the presence of a duty of care between a particular nurse and the patient to whom she has been assigned. Once the courts determine that the relationship of undertaking and reliance exists, the question to be determined subsequently, is the nature, scope or extent of the duty.

2. Critical Element # Two: Breach of the Duty of Care:

If the duty of care does not exist between the particular plaintiff and the particular defendant the latter may be as negligent as he or she pleases and the plaintiff will have no recourse by way of a private remedy in a negligence action. However, once a duty is found the plaintiff then has the burden to show that there was a breach of duty by the defendant. The plaintiff must identify the *standard of care* owed, and prove that the defendant *breached the standard of care*. (The plaintiff may allege that the accident itself speaks of negligence, i.e. *res ipsa loquitur*.) The defendant, in his or her defence, will claim that the required standard of care was not breached because he or she complied with approved *custom*. Alternatively the defendant may claim, that the omission or commission was due not to negligence but to an *error in judgment* or a *nursing misadventure*.

Under the critical element of breach of the duty of care, the foregoing concepts are analyzed as they have been applied in Canadian nursing negligence cases:
(a) Standard of Care
(b) Res ipsa loquitur
(c) Custom
(d) Error in Judgment and Nursing Misadventure.

(a) Standard of Care

In actionable negligence the offending conduct is measured against a yardstick or standard known as *the reasonable and prudent man standard*. This standard was articulated in 1856, and may be transposed to the *reasonable and prudent nurse standard* as follows:

" The omission to do something which a reasonable man (nurse), guided upon those considerations which ordinarily regulate the conduct of human (nursing) affairs would do, or doing something which a reasonable and prudent man (nurse) would not do. " [19]

The nurse may be unreasonable or imprudent in the carrying out of certain actions, or in the omission of reasonable and prudent acts. It is the judge who determines what standard of care is to apply (and if the trial is heard by judge and jury, it is the latter who will determine whether the appropriate standard has been met). The court will not exact the highest standard:

" nor should they be content with a very low standard. The law requires a fair and reasonable standard of care and competence. " [20]

The courts have determined that the professional:

" ...does not undertake, if he is...a surgeon...that he will perform a cure, nor does he undertake to use the highest possible degree of skill. There may be persons who have higher education and greater advantages than he has but he undertakes to bring a fair, reasonable, and competent degree of skill... " [21]

By 1956 the Supreme Court of Canada concluded that the professional concerned undertakes that he possesses the same degree of *knowledge and skill* and an *honest, and intelligent exercise of judgment* as the average of the special group of class of technicians to which he belongs.[22]

There are two nursing negligence cases which point out the content of the reasonable and prudent nurse standard, and the impact of compliance and non compliance with the standard, to the outcome of the case. The cases to be analyzed are:
— Wilcox v. Cavan
— Huber v. Burnaby General Hospital

Wilcox v. Cavan[23], which was heard by the trial division and the appeal court of New Brunswick and finally by the Supreme Court of Canada in 1975, concerned an injection administered by the defendant registered nurse.

The plaintiff had developed pneumonia. After examination and x-ray the attending physician ordered an injection of bicillin. The nurse worked in the outpatient department of the hospital to which the plaintiff had been directed for the injection. She prepared the injection and approached the patient, requested that he lower his trousers and lie on the examining cart so that she could inject the antibiotic in the gluteus maximus muscle of the buttocks. The plaintiff did not cooperate with the request. The nurse then chose to inject the patient in the deltoid muscle of the left arm, a site which the court determined was an acceptable alternate site at the time.

The plaintiff returned home after the injection, but immediately experienced extreme pain in the left arm and blanching of the fingers. The physician examined the plaintiff the next day and noted that gangrene had set in. He then admitted him to hospital both because of the condition of his hand and because of the pneumonia. Due to the deterioration of the patient he was not operated on until twenty days after the injection. At that time parts of five fingers were amputated.

The plaintiff sued the nurse (and the physician for his failure to see the patient until twenty-four hours after the injection. The latter defendant was not found to be liable). The plaintiff alleged that the nurse administered the injection in a negligent manner in that she injected the needle below the deltoid muscle and in so doing plugged the circumflex humeral artery causing impaired circulation and consequently, gangrene. Evidence from the pathologist at trial confirmed that the actual cause of the gangrene was the plugging of the circumflex artery with the antibiotic. The plaintiff's wife contended that she was present when the injection was administered and that it had been given below the deltoid muscle. Two physicians who had examined the patient on admission to the hospital the day after the injection, gave evidence about the location of the needle mark and placed the needle mark over the deltoid muscle. The defendant nurse took

the stand. She demonstrated the technique for injections which she had been using in her ten years of practice. (Her testimony was as to the manner in which she was accustomed to giving injections and was not an actual recollection of the events on the day in question.) Her recounting of the technique stated that she would prepare the site, inject the needle, withdraw on the plunger to determine she was not in an arterial or venous area, and then inject the drug and withdraw the needle. The defence then called expert nursing witnesses who gave the opinion of the appropriate method of giving injections. They stated that knowledge of the location of the circumflex artery had not to that date been included in basic nursing texts; such knowledge was not, to that date, part of the expected knowledge of nursing practitioners. The experts confirmed that the method of injection described by the defendant nurse complied with the method approved and accepted by the nursing profession. The trial judge noted at one point in the judgment:

> " Considerable importance attaches to the fact that the proper practice in giving such an injection, and the one which Mrs. W said she followed coincided . " [24]

The court held that the nurse's technique was faultless and she did not breach her standard of care, and therefore was not negligent. (On appeal at the next two levels of court the issue was one of res ipsa loquitur.) At the trial the judge was satisfied because the evidence of the defendant nurse, although not based on recollection of the specific event, was corroborated by two physicians who had noted the location of the injection site. The defendant nurse was found to be negligent on appeal to the New Brunswick Court of Appeal but was exonerated by the Supreme Court of Canada. (This case is further analyzed under the concept of res ipsa loquitur.) The Supreme Court of Canada set out the principle of compliance with the aproved standard which when transposed from the medical standard to the nursing standard is as follows:

"Certainly [nurses] should not be held responsible for unforeseeable accidents which may occur in the normal course of the exercise of their profession. Cases necessarily occur in which, in spite of exercising the greatest caution, accidents supervene and for which nobody can be held responsible. [The nurse] is not a guarantor of the . . . attention she gives. If she displays normal knowledge, if she gives the [nursing care] which a competent [nurse] would give under identical conditions, if she prepares her patient before the [treatment] according to the rules of the art, it is difficult to sue [her] in damages . . ."[25]

In contrast to *Wilcox v. Cavan*, an unreported case of the British Columbia Supreme Court, that of *Huber v. Burnaby General Hospital*[26] held the hospital to be liable for the negligence of its registered nurse employee.

The plaintiff sued the hospital alleging the registered nurse had injected the plaintiff in the hip area, causing temporary injury to the sciatic nerve and subsequent pain and numbness. The plaintiff contended the nurse administered the injection in the early morning hours and while the room was in darkness. The court accepted the plaintiff's evidence and that of another patient who had been in the room at the time.

If one administers an injection in the buttocks without using proper lighting, such would be contrary to the reasonable nurse standard. The reasonable and prudent nurse is expected to know that the sciatic nerve travels down the spinal column, through the inner quadrant of the buttocks and down into the legs. For this reason, customary and approved nursing practice requires that the area be well lighted, and that the buttocks be "divided" into four quadrants. This is a prerequisite in order to ensure that the needle is injected in the upper outer quadrant well away from the path of the sciatic nerve. Without proper lighting of the area, and careful marking of the site, it is foreseeable that the needle may enter the wrong quadrant and cause temporary or permanent damage of the nerve concerned.

(b) Res Ipsa Loquitur:

In an action grounded in negligence the plaintiff has the legal burden of proving that the injury or loss was caused by the defendant's negligence. This legal burden does not shift and at the conclusion of the evidence the court must be satisfied that, on a balance of probability, the defendant's negligence "caused" the loss. If the plaintiff is unable to so prove, his case will fail.

In certain situations the plaintiff may be unable to say how or why the loss occurred. He may only know that he was injured. If he does not know he is unable to plead any particular negligent act or omission on the part of the defendant. This is a common problem in medical and nursing negligence actions. The law of evidence has evolved to accommodate this burden in certain restricted situations. The latin maxim *res ipsa loquitur* translated to mean "the thing speaks for itself" may apply to assist the plaintiff. Res ipsa loquitur is a circumstantial rule of evidence based on the principle that if an accident occurs under circumstances where it is so improbable that it could have happened short of negligent conduct, the mere happening of the incident may give rise to an inference that the defendant was negligent. If the nature of the case is such that res ipsa loquitur applies, the effect is that the defendant must rebut the presumption or inference of negligence by introducing a reasonable explanation of the occurrence consistent with no negligence as with the inference of negligence. (He does not have the burden of proving non-negligence on his part.)

In the previously mentioned *Wilcox v. Cavan*, the appeal court of New Brunswick overturned the decision of the trial judge and held the nurse to be negligent. Their rationale for so finding was that an injection of a drug shown to cause a blockage and gangrene raised the maxim of res ipsa loquitur, creating an inference of negligence on the part of the nurse in administering the drug. The appeal court concluded that the nurse did not rebut this presumption of negligence and that the evidence was sufficient to support the conclusion that gangrene would not have developed in the absence of fault in the administration of the injection. On appeal to the Supreme Court of Canada the court determined that the nurse had discharged the burden placed on her to rebut the presumption raised by the doctrine of res ipsa loquitur.

In order for the doctrine to be applicable three requisites must be met:
(1) The plaintiff must not know how or why the accident occurred.
(2) The accident must be one which would not ordinarily happen in the absence of negligent conduct.
(3) The defendant must have been in exclusive control of the event or situation.

(1) *The plaintiff must not know how or why the accident occurred:* When the facts of the case are known the doctrine is not applicable. In *Kolesar v. Jeffries et al,*[27] (1974) the Ontario court ruled that res ipsa loquitur did not apply because the cause of death was known. (This case involving the death of a patient following surgery is discussed in detail in chapter four: Tort of Negligence and the Nursing Process.) The actual cause of death was the inhalation by the patient of his stomach contents during the first night following surgery. (In this case the court did make a finding of nursing negligence.) In *Johnston v. Wellesley Hospital*[28] (1971) the Ontario court refused to apply the doctrine because the cause of the plaintiff's facial scarring (due to use of a carbon dioxide slush treatment) was known to the plaintiff. In *MacDonald v. York County Hospital Corporation*[29] (1973) the doctrine was applied by the Ontario court in the case where the plaintiff was hospitalized for treatment of a fractured ankle and in the process had his leg amputated because of irreversible gangrene. The plaintiff did not know how the damage occurred. The only reasonable inference that could be drawn was that the damage must have arisen out of the treatment or failure to treat the patient. The court ruled that the damage could

not have occurred without negligence. The orthopedic surgeon was unable to offer an explanation of the injury that was as consistent with no negligence as with negligence. Liability was therefore imposed.

(2) *The accident is one which would not ordinarily happen in the absence of negligent conduct:*
The doctrine of res ipsa loquitur comes into play when common experience (or the evidence itself) indicates that the mere happening of the injury itself may be considered as evidence that reasonable care was not used. For example, in *Eady v. Tenderenda,*[30] a decision of the Nova Scotia court, (ultimately appealed to the Supreme Court of Canada in 1973), the doctrine of res ipsa loquitur was applied in the situation where the defendant surgeon performed a mastoidectomy using the obsolete hammer and chisel method. Bone chips became imbedded in the plaintiff's facial nerve causing facial paralysis. In *Holmes v. The Board of Hospital Trustees of London*[31] the doctrine also applied where the defendant anesthetist performed a transtracheal ventilation in which the plaintiff suffered massive tissue emphysema and eventually became quadraplegic. Neither of the defendants in the foregoing cases were able to advance a reasonable explanation as to how the plaintiff's injuries could have occurred without fault on the part of the defendants.

The basic question is whether the anatomical area or part so injured, is ordinarily damaged in the course of the particular therapy or nursing care. For example, if a physician is engaged to remove the plaintiff's tonsils and does so successfully but in the process injures the plaintiff's tongue, an undiseased organ, which the physician was not engaged to treat, such injury would likely raise an inference of negligent conduct on the part of the physician.

In nursing the performance of injections, is usually carried out without blocking arteries and without injuring sciatic nerves. It is a matter of common knowledge and observation that such injuries do not ordinarily accompany the nursing technique of one possessing ordinary skill and experience. In such instances the failure of a defendant nurse to advance an explanation of the accident that is as consistent with no negligence as with negligence, will likely permit the court to conclude from the inference that the nurse was negligent.

However, not each and every accident will speak of negligence by its very occurrence. *Videto v. Kennedy*,[32] a 1980 decision of the Ontario courts involved an accident in which the physician perforated the plaintiff's bowel during a sterilization procedure. The reason for the perforation was unknown. The plaintiff had been positioned properly on the O.R. table but the bowel did not move out of place as it should have done. There was no evidence that the physician did not carry out all the procedures correctly. The court determined that the occurrence (the perforation) was not one that could not have happened, except for negligent conduct and therefore the doctrine would not be applied on mere suspicion only.

(3) *The defendant must have been in exclusive control of the circumstances leading up to the injury*:

The plaintiff, in order to avail of the res ipsa loquitur doctrine, must be able to point to the single defendant who had the management and control of the offending event. If the plaintiff's evidence points to two or more likely creators of the injury, the doctrine will not apply. In the hospital situation the physician or the nurse may not have that exclusive control. One author cites, under this prerequisite, the case of *Morris v. Winsbury-White*.[33] In that case, the defendant surgeon inserted certain tubes during a surgical procedure. Post-operatively a number of physicians and nurses were involved in the replacement of the tubes. Sometime following discharge from the hospital the plaintiff discovered a remnant of tube had been left in the bladder. The court held that res ipsa loguitur did not apply because the defendant surgeon was not in exclusive control and management for the period of treatment.

Once the foregoing prerequisites are met the defendant must offer a reasonable explanation in order to exonerate himself. In *Finlay v. Auld*[34] the defendant surgeon had performed a scalene node biopsy which confirmed a diagnosis of sarcoidosis. Following the procedure the plaintiff suffered a paralyzed vocal cord. Res ipsa loquitur was argued successfully. However the defendant then offered an explanation that the paralyzed vocal cord could have resulted from the disease itself. The court agreed that the physician had produced an explanation equally consistent with no negligence as with negligence. As a consequence the plaintiff was unable to discharge the ultimate burden of proof.

(c) Custom:

Concerns the traditional ways of behaving exhibited by members of a particular community group or profession, and may be an absolute defence to allegations of negligence:

> " ... The customs followed by a group are its collective habits, analogous to the individual habits of a person, whereby there is a tendency to repeat an act in the same way time after time." [35]

Evidence of custom has been admitted at trials of nursing negligence and medical negligence on the ground that the custom reflects the reaction of the profession to a similar danger indicating a composite judgment about the reasonable precautions to be taken. The nurse may successfully defend herself by evidence showing she conformed to the practices accepted as proper by a responsible sector of her profession. The courts have tended to accord great respect to "custom" in health care practice, possibly because of "greater judicial trust in the reasonableness of the practice of a sister profession than there is in the methods of commercial man". The courts have placed varying values on the fact of adherence to approved custom. Some courts have considered the fact relevant; others have considered it to be conclusive evidence; yet other courts have stated that approved custom is prima facie evidence of reasonable and prudent behavior on the part of the professional person.[36]

There is a heavy burden on the plaintiff who wishes to challenge established approved professional practice. The court will be reluctant to classify as negligent "the custom of the trade". However, the court will evaluate the custom in question, and if it finds that the practice is unsafe, such conduct will not be countenanced. In 1962 and 1964, two western Canada cases exonerated hospital staff on the basis of compliance with good custom. In the first case, the nursing staff failed to apply siderails and the pre-operative, elderly patient attempted to get out of bed, fell and fractured her hip. She subsequently died from a pulmonary embolism. The court accepted that good hospital practice had determined it was not necessary to use siderails in the circumstances. In the second case, the patient suffered from multiple sclerosis, a condition characterized by lack of muscle coordination. The patient fell out of bed. The nursing and medical personnel stated that a decision had been made to leave siderails down and the court concluded that the decision accorded with approved practice, (which approved practice had been set out for the court by uncontradicted expert evidence).[37] Review of the *Wilcox v. Cavan* case demonstrates the effect of compliance with custom. The nurse stated she had given the injection in accordance with accepted and approved method. In *Huber v. Burnaby Hospital* it appeared that the nurse did not adhere to the customary and approved method of administering injections.

(d) Error in Judgment and/or Nursing Misadventures:

Every phase of the nursing process calls for the exercise of independent nursing judgment. The nurse owes a duty to the patient not only to have reasonable knowledge, skill and care, but also to apply an *honest and intelligent exercise of judgment*. In a nursing negligence action, the defendant nurse may, in her defence, admit she made a mistake but state that such error was not due to "negligence" but to an *error in judgment*.

In determining whether a defence of *error in judgment* can prevail the court will have regard to all the circumstances existing at the time of the incident and may seek the answers to a series of questions including:

— What pertinent facts existed at the time of the nursing contact of which the nurse knew, or, in the exercise of due care, should have known?

— Was there an incorrect belief as to the existence or effect of matters of certain fact? If a determination of certain physical facts resolves itself into a question of judgment alone the nurse will not be held liable in negligence.

— Was the nursing decision made, one that was required to be made without delay and based on limited known or unknown facts?

— If there was an incorrect determination of a physical condition was there a reasonable opportunity for examination and was the true physical condition so apparent that such could have been ascertained by the exercise of the required care and skill?

— Did the nurse honestly and intelligently apply her mind to the problem presenting itself and arrive at a conclusion or judgment upon which she acted and which judgment subsequently proved to be wrong?

— Was the decision made by the nurse such that at least the preponderant opinion of nurses would have been against the decision or would the substantial opinion support the decision made?

In the previously mentioned *Dowey v. W.O. Rothwell and Assoc.*[38] the defence attempted unsuccessfully to convince the court that the nurse's decision to place the patient on an examining table and not supervise her (when the patient was a known epileptic, had stated she was experiencing an "aura" and had not taken her epileptic medication) was no more than error in judgment. The court applied the test of Rand J. in the 1956 decision of the Supreme Court of Canada in *Wilson v. Swanson*:[39]

" . . . The test can be no more than this: was the decision the result of the exercise of the surgical intelligence professed? Or was what was done such that disregarding it may be the exceptional case or individual, in all the circumstances, at least the preponderant opinion of the group would have been against it? "

The court in the previously analyzed *Dowey v. W.O. Rothwell* case concluded on its facts that what happened at the clinic was more than an error in judgment; it was a failure to provide that minimum standard of care that the patient had a right to expect. In *Haines v. Bellissimo*,[40] however, the defence was successful. The defendant psychiatrist and psychologist had treated the deceased who suffered from chronic schizophrenia and depression. The deceased had purchased a gun and when this fact was reported to the psychiatrist a complete assessment was carried out. On the basis of the assessment the defendants judged that the deceased did not have sufficient suicidal intentions as to require hospitalization. Later the deceased purchased another gun and shot himself. In a negligence action against the psychiatrist and psychologist the court concluded that the defendants had exercised reasonable skill and care and had made a diagnostic error in judgment. In *Meyer v. Gordon*[41] the defence was successful for one of the defendants who intervened to resusitate a newborn infant in an emergency situation created when the mother gave birth quickly (and without proper supervision from the nursing staff). (This case is analyzed in chapter four: Tort of Negligence and the Nursing Process.) The successful defendant was Dr. C an anesthetist who responded to the emergency and found the newborn infant was flaccid, pale and not breathing. The anesthetist proceeded to resusitate the newborn using the following procedures in the following order:
— Intubation
— Suction through the trachea
— Use of a positive pressure ventilation through a mask.
Medical experts disagreed on whether the procedure was appropriate and whether it caused further damage. One expert testified that the procedure used was not an accepted technique but the choice of procedure was a matter of judgment of the doctor and that time was of the essence. The court viewed the matter as Dr. C was

obliged to view the matter, namely as an emergency situation with a desperately ill, flaccid, pale newborn child who was not breathing. The court went on to note a principle set out in *Challand v. Bell*[42] to the effect that:

" " When the experts disagree but some of them support the treatment given, then surely the treatment given by the general practitioner should not be criticized, and one must always keep in mind the importance of viewing the treatment and seeing matters through the eyes of the attending physician. "

The court made a finding in *Meyer v. Gordon*[43] that the physician used an inappropriate technique which caused some delay but that such was an error in judgment and did not amount to negligence under the circumstances.

In *Elverson v. Doctors Hospital (1974)*[44] the defence of the defendant hospital was successful. In this case, the plaintiff's husband took his pregnant wife to the defendant hospital because she was bleeding and immediate nursing care was required. Two of the nurses employed by the hospital proceeded to elevate the foot of the patient's bed on blocks. The husband volunteered to assist in lifting the bed and thereby aggravated an old back injury. His action against the hospital alleged the nurses were negligent in failing to call for an orderly. Both at trial and on appeal the courts held there was no negligence but that, at most, the failure to call for an orderly was in the circumstances an error in judgment.

When an injury is due to an *error in judgment* by the nurse the event may be referred to as a *nursing misadventure*. Such is not negligence. The availability of this defence recognizes the concept that the practice of medicine (and nursing) is not an exact science and physicians and nurses are not guarantors or insurers that their cures and care will bring totally effective results:

" ... A proper sense of proportion requires us to have regard to the conditions in which hospitals and doctors (and nurses) have to work. We must insist on due care for the patient at every point, but we must not condemn as negligence that which is only a misadventure. "[45]

3. Critical Element # Three:
Presence of a Material Injury:

Without proof of material injury the court will not make a finding of "negligence". (In contrast, an action in assault, to succeed, does not require proof of injury.) This is so because it is the object or purpose of negligence law to place the plaintiff back in the position he was in prior to the occurrence of the negligent act. The injury must be "material" in the sense that it must be the type of loss or injury to one's person or one's property that is acknowledged by the courts. For example, the court does not acknowledge hurt feelings as a loss or injury to be compensated. In a case involving a severing of the uvula during a tonsillectomy, the court refused to acknowledge the loss of the structure (which had no known function) as a material loss. A nurse may be negligent every day of the week but an offended patient will not have a remedy sounding in negligence unless there is a material injury. If a material injury is present, the court will then have to quantify the amount of the appropriate award in money. Consider this example of a patient who is admitted to hospital for treatment of a myocardial infarct. He becomes mentally confused because of the pain. He falls from his bed causing a head injury and dies shortly after. The autopsy reveals the cause in fact of death to be massive coronary artery disease and that the head injury did not cause or accelerate the death. Assuming the hospital had a duty of care to this patient and the duty was breached because the assigned nurse failed to properly supervise the patient, the question becomes whether or not there was a material injury? The material injury the patient suffered due to negligence was a head injury which caused pain for certain minutes prior to death. The quantum of damages available for such a loss would be miniscule and certainly would not warrant commencing a costly action in negligence.

In determining the injuries or losses to be recognized the courts may approach the question from the "foreseeability" perspective. In 1978, a surgeon was sued in negligence for surgically removing the plaintiff's only kidney, having mistaken the structure for an ovary. The plaintiff's father subsequently donated his kidney. The Manitoba court held that the transplant was a foreseeable consequence of the surgeon's negligence, and that the father was entitled to have his loss compensated.[46]

4. Critical Element # Four:
Causation:

— Under what circumstances can it be said that a wrongdoer's conduct "caused" the injury or loss?
— Under what circumstances can it be said that more than one wrongdoer "caused" the injury or loss?
— Under what circumstances will the court likely hold one wrongdoer liable for the entire loss when other wrongdoers were also involved?
— Under what circumstances will the court allow one wrongdoer to be compensated by another wrongdoer, for part or all of the damages the former is required to pay to the injured plaintiff?
— Under what circumstances can it be said that the plaintiff himself contributed to his own loss?

All of the foregoing considerations may enter into the problem and legal effect of proof of causation of the injury or loss complained of by the plaintiff. Before there can be a finding of negligence on the part of a wrongdoer who has been named as a defendant, the plaintiff must prove a causal link between the defendant's act and the injury or loss. The courts approach the causation question by requiring the answer to the two following questions:

a. What was the cause in fact of the injury or loss?
b. What was the proximate cause of the injury or loss?

The first is a factual question which depends for its answer on the evidence brought before the court, and the second is a legal question which the court will determine through a rather complicated legal analysis. The latter involves the court in the use of certain formulas for the purpose of placing limits on liability

(a). Cause in Fact:

If the defendant's conduct did not cause the particular loss there is no liability. The burden is on the plaintiff to prove by a preponderance of evidence that the defendant's negligence was the effective cause of the loss, and if the burden is unable to be met, the negligence action will fail for the want of a causal connection. The question of what was the cause in fact, must be answered before answering the legal question of what is the proximate cause. Sometimes it is difficult to determine what the actual physical cause of the injury was, because it may not be automatically concluded that every negative body change or negative response to medical or nursing care was "caused" by defective intervention on the part of the physician or the nurse. To determine the cause in fact, the "but for" test is applied. The defendant's fault is a cause of the plaintiff's injury if such harm would not have occurred without, or *but for* the alleged defective conduct. Conversely it is not a "cause" of the harm, if the harm would have happened whether the fault was present or not. The court will conclude, in such instant, that the defendant's conduct was irrelevant to the causation of the injury. In the previously analyzed *Wilcox v. Cavan*[47] case the plaintiff suffered blockage of circulation to his hand following an injection of antibiotic. The blockage resulted in gangrene and subsequent amputation of part of his fingers. The plaintiff was unsuccessful in his allegation that the physician's negligence caused his injury because he exercised undue delay in attending him following the injection. The court dismissed the action against the physician on the basis that the evidence failed to prove medical follow-up could have prevented the subsequent gangrene, and was, therefore, of no causal relationship to the loss suffered by the plaintiff.

In the more recent case *Yepremian v. Scarborough General Hospital et al*[48] the courts used the language of "insulation from liability". The facts of the case suggest that the first two physicians who intervened in the plaintiff's care did so negligently, but their negligent acts did not factually cause the plaintiff's cardiac arrest which reduced the plaintiff to a vegetable state.

In October 1970 the plaintiff, who at the time was nineteen years of age, had been feeling unwell. He complained specifically of increased urination and polydipsia (excessive thirst). His family physician was on holiday when the plaintiff's parents brought him to the office. Dr. G, a physician who had graduated a year previously, and was then in research was relieving for the family physician. Dr. G diagnosed the plaintiff's condition as tonsillitis, gave him a prescription and stated it was not necessary for him to go to hospital. Later in the night the plaintiff hyperventilated so the parents took the young man to the emergency department of the defendant hospital. There he was seen by a Dr. C, who did not complete a proper medical assessment and ordered valium for the already semi-comotosed patient. The plaintiff was then transferred to the intensive care unit where Dr. R attended him. Dr. R was an internist and specialist in endocrinology. Diabetes mellitus was his specialty. He was not an employee of the hospital but was an independent contractor with admitting privileges to the institution. Dr. R failed to diagnose the condition. Eleven hours after admission to the unit a registered nurse diagnosed the condition as possible diabetes mellitus on the basis of the characteristic fruity odour of the breath. To this point no urinalysis had been done (which test would have identified the condition). When Dr. R learned of the diagnosis he calculated the amount of sodium bicarbonate inaccurately. He ordered an excessive injection of insulin the natural result of which was to reduce the level of blood potassium. Once this blood product falls to a certain level the expected effect, if left untreated, is cardiac arrest. The plaintiff did arrest and suffered severe brain damage.

The plaintiff, through his next friend sued the hospital, and Dr. G. Neither Dr. C or Dr. R were sued.

The court determined that the cause in fact of the plaintiff's loss was the cardiac arrest which in turn was caused by the negligence of Dr. R in failing to diagnose the diabetic condition earlier, and on diagnosis, his failure to administer sufficient potassium soon enough to counteract the known effect that insulin has on the blood potassium level. The court went on to conclude that Dr. R's negligence was the factual and legal cause of the plaintiff's loss. It also dismissed the action against Dr. G on the basis that although Dr. G's conduct was negligent his negligence was *insulated* from liability by the subsequent negligence of Dr. R. The court also suggested that if wrongdoer Dr. C had been sued (i.e. made a defendant) he would not have been found liable, because his conduct was also *insulated from liability* by the ultimate negligence of Dr. R.

The difficulty in the case was that wrongdoer Dr. R had not been sued. Counsel for the plaintiff had the task of persuading the court that the defendant hospital should be held liable for Dr. R's negligence. Since Dr. R was not a hospital employee, the plaintiff could only obtain a remedy if the defendant hospital was found to be liable in breach of its contract to the patient, or because it was personally negligent by some failure of its corporate duty to the patient, or on the basis of vicarious negligence. (The court's consideration of the foregoing is discussed under the concept of corporate negligence later in the chapter.)

Despite the use of "insulation of liability" language in the Yepremian case it cannot be said that a series of negligent actors whose conduct constitute, in combination, the cause in fact of the plaintiff's injury, will be protected from liability for their negligence because of the negligent activity of subsequent wrongdoers in the chain of events. On the contrary, the courts have used the *substantial factor test* and the concept of *materially increasing the risk* to determine how long the causation chain is to be extended and which of the defendants will be held to have "caused" the loss. The courts use labels such as *joint tortfeasors joint and several liability, vicarious liability,* and *contributory negligence.* These suggest what defendants are to be held to have caused the loss, and how much of the loss any one defendant is to be required to pay, and whether or not the defendant who actually pays the plaintiff's loss, can look to any of the other defendants in the causation chain (or to wrongdoers who were not sued and therefore not defendants) to reimburse him.

In terms of causation there is commonly an involvement or interaction of several (though independent) causes producing a single indivisible result for which a number of wrongdoers will be answerable for either the whole or a part of the damages. The conduct of two or more wrongdoers might have been simultaneous, as when two nurses are performing a nursing procedure which injures the patient. The conduct of the two or more wrongdoers might have been successive. For example, a physician gives a defective medical order thereby creating a situation fraught with danger which does not culminate in injury until a nurse intervenes and carries out the defective medical order, as in *Meyer v. Gordon.* Alternatively the acts of a series of wrongdoers may be quite separate in time, and result in a single injury or in more than one injury, as will be seen in the *Kolesar case.* The effect of the foregoing, on a particular defendant, and the amount of the loss he will have to pay has a number of interesting permutations. Basically, if the acts of two or more people are both *substantial factors* in bringing about the result, liability will be imposed on both.[49]

Sometimes there may be a question as to the actual physical cause of the injury complained of, as in *Meyer v. Gordon.* The court disposed of the question this way: In their suit the plaintiffs, on behalf of their severely brain damaged newborn, alleged the damage was caused by lack of supervision of the mother during active labour, and a consequent rapid delivery without the assistance of the defendant physician. The court held the defendant hospital to be seventy-five percent liable (on a vicarious liability basis) for the personal negligence of its nursing staff. The defendant physician was held to be twenty-five percent liable for the same injury. The courts applied a principle from a 1972 decision of the House of Lords. The latter set out the rule that:

" A defendant is liable in negligence if his breach of duty has materially contributed to the injuries suffered by the plaintiff notwithstanding that there were other factors, for which the defendant was not responsible, which had contributed to the injury. "[50]

The court in *Meyer v. Gordon*, in applying the above principle concluded that:

" ...the failure of the nursing staff to examine Mrs. Meyer and render proper care and their leaving her unattended in the supine position *materially increased the risk of injury* to the child and materially increased the risk of fetal distress and the resulting hypoxia. "[51]

The Meyer court noted that the foregoing principle expressed by the House of Lords was applied in Canada by the Manitoba Court of Appeal:

" ...I think the law in Canada is that, where a tortfeasor creates or materially contributes to a significant risk of injury occurring and injury does occur which is squarely within the risk thus created or materially increased, then unless the risk is spent the tortfeasor is liable for injury which follows from the risk, even though there are other subsequent causes which also cause or materially contribute to that injury. "[52]

(b) Proximate Cause

Once it is determined that the nurse's negligent conduct was the actual physical cause or "cause in fact" of the injury, the second branch of causation must be met before the plaintiff can succeed. This second branch is referred to as the *proximate cause* and is an artificial device constructed by the courts to limit liability; for courts have determined, as a principle, that negligent persons shall not be liable for any and all consequences of their negligent conduct. As one author described the problem:

" The matter under consideration is the extent to which an actor will be held liable for his substandard conduct. If he drops a lighted match into a waste basket, will he be held

liable for the building if it burns down, for the entire block if it goes, for the whole city if it is destroyed? Must he compensate someone who is burned in the neighbouring building? What if the victim becomes mentally deranged because of his disfigurement? What if a rescuer is hurt trying to extricate him? What if the doctor who treats him bungles the operation? What if he commits suicide?... "[53]

If there aren't some limits imposed by the courts the causation chain would stretch into infinity, with each act being linked to every other act. Thus, the courts have devised a test to limit the chain of consequences for which the actor will be liable. The test is commonly referred to as the *foreseeability test*: The defendant will be liable only for those consequences which were foreseeable to a reasonable person in the defendant's position at the time. Any loss which falls outside of that which is reasonably foreseeable would be considered by the court to be *too remote* and therefore not compensable.

This concept is not a simple one nor is its legal application easily predicted. At its simplest it may be said that the foreseeability test both determines whether negligence will be found, and if found, what injury or loss will be recognized. In an Alberta case in 1965, the court considered the situation where the plaintiff asked to ride in the defendant's car. At one of the stops the defendant drank a considerable amount of alcohol. Later, while the plaintiff drove, the defendant grabbed the wheel and forced the car out of control. As a consequence of the defendant's actions, the plaintiff was forced to walk several miles in sub-zero weather. He suffered frostbite and required amputation of his feet. The defendant was found to be liable as he should have foreseen the dangerous consequences likely to flow from grabbing the wheel. The plaintiff's wife left him because he was disabled. The court determined that the plaintiff's loss of consortium was *too remote* a loss for it to be compensable, but the other more foreseeable losses were allowed.[54]

In the case where the defendant surgeon

removed the plaintiff's only kidney when he mistook it for the woman's ovary, the plaintiff's father donated his kidney. The court held that the transplant was a foreseeable consequence of the negligent act for which the defendant was required to compensate.[55]

c. Joint Tortfeasors, Joint and Several Liability and Contribution:

When is it fair to hold one wrongdoer liable when the conduct of the other wrongdoers are involved in causing the injury? And what is the legal effect?

Following is a brief examination of how the courts distributed the losses in *Kolesar v. Jeffries, Joseph Brant Memorial Hospital et al*[56]

On January 2, 1969, the late Mr. Kolesar suffered a back injury due to a motor vehicle accident caused by the defendant Jeffries. (It was admitted that the collision was due solely to the latter's negligence.) A year later the defendant's surgeon performed a spinal fusion to correct the back injury. After the surgery, Mr. Kolesar was placed on a Stryker frame and transferred to the surgical ward of the defendant hospital. At five a.m. the following morning he (the patient) was found dead by the nurses on the night shift.

The family sued the motorist, the surgeon (against whom the action was dismissed), the defendant hospital and the nurses.

The court stated that the motorist, whose negligent operation of the car caused the injury and surgery, was also liable for the death since the nursing error was not completely outside the range of normal experience. Essentially the court is saying that it is foreseeable that the repair of the injury due to the negligence of the first tortfeasor, could be done negligently. If such happens the first tortfeasor may be liable to the plaintiff for the entire loss.

In the Kolesar case the court rendered judgment of liability as follows:
— Against the motorist for damages sustained by the late Mr. Kolesar up to the time of his death: $11,679.09
— Against the motorist, the hospital and one nurse employee for damages sustained to the estate by the death of Mr.

Kolesar: $101,901.09
— For the motorist, entitlement to be reimbursed by the other judgment defendants to the extent of any portion of the $101,901.09 the motorist is called on by the plaintiff to pay. (Entitlement to contribution). The foregoing points up the fact that when one and the same injury or loss is attributable to the negligence of two or more wrongdoers the liability may be:
— **joint or**
— **joint and several**.

Participation in a joint tort results in collective responsibility for the resulting harm in the sense that the negligence of one is imputed to the other. Wrongdoers, if sued, may become joint tortfeasors if the evidence shows they acted *together, in concert,* in some common enterprise in which their collective negligent behaviors form the proximate cause of the resulting loss. If the resulting harm to which both tortfeasors contributed, is considered by the court to be indivisible, each of the wrongdoers will be answerable for all of the damage and the plaintiff may choose which of the defendants is better able to pay for the losses awarded by the court and proceed to collect from that defendant.

If the loss can be divided the court may hold each defendant liable only for the amount of the damage that he has inflicted. In *Meyer v. Gordon* recall that the court assigned seventy-five percent of the liability to the hospital and twenty-five percent to the physician.

Tortfeasors may be found to have joint and several liability when they, in independent negligent acts, cause the one injury:

" The only nexus between the defendants is that the damage would not have occurred without the negligence of both of them ... They are admittedly both liable for the total damage, but their liability is several, not joint, and therefore spares them from the peculiar consequences of joint liability. "[57]

When the liability is "several" and the plaintiff has collected from one of the tortfeasors for the total amount of the judgment, legislation now provides a right to the defendant to apply to the courts for a *contribution* from the other wrongdoer (who may or may not have been sued by the plaintiff). Commonly, if the plaintiff has not sued one of the wrongdoers involved in the chain of events, the named defendant may apply to have the person joined as a *third party*, for the purpose of obtaining possible reimbursement for any losses he will be called on to pay. For example, in the health care institutional setting, the employer may be called on as a defendant, not because of any personal negligence on the part of the employer, but because courts may find him to be *vicariously liable* for the personal negligence of its servants. In such an instance (as in the Kolesar case) the courts may make a finding of *joint liability*.

5. Critical Element # Five:
Absence of:
(a) Contributory Negligence
(b) Voluntary Assumption of Risk

The courts have recognized that plaintiffs owe certain duties of care to themselves, and it may well be that a plaintiff's conduct in the chain of negligent events will, partially or completely, defeat his claim. The onus is on the defendant to plead and prove any such defences, as for example that the plaintiff contributed to his own loss, or that the plaintiff voluntarily assumed the risk. A defendant nurse in a negligence suit would have the burden of proving that the patient who sued her was not a reasonable and prudent patient in the circumstances. The first of the two defences offered above has been successfully pleaded in medical negligence suits in Canada.

(a) Contributory Negligence:
Refers to the plaintiff's failure to adhere to that standard of care required of the reasonable and prudent man. If such failure is proven to be one of the contributing causes in fact of the injury together with the defendant's negligence, the court will find that such contributory negligence constitutes one of the proximate causes in law. Such a finding will have a bearing on the quantum of net damages flowing to the

plaintiff in the event negligence is found to be present by the court. It is suggested that the plaintiff's negligence will not make a causal link in the negligence chain unless it is shown by the defendant that *"but for"* the contributory negligence the accident would not have happened, or the injuries would not have been as severe. Once the cause in fact is established, the courts will then determine the plaintiff's negligence to be a proximate cause if the loss complained of "resulted from the type of risk to which the plaintif exposed himself". For example a plaintiff who drives without a licence is not precluded from recovery if this omission is not a proximate cause of the accident.[58] The plaintiff is not necessarily barred by virtue of the fact that he or she has engaged in an unlawful act.

The legal effect of a court finding contributing negligence is the apportioning of the liability as provided by the contributory negligence statute of the province concerned. If the portion of liability can be clearly severed from that of the defendant the courts will so sever it and if not the division may well be on a fifty-fifty basis. In *Crossman v. Stewart*[59] the court made a finding of contributory negligence on the part of the patient who suffered eye damage due to extended use of a drug which she obtained from a drug salesman. The court determined that although the physician was liable for failure to warn of the side effects of the initial prescription, the plaintiff herself was also liable and to the extent of $66^2/_3$ percent. This distribution of the liability effectively reduced any damages awarded to the plaintiff by that percentage. The Supreme Court of Canada in *Hopital Notre Dame De L'Esperance v. Laurent*[60] found the plaintiff to be contributorily negligent. The plaintiff had fallen and injured herself while curling. The defendant physician had examined her but failed to x-ray her bruised hip. The plaintiff continued to walk around for some three months while experiencing severe pain. When she consulted another physician, he diagnosed a fracture of the hip with complications due to the delay in treatment.

In *Dowey v. Rothwell*[61] the plaintiff had

stopped taking her anti-epileptic drugs because of her religious affiliation. She consequently suffered a grand mal seizure which caused loss of consciousness. The latter was the effective cause of her fall from the examining table while in the care of the defendant nurse. Apparently the defence of contributory negligence was not raised in that case.

(b) Voluntary Assumption of Risk:

No wrong is done to one who consents. The principle of voluntary assumption of risk states that the plaintiff, in consenting (expressly, or impliedly) to assume a particular risk, will insulate the defendant from any liability in the event of injury or loss suffered by the consenting plaintiff.

This defence places the burden on the defendant to prove that the plaintiff had knowledge of the risk, understood its nature, undertook the risk voluntarily, and finally, exempted the defendant. (This defence is basic to the concept of failure to inform in negligence and assault discussed in Chapters three and four.)

V. Direct and Vicarious Liability in Negligence:

The foregoing concerns the nature of the legal accountabilities of the *corporate authority* in health care institutions, which authority commonly has an employer-employee relationship with registered nurses. Examination of the duties of the corporation reveal that it can be held "personally" liable for breach of its duties to the patient. As well it will be seen that the corporation may be held *vicariously liable* for the breach of legal duties owed to the patient by certain users of the health care facilities. This latter liability is not based on a breach of the corporation's personal duties but on the basis of *respondent superior*: Let the master answer.

1. Direct Liability:

A corporation is the artificial creation by statute, of a legal entity whereby the entity becomes endowed with certain powers, rights and duties. "Incorporation" associates a number of people, in succession, in such a way that the people making up the members of the corporation are legally separate and distinct from the personality and existence of the corporation itself.

The statute vests the powers, rights and duties of the corporation in the *board of trustees* of the corporation for the purpose of governing, controlling and managing the health care institution. The board of trustees becomes the "master" and is held accountable for:
— Statutory duties
— Contractual duties
— Certain common law duties to avoid foreseeable harm to patients recognized in a doctrine of direct negligence
— Certain common law duties to indemnify the patient who is harmed by the negligent acts or omissions of the corporation's employees and servants recognized in the doctrine of vicarious negligence.

The direct duties owed by the corporation to the patient, a breach of which would constitute corporate negligence, are "non-delegable". This means that responsibility for the duties cannot be gotten rid of by the board even though the function itself was assigned to an employee of the board. If the direct duty of care falls below the required standard, the corporation must answer to the patient for any damage due to such breach. Those *direct* corporate duties remain with the corporate authority whether the corporation acts through its employees or through such independent contractors as physicians using the facilities through the route of "admitting privileges".

The duties owed by the corporation directly to the patient include:
— A duty to select professional staff, using reasonable care
— A duty to review staff performance on a periodic basis
— A duty to provide reasonable supervision of staff
— A duty to provide for adequate staffing, equipment and resources, and appropriate work scheduling, and organization.

The foregoing does not imply that the board of trustees involves itself in the day to day management of the institution. Rather it requires that the board of trustees identify the "mission" of the institution, and exercise care in the appointment of the "administrator" or the chief executive officer of the institution, delegate to him responsibility for ensuring the foregoing duties are attended to and require that he account to the board of trustees on a regular basis on the status of the situation.

The most recent case concerning liability of hospital corporations for breach of a direct duty of care is that of *Yepremian v. Scarborough General Hospital*[62], the facts of which case were set out in this chapter under the concept of "Insulation from Liability". In addition to that concept, the case dealt directly with the issue of whether the hospital corporation was accountable for the injury caused by the negligence of Dr. R, an independent contractor on staff at the hospital who had not been sued by the solicitor for the plaintiff. Consequently counsel was faced with the challenge of proving to the court that on the particular facts of the case, the hospital corporation was liable.

At trial the court noted that the *Public Hospitals Act of Ontario* imposed a duty on the hospital to admit a patient in need of active treatment and that the intent of the particular wording of the act was to make the hospital authority responsible for the quality of medical care provided in the hospital. The trial judge went on to acknowledge that:

— A hospital is not responsible for the negligence of a physician not employed by the hospital when that physician was personally retained by the patient
— A hospital is liable for the negligence of a physician where the latter is an employee of the hospital
— Where the physician is not an employee and is not personally retained by the patient, all of the circumstances must be considered in order to decide whether the hospital was under a non-delegable duty of care to the patient concerned.

The court stated that the Yepremian case fell within the last-named situation. The semi-comatosed patient was taken to the hospital by his parents because he was seriously ill and in need of treatment. The plaintiff was assessed in the emergency department by a physician not of his choice. Rather the patient "got the luck of the draw". When the patient was later admitted to the intensive care unit, again, he did not select or engage the physician who attended him and whose negligence caused him to arrest and suffer irreversible brain damage. The trial judge determined that in the circumstances, by accepting this patient, the hospital undertook toward him a duty of care that could not be delegated.

On appeal the court with five judges considered whether the hospital undertook to provide competent medical care, or did it only undertake to select competent physicians. (It was not alleged that the hospital breached any duty in the process of selecting the physician and granting him admitting privileges to the institution.) Three of the five judges concluded that the corporation did not have such a non-delegable duty. Rather, that its duty was restricted to the reasonable selection of professional staff, which duty the corporation had met.

Two of the remaining judges on the appeal court dissented, contending there was such a duty of care owed by the board. They acknowledged the profound changes in social structures and public attitudes relating to medical services and the changing role of hospitals in the delivery of health care. The duty was deemed to have been created by several factors: the public's increasing reliance on hospitals for medical treatment, and in particular, emergency services, and the fact that the defendant hospital held itself out as offering such services. The second dissenting judge concluded that the duty owed should be consistent with the role that the hospital takes on. If the hospital functions merely as a provider of medical care facilities no responsibility for independent contractors would then exist. However, if the hospital functions as a place where a person in need of treatment goes to obtain it, such circumstances create that extended duty of care.

Leave to appeal the decision to the Supreme Court of Canada was granted. Prior to hearing of this important appeal, the insurers for the defendant negotiated a multi-million dollar settlement and the action was discontinued.

In the event a health care institution is found directly liable for the omissions of its servants, such will preclude the employer from turning to the employee to indemnify the employer for the negligence concerned (which the employer in theory could do under the umbrella of vicarious negligence). The movement in this direction has a negative repercussion by insulating the employee from the consequences of his substandard behavior. Such cancels out a policy basis of negligence, that of educating the public and the tortfeasor that substandard behavior is not to be tolerated. However such a movement does acknowledge the reality, that health care institutions today offer comprehensive service in a system in which the patient often has no freedom of choice about the person who delivers that care to him.

2. *Vicarious Negligence:*

" In my opinion authorities who run a hospital be they local authorities, government boards or any other corporation are in law under the self same duty as the humblest doctor. Whenever they accept a patient for treatment they must use reasonable care and skill to cure him of his ailment. The hospital authorities cannot do it by themselves. They have no ears to listen through the stethoscope and no hands to hold the knife. They must do it by the staff which they employ and if their staff are negligent in giving the treatment they are just as liable for that negligence as anyone else who employs others to do his duties for him ... Once they undertake the task they come under a duty to use care in the doing of it and that is so whether they do it for reward or not. It is no answer for them to say that their staff are professional men and women who do not tolerate any interference by their lay masters in the way they do their work ... *The reason why the employers are liable in such cases is not because they can control the way in which the work is done, they often have not sufficient knowledge to do so but because they employ the staff and have chosen them for the task and have in their hands the ultimate sanction for good conduct —the power of dismissal ...* " [63]

In its meanings "vicarious" includes "suffered in place of another person or thing".

Vicarious Negligence, in law, holds one person responsible for the misconduct of another although the person is, himself, free from personal blameworthiness or fault. The consequence is that the person or corporate entity may be required to pay the damages in place of the actual tortfeasor. Canadian law recognizes a vicarious liability of employers for the negligence of its or his employees if and when the servant or employee was acting within the scope of his employment or authority at the time of the incident complained of. Whether or not vicarious liability will be said to exist depends upon the nature of the relationship between the tortious servant and the employer. The courts may apply the organizational test to determine whether the tortfeasor was part of the employer's organization: was his work subject to the coordinated control as to the where and when rather than the how? Evidence of the employer's efforts to control the activities of such employees is evidenced by written job descriptions and policy and procedure manuals in the health care institutions.

VI. Limitation Periods:

Refer to the time within which a legal action must be commenced, after the expiry of which time period it will be said that the matter is time barred. By statute there are procedural rules governing the limitation periods affecting certain causes of action and certain types of defendants. These statutes are called statutes of limitation and their purpose is to effect an "act of peace". They are designed to protect defendants from a never-ending threat of liability, and to induce the plaintiff not to sleep on his rights. Through such statutes the courts guarantee the defendant that after passage of a certain period of time the incident will be closed as a matter of law.

In order to determine the limitation period it is important to know when a right of action arises and the nature of the right of action. The limitation periods will vary in accordance with whether the cause of action is founded in:

— Breach of Contract
— Negligence
— Assault
— Defamation
— False Imprisonment.

Nurses commonly have a contractual relationship with health care institutions. Less frequently, the nurse is engaged directly by the patient in a contractual relationship to render nursing care in consideration of a certain fee per shift. If the nurse sues the employer, or the patient, or alternatively, the patient sues a hospital or a nurse in contract, the question becomes: when does the time begin to run and when does the limitation period expire, and what if any activity or event will cause the limitation period to be extended?

Depending on the wording of the particular act one may be barred from obtaining a remedy for breach of contract after six years have elapsed from "the time the right of action" arises. A right of action does not arise in contract until there has been a *breach* of the contract. If the employer, for example, refuses to pay the nurse the salary owed for a particular work period, a breach will have occurrred. The nurse may be required to initiate an action within six years from the date of the breach in order to obtain legal redress. However, although the nurse loses her right to the remedy, the cause of action itself is not necessarily extinguished. Consequently, the debtor might cause an entirely new limitation period to commence to run, if, for example, the debtor, makes a part payment of the debt, or makes a new offer in writing to pay the debt.

The applicable time period in a negligence action is determined by whether the defendant is an ordinary member of the public and thereby subject to a general statute of limitations or is a member of a hospital, or a profession of nurses, or physicians, or pharmacists etc. There may be a special protection built in to the limitation statute itself or, in the statute regulating the particular profession in the province concerned. For example sec. 31 of the *Saskatchewan Registered Nurses, Act* provides that:

" No registered nurse or certified nursing assistant shall be liable in any action for negligence or malpractice by reason of services requested or rendered by the person unless the action is commenced within one year from the date of the occurrence of the incident which gives rise to the cause of action. "[64]

In Ontario, the *Health Disciplines Act* provides for an abbreviated time period governing suits against nurses and physicians coming within the aegis of that act:

" No duly registered member of a College is liable to any action arising out of negligence or malpractice in respect of professional services requested or rendered unless such action is commenced within one year from the date when the person commencing the action knew or ought to have known the fact or facts upon which he alleges negligence or malpractice. "[65]

In contrast the limitation periods provided within general statutes of limitations, and governing the members of the general public could expose a person to liability for negligence for as much as six years from the date when the damage occurred. The special limitations provided for physicians in some jurisdictions is even more restrictive, requiring the patient to institute action, in some instances, within "one year from the cessation of the treatment". British Columbia, in its Medical Act provided such a limitation. It protected the physician in the 1979 case of *Whiston v. Deane*.[66] The Supreme Court dismissed the plaintiff's action against the defendant surgeon for alleged negligent tubal ligation. The plaintiff became pregnant three years following surgery. The court concluded that the matter was statute barred since the action was not commenced within "one year from cessation of treatment". (The wording of the Ontario *Health Disciplines Act* would suggest that the Whiston type of situation might have better prospects if it occurred in Ontario since there, the plaintiff has one year from "the date that the person . . . knew or ought to have known the fact".)

If the defendant nurse or physician is an employee of the hospital, and the province provides a special limitation period for hospitals, the question becomes: Is the nurse employee protected under the limitation period for the hospital or, where provision is made in the Nurses Act, by the latter. This was raised in *Dobson et al v. Wellington Tavern (Windsor) Ltd. et al; Paolotto et al, Third Parties*:[67] The defendant hospital and its nurses applied to set aside a court order adding them as defendants. The application was denied. On appeal to the motions court judge, the latter allowed the application on the basis that the two year limitation period, set out s. 28 of the *Public Hospitals Act*, R.S.O. 1980 c. 410, was applicable and barred the action. On further appeal the application was disallowed. The issue of whether the plaintiff's action was statute barred was left to be resolved at trial. (There was apparent conflict between section 37 of *Ontario's Public Hospital's Act* and section 17 of the Province's *Health Discipline Act*. At issue was which of the statutes applied with respect to the nurse employed by the public hospital. If section 37 applied, the factual issue of when the plaintiff "ceased to receive treatment" within the meaning of the act had to be resolved. If section 17 applied, the factual issue to be resolved was when the plaintiff "knew or ought to have known" the facts upon which the allegation of negligence was being made. There could be a wide variation in the times available to the plaintiff.)

If the hospital, physician or nurse provides services to the patient after the applicable limitation period has expired, the subsequent services may cause the limitation period to start running once again. For example, limitation periods governing hospitals and physicians usually provide for the period to expire one or two years from "cessation of treatment" or from "date of discharge". In the 1977 Nova Scotia case *MacKenzie v. Vance*,[68] the plaintiff had been admitted to the hospital and the defendant surgeon treated his fractured elbow. The plaintiff alleged he suffered permanent damage caused by the physician's negligence. The limitation period expired. Subsequently, the physician completed a physical examination of the plaintiff and completed forms for worker's compensation. This service caused the limitation

period to commence again. The defendant was then successful in his application to have the hospital and the nurse employee joined as *third* parties for purposes of *contribution* to any damages the defendant surgeon might have to pay the plaintiff. This was permitted by the court despite the fact that the limitation period had expired against the hospital and the nurse. The decision was rationalized on the facts of the case and the rights available to the defendant pursuant to the province's *Tortfeasor's Act*. The right to contribution would only arise if and when a judgment was rendered against the defendant, which right, concluded the court, should not be barred before it arose.

In *Abbott et al v. Cook*,[69] another Nova Scotia case, the plaintiff sued two physicians for alleged negligent diagnosis of a serious thyroid condition and mistreatment by use of improper and injurious medication. The plaintiff contended that one limitation period, which would have otherwise expired, was reactivated because the defendants continued to treat her after the injury, in that she continued to take medication prescribed and, or, recommended by the defendants. At issue was whether the continuing of medication constituted continuing of "professional services" within the meaning of Nova Scotia's Statute of Limitations.

In summary, for those persons at risk because of alleged negligent, assaultive or other tortious conduct (such as defamation, and false imprisonment), it is advisable to consult counsel regardless of the preconception one has with respect to limitation periods. It may well be that, on the facts of the case, the limitation of time is not easily determined. In *Perrie v. Martin*[70] (1982) the Ontario High Court ruled sec 17 of the *Health Disciplines Act* applied so that a negligence action for surgery performed in 1969, was not statute barred.

For persons within health care institutions involved in designing policies directed to the reduction of risks in negligence, assault and other torts, etc., direction should be received from the institution's legal counsel concerning the impact of current legislation and case law on point.

VII. Use of the Jury in Civil Trials:

Juries are available in Canada for use in criminal trials. However, their use in civil trials is somewhat more limited and their use in trials of medical and nursing negligence is again much more circumspect. Commonly, if either the plaintiff or defendant wishes to avail of a jury, he or she is required to serve notice of such intention to the parties on the other side. If the other party wishes to oppose the application, he may apply to a judge to have the jury notice struck out.

Generally there is a tendency on the part of the courts to refuse jury trials for negligence actions against health care professionals on the policy basis that malpractice actions involve highly technical and complex issues beyond the comprehension of the minds of ordinary men and women making up the jury. The courts were concerned that physicians not be left entirely at the mercy of juries. There was a hesitancy on the part of the courts to permit juries to be involved in the determination of simple questions such as whether the leaving of gauze in a surgical wound could constitute reasonable surgical practice.[71] Such refusal was common in Ontario until 1976 when the courts refused to strike out the jury notice if the issue was not the surgeon's liability in negligence, but the restricted question of the amount of damages to be assessed against him. At that time the court stated:

> " ...there is no good reason why a member of the medical profession should be automatically insulated from the judgment of members of the public so far as cost of his mistake or his negligence is concerned. "[72]

In 1978 the appeal courts of British Columbia upheld the decision of the trial court to refuse to strike the jury notice in a trial regarding the alleged failure to diagnose an infection.[73] The Nova Scotia courts struck out the jury notice in *Marshall v. Curry*[74] but refused to do so in the later case of *Eady v. Tederenda*[75] in 1975 and refused to do so in *Hearn v. Bear and the Halifax Infirmary*, on which point the court stated:

> " ...the judge must exercise his discretion in each case bearing in mind the plaintiff's right to a jury trial and the nature of the action... having regard to the issues involved and the nature of the medical evidence I am satisfied that the issues can properly be tried by a jury. The issues in this case appear to be no more complex or difficult than in many other jury cases. "[76]

In 1978 the Prince Edward Island court of appeal refused to strike out a jury notice (in an action against the physician alleging that surgery was performed on the wrong limb).[77] In 1982 the British Columbia Supreme Court did strike out a jury notice in *Foote et al v. Royal Columbian Hospital et al.*[78] The plaintiff had sued a physician and a hospital in negligence and the co-defendants alleged negligence against each other. The trial was expected to last at least five weeks and the discoveries for trial had lasted twenty days. The court held that although the plaintiff had a *prima facie* right to a jury, the issues in the case were of an intricate and complex character and a judgment would require prolonged examination of documents of a scientific nature. The court ordered that the jury notice be struck.

The whole thrust behind the arguments for and against jury trials in health care negligence in Canada is the awareness of the American system and trends. The presence of juries are commonplace in the United States and the effect of the jury system is that higher damages are frequently awarded than are usually available in a trial before a judge alone. The question becomes whether it is fair, in the Canadian system, to continue to confer an exceptional privilege upon members of health care professions and institutions, particularly in this time of increasing sophistication of community members making up the jury systems.

Any concern on the part of the Canadian health care establishment that the number and scope of negligence actions against their members is taking on proportions of a service industry similar to the American scene, is not well founded. One has only to peruse the relatively few cases reported in the Canadian jurisdictions, cull from those, the numbers in which patients successfully proved liability in negligence, and examine the conservative quantum of damages awarded, to know that the system is not well weighted in favour of patient plaintiffs.

VIII. Endnotes:

1. Blyth v. Birmingham Waterworks Co. (1856) ll Exch. 781 at p. 784
2. See Fleming J.G. The Law of Torts, Law Book Co. Ltd, (Sydney, Australia, 1983), and Linden A.M. Canadian Tort Law, 3rd ed. (Toronto, Butterworths & Co. Canada Ltd. 1982).
3. Nova Mink Ltd. v. T.C.A. [1951] 2 D.L.R. 241 at 254
4. Supra n. 3 at p. 254
5. Donoghue v. Stevenson [1932] A.C. 562 at p. 580
6. Dowey v. Rothwell [1974] 5 W.W.R. 311
7. Black H.C. Black's Law Dictionary, (St. Paul's, Minn. West Publ. 1979)
8. Rex v. Bateman [1925], 41 T.L.R. 557 at p. 559
9. Harmer v. Cornelius (1858) 141 E.R. 94
10. Supra n. 6
11. Supra n. 6 at p. 318
12. Supra n. 6 at p. 319 citing Rex v. Bateman Supra n. 8
13. Supra n. 6 at p. 319
14. Supra n. 6 at p. 313
15. Supra n. 6 at p. 321
16. Linden A.M. *Canadian Tort Law* (3rd.ed), Toronto (Butterworths & Co. Canada Ltd, 1982 p. 102)
17. Supra n. 5 at p. 580
18. Supra n. 5 at p. 580
19. Supra n. 1
20. Supra n. 8 at 48
21. Lamphier v. Phipos (1838), 8 C & P. 475 at 478
22. Wilson v. Swanson [1956] S.C.R. 804 at p. 811
23. Wilcox v. Cavan [1975] 2 S.C.R. 663. 9 N.B.R. (2d) 140, 2 N.R. 618, 50 D.L.R. (3d) 687 reversing 7 N.B.R. (2d) 192, 44 D.L.R. (3d) 42. See also Fiege v. Cornwall G. Hosp. (1980) 3 O.D.R. (2d) 691
24. Supra n. 23 (1975) 50 D.L.R. (3d) at p. 691
25. Supra n. 23 at p. 696
26. Huber v. Burnaby General Hospital (1973) unreported (B.C.S.C.) Notated in D.R.S.) 0857/72 at 653
27. Kolesar v. Jeffries (1974) 9 O.R. (2d) 41, 59 D.L.R. (3d) 367; (varied 12 O.R. (2d) 142, 68 D.L.R. (3d) 198; affirmed (sub nom. Joseph Brant Memorial Hospital v. Koziol) 2 C.C.L.T. 170, 15 N.R. 302 (sub nom. Kolesar v. Joseph Brant Memorial Hospital) 77 D.L.R. (3d) 161 (S.C.C.)
28. Johnston v. Wellesley Hospital [1971] 2 O.R. 103, 17 D.L.R. (3d) 139 (Ont. High Court)
29. MacDonald v. York County Hospital (1973) 1. O.R. (2d) 653, 41 D.L.R. (3d) 321; affirmed (sub nom. Vail v. MacDonald) [1976] 2 S.C.R. 825, 8 N.R. 155, 66 D.L.R. (3d) 530
30. Eady v. Tenderenda [1975] 9 N.S.R. (2d) 444, 3 N.R. 26, 51 D.L.R. (3d) 79 reversing 41 D.L.R. (3d) 706
31. Holmes v. Board of Hospital Trustees of London (1977) 17 O.R. (2d) 626, 81 D.L.R. (3d) 67
32. Videto v. Kennedy (1980) 27 O.R. (2d) 747. (1981) 33 O.R. (2d) 497 Ont. C.A.
33. Supra n. 16 at p. 262
34. Finlay v. Auld [1975] S.C.R. 338 affirming 3 N.S.R. (2d) 464, which affirmed 2 N.S.R. (2d) 483
35. Supra n. 16 at 157
36. Supra n. 16 at p. 158
37. Supra n. 16 at p. 165-166
38. Supra n. 6 at p. 311
39. Supra n. 6 citing Wilson v. Swanson (1956) S.C.R. 804
40. Haines v. Bellisimo (1977) 18 O.R. (2d) 177 (Ont. High Court)
41. Meyer v. Gordon (1981) 17 C.C.L.T. 1 at p. 56
42. Supra n. 41 citing Challand v. Bell [1959], 18 D.L.R. (2d) 150
43. Supra n. 41 at p. 56
44. Elverson v. Doctors Hospital [1974] 4 O.R. (2d) 748, 49 D.L.R. (3d) 196; affirmed 65 D.L.R. (3d) 382 (S.C.C.)
45. Roe v. Minister of Health [1954] 2 Q.B. 66 at p. 86-87
46. Urbanski v. Patel (1978) 2 L.M.Q. 54
47. Supra n. 23
48. Yepremian et al v. Scarborough General Hospital et al (1978) 20 O.R. (2d) 510 (1980) 28 O.R. (2d) 494
49. Supra n. 41 at p. 41-42
50. Supra n. 41 at 42. Man. C.A. in Powell v. Guttman applied McGhee v. Nat. Coal Bd. [1972] 3 All E.R. 1008 (H.L.)
51. Supra n. 41 at p. 43
52. Supra n. 41 at p. 43

53. See Linden Canadian Negligence Law, Toronto, Butterworths & Co. Canada Ltd, 1972, at 261, and n. 16 at 340
54. Discussed Supra n. 16 at p. 345-346
55. Supra n. 46
56. Supra n. 27
57. Supra n. 42
58. Supra n. 16 at p. 468
59. Crossman v. Stewart (1977) 5 C.C.L.T. 45 (B.C.S.C.)
60. Hopital Notre Dame de L'Esperance v. Laurent [1978] 1. S.C.R. 605 affirming (1974) C.A. 543
61. Supra n. 6
62. Supra n. 48
63. Cassidy v. Minister of Health [1951] 2 K.B. 343 [1951] 1 All E.R. 574 (C.A.) (Lord Denning)
64. Sask. Reg. Nurses Association Act R.S.S.R. —12.1 sec. 31
65. Ont. Health Disciplines Act R.S.O. 1980 c. 196
66. Whiston v. Deane [1979] 15 D.L.R. (3d) 184 (B.C.S.C.)
67. Dobson v. Wellington Tavern (Windsor) Ltd. et al, Paolotto et al Third Parties [1982] 124 D.L.R. (3d) 131; 139 D.L.R. (3d) 255
68. MacKenzie v. Vance [1977] 74 D.L.R. (3d) 383
69. Abbott et al v. Cook (1980) 11 C.C.L.T. 264
70. Perrie v. Martin (1982), 26 C.P.C. 198, 135 D.L.R. (3d) 187
71. Gerbracht v. Bingham [1912] 7 D.L.R. 259
72. Law v. Woolford (1976) 7 C.P.C. 197
73. Nichols v. Gray (1978) 9 B.C.L.R. 5, 8 C.P.C. 141 (B.C.C.A.)
74. Marshall v. Curry [1933], 3 D.L.R. 198 and 260 (N.S.S.C.)
75. Supra n. 30
76. Hearn v. Bear and The Halifax Infirmary (1976) 16 N.S.R. (2d) 62
77. Barry v. Lee [1978] 84 D.L.R. (3d) 200, 14 N & P.E.I.R. 446 (P.E.I.C.A.)
78. Foote et al v. Royal Columbian Hospital et al [1982] 134 D.L.R. (3d) 736 B.C.S.C.

Chapter Three:

The Tort of Battery and Consent to the Nursing Process

1. Concept Objectives:

This chapter recognizes the historic differences between the orientation of health care delivery, which is designed to meet perceived health needs of persons, and the orientation of law, which is directed to the protection of rights. Within the framework of the health care system there are occasions when rights and needs may come into conflict. Of major concern to patients, for example, is the right to refuse or consent to care offered to meet their health needs. This well-recognized legal right places a definite duty on health care personnel not to breach that right in the process of delivering care. The intent in this chapter therefore is to:

— examine the tort of battery and the role of consent in authorizing otherwise unlawful acts
— identify the criteria inherent in legally effective consents to treatment
— examine the content of the duty to inform within the context of the tort of battery and the tort of negligence
— identify consent options for policy consideration by managers of health care institutions
— encourage the advocacy of patients' rights to engage in the consent to medical treatment and nursing care.

II. Introduction:

Historically, the courts have protected the individual's right to be free from bodily interference. This right has been recognized at common law since the thirteenth century in various forms of action known as trespass to the person. The most common forms of such action include false imprisonment, malicious prosecution, and battery.

The tort of battery is a form of trespass involving an intentional touching of a person without legal justification. Unlike the tort of negligence which cannot succeed without proof of damage battery is actionable without proof of actual damage.

Within the framework of health care, every medical and nursing procedure involves touching. Without legal justification, such touching constitutes battery. Nursing care involves almost constant contact with the patient: physical examination, administration of intravenous therapy, catheterizations, medications, injections and dressings are but a few examples. Without a legal justification, such touching constitutes battery and the fact that the touching was beneficial is irrelevant. It is the presence of the patient's consent which justifies this otherwise unlawful act. (In certain situations there may be justification other than that of consent, as is described further in the chapter.)

An offended patient may succeed in an action based in battery by merely proving that he was touched without his authorization. The burden then shifts to the defendant to prove that a legally effective consent was present, or some other legal excuse was in place, such as a legislative right, emergency, self defence, or order of the court. However, for all practical purposes, a patient will not likely initiate a legal action against a health care worker unless he has suffered a significant negative result from the health care provided.

Depending on the facts of the particular case, the patient's solicitor may choose to commence a legal action in negligence, battery and breach of contract. Whether the facts of the case can support a finding in contract, or negligence rather than battery has important practical significance. In particular, there are important distinctions between negligence and battery such as the issue of causation, the matter of proof, the importance of medical expert evidence, the significance of the physician's judgment, proof of damage and the substantive basis upon which liability may be found.[1] Whether the action succeeds in negligence or in battery is also affected by the limitation periods governing negligence versus assault. In terms of the financial burden of the defendant it may also have implications for the availability of insurance to meet the loss. The particular malpractice insurance policy may or may not insure against assault.[2] It is recommended that the owners of the health care facility and persons practicing health care, review their insurance coverage and confirm that the probable risks are adequately provided for.

III. Common Nursing Concerns in the Matter of Consent:

In recent years registered nurses have raised the following questions concerning the consent issue. These questions reflect the awareness by nurses that their independent nursing functions and the wide variety of dependent functions in which they carry out nursing activities pusuant to physician's orders, bring the right of the patient to consent into play:
— Who is the consent meant to protect?
— Is the patient's consent necessary in order to render emergency care?
— Of what legal value is a general consent form signed in the admitting office?
— Is the duty to inform the patient about medical and surgical treatment a nursing function or a physician function?
— What is the legal significance of a nurse witnessing the signature of the patient on a consent form?
— Are consents to treatment obtained by telephone legally effective?
— If the patient is intoxicated at the time of obtaining a written consent is such consent legally effective?
— When a patient is transferred from hospital A to hospital B is the consent signed in hospital A transferrable to hospital B for the protection of the latter?
— What is the legal age limit required in order for the patient to give a legally effective consent? Is there an upper age limit?
— Who may give a legally effective consent for an elderly person whose mental competency is in question, and who requires elective treatment?
— Is a wife's consent required when the husband is scheduled for a vasectomy? Is the husband's consent required when his spouse wishes to have a tubal ligation or an abortion?
— May a common law wife or husband consent to or withhold consent to treatment of the other party?
— May a mentally depressed person be forced to undergo electro-convulsive shock therapy against his or her wishes?
— May a parent under the age of majority provide a legally effective consent for medical treatment of his or her child?
— May a child be treated against his parents' wishes?
— What legal risks exist for the physician prescribing birth control measures for minors, without parental consent or contrary to their expressed wishes?
— What legal risks exist for the nurse who counsels minors regarding birth control measures and, or assists the physician in the issuance of birth control pills, or application of intrauterine devices in minor patients?

The type of consent problems vary with the nature of the health service being offered. It is important that managers identify the risks associated with the particular service and client, and strike reasonable, written policies for the guidance of the staff who provide the treatment and care. Policies are expressions of the balance between the risks of the treatment and the goals of the service.

IV. Battery: (defined)

The intentional offer to use force directed at another person under circumstances which create a reasonable apprehension of imminent peril coupled with the apparent ability to carry out the threat is termed *assault*. The actual use of force in actualizing the threat is termed *battery*. Commonly the two terms are used together.

An assault incident may give rise to a charge under the Criminal Code of Canada. The offended victim may also choose to initiate a civil action for damages. This chapter will focus on the civil rather than the criminal dimensions of assaultive behavior because medical and nursing practice commonly has more civil than criminal repercussions.

In an *action for negligence*, the plaintiff has the burden of proving the defendant owed him a duty of care, and that the defendant breached the duty which caused the plaintiff a material injury. The task for the plaintiff in an *assault action* is much less onerous. He merely has to prove that he was touched. If the defendant is unable to prove the presence of consent, or some other justification, damages will be awarded. In addition to general damages the plaintiff may obtain punitive damages, the purpose of which award, is to punish the defendant for invading the plaintiff's right to personal autonomy.

In the following three cases a consent form had been signed. In each case the court made a finding of battery. The cases are significant in that they indicate that consent is for a limited purpose, and if the defendant exceeds the consent, his behavior is assaultive. The cases also show that the presence of a true emergency *may* eliminate the need for the patient's expressed consent to intervene in an unexpected and life-threatening situation.

In *Murray v. McMurchy*[3] (1949), the British Columbia Supreme Court made a finding of liability for assault against the surgeon on the following facts. The surgeon had obtained a written consent from the plaintiff's husband, to perform a caesarian section, and any further surgical procedure found to be necessary. During the surgery the physician performed a tubal ligation. The court determined that although the sterilization may have been *desirable* it was not *essential* for the preservation of the plaintiff's life or health. (The defendant had discovered fibroid tumors on the uterine wall during the surgical procedure which condition was believed to increase the possible hazards in subsequent pregnancies.) The court made the point that if the surgical procedure had been found to be necessary at the time of the caesarian section for the protection and preservation of the patient's life and health, the defendant would have been entitled to proceed. In this instance however, the tubal ligation was a matter of convenience and the surgeon did not have the consent of the plaintiff for it. The consent had been limited to authorization of a caesarian section.

In 1974 an Ontario Court reached a similar conclusion in *Schweizer v. Central Hospital*[4]. The plaintiff had been admitted to the defendant hospital for surgical treatment of his toe. At the time the plaintiff also suffered from a spinal disability. In error the surgeon performed a spinal fusion. Even though the surgery was skillfully performed the surgeon was not justified in doing it without the patient's consent, except in an emergency situation which was not a consideration in the particular case.

In *Allen v. New Mount Sinai Hospital*[5] (1980), the Ontario court made a finding of battery on the following facts: The plaintiff was scheduled for surgery in the defendant hospital. The night prior to the surgery she was visited by the resident. She informed him that she wished to speak to the anesthetist before the surgery. She did not see him until immediately prior to the surgery as she was waiting outside the operating room. At the time she had been sedated with ten milligrams of valium. When she saw the anesthetist she allegedly told him not to use her left arm for the anesthetic injection. This was apparently based on previous experience where a physician had found it difficult to locate and use the necessary vein in that arm. The plaintiff alleged that when she told the anesthetist not to use her left arm he replied: "We know what we are doing". In the operating room she saw the physician proceed to use her left arm. When she recovered from the anesthetic her left arm had been injured apparently due to infiltration of the intravenous anesthetic causing breakdown of surrounding tissue. She suffered pain and economic loss for a number of months. Subsequently, she sued in battery and in negligence. The court determined that the physician had administered the anesthetic in a reasonably competent manner and dismissed the matter of negligence. The court did, however, hold the physician liable in battery because the plaintiff had not consented to the use of her left arm. The defendant used the particular arm over the objections of the plaintiff. To so disregard such objections, even for the best of professional reasons, constituted battery. The defendant was liable for all consequential damage whether foreseeable or unforeseeable.

In the foregoing case the patient had

expressed her non-consent to the touching of a particular part of her body for the purpose of giving the anesthetic. The legal repurcussion reaffirms the principle that to treat an adult in the presence of non-consent is a trespass to the person giving rise to potential liability. (In the Murray and Schweizer cases it was not a matter of treating in the presence of expressed non-consent. Rather the defendant surgeons exceeded their authority in treating parts of the body for which consent had not been rendered. The foregoing instances reaffirm the principle that consent to treatment is for limited purposes only and to view it otherwise is to subject oneself to potential liability.)

V. Defences to Battery:

Fleming[6] raises a number of defences of varying benefit to a defendant sued by a plaintiff in battery or in one of the other trespasses to the person.

Two common defences in the health care system include:

1. Privilege in emergencies or in self defence and
2. Consent.

1. Privilege:

(The matter of emergency has been referred to briefly and is discussed again later in the chapter.)

There are occasions when patients with emotional problems may become aggressive toward other patients, visitors, and staff and it is necessary to defend against such behavior. (However, these occasions are fewer in situations where professional staff have the necessary therapeutic skills and are sensitive to factors which trigger aggressive behavior.) A victim of an attack has the privilege of warding off his attacker by means necessary for his own protection. The privilege arises when there is a reasonable apprehension of physical aggression. It is not necessary for the would-be victim to wait until he is actually struck. If a person raises his hand against the victim and is within reasonably proximity of the victim the latter may strike to prevent the attack, but may not use excessive force.[7] The fact

that a patient uses abusive language causing one to be enraged will not justify excessive force.

Neither does the privilege sanction blows struck in revenge. There is no defensible excuse, ethically or legally, for health care workers to strike a patient because the latter's behavior is antagonistic or inappropriate. There have been a small number of instances in which health care workers were convicted of criminal assault resulting from physical abuse of persons who were mentally or physically handicapped. A conviction for such criminal assault will likely be followed by termination from employment of the persons concerned.

Persons who demonstrate assaultive behavior are not necessarily excused because they suffer from mental illness. They may be held accountable both in a court of criminal jurisdiction and in a civil action initiated by an employee, visitor, family member, or another patient. For example, in Nova Scotia, in 1982, a wife sued her husband in battery after he had stabbed her. His defence, based on insanity, was not successful. Prior to the stabbing incident the defendant had been receiving psychiatric treatment. Following the incident he was diagnosed as psychotically depressed with suicidal tendancies. However medical evidence at trial did not indicate that the defendant was unable to form the necessary intent to commit the assault. The court concluded that he was capable of forming the intent and understood what he was doing even if he did not realize that it was wrong.[8]

2. Consent:

"Volenti non fit injuria": No wrong is done to one who consents. The presence of consent is the most commonly cited defence to allegations of assault against a health care worker. The fact, however, that the patient has gone through the physical exercise of signing his name to the bottom of a consent form presented to him in the admitting office of the health care institution, is no guarantee that the patient consented to a particular treatment or nursing care about which he complains at a later date. The signed form is evidence, and sometimes not very explicit evidence, of the patient's authorization to treatment. The act of signing the form is not a comprehensive consenting to the whole hospital world touching him for care and treatment of any and every kind irrespective of how beneficial such care and treatment might be.

VI. Consent: Defined and Types:

1. Consent (defined)

" An act of reason accompanied by deliberation wherein the mind weighs, as a balance, the good or evil on either side. " [9]

2. Types of Consenting Behaviors:

(a) **Expressed**
(b) **Implied**
(c) **Inferred or Deemed**

One expresses consent when he authorizes an act *verbally* or in *writing*. The patient may say to the physician: "Yes, I agree to have the surgery" or he may express his consent by signing a form. Consent may be *implied* by the patient's non-verbal behavior. His actions may speak louder than words but not necessarily as clearly. Depending on the circumstances the patient's silence, inactivity and failure to resist or protest may be said by the courts, to imply consent. Consent may be implied from the circumstances or from prior conversations with the patient. The person who presents himself to the hospital with a broken limb, is likely implying consent to treatment of the injury. The practical and legal difficulty with implied consent is the identification of the boundary or limit placed on persons and procedures by implied authorization. Is the patient implying consent to the attending physician? To the nurse carrying out the orders written by the attending physician in the preparation of the patient for the medical or surgical intervention? To the student nurse who is administering the pre-operative medication as part of her educational program? Is the patient implying consent to the use of any anesthetic the anesthetist chooses to use? To any combination of therapeutic measures, regardless of how radical, regardless of the risks and regardless of the questionable benefit of the particular therapy?

Implied consent is defined as:

" That manifested by signs, actions, or facts, or by inaction or silence, which raise a presumption that the consent has been given. " [10]

Health care workers who rely on implied consent in the absence of emergency, and in the presence of high risk procedures are exposing patients to prospects of unauthorized invasions, and themselves, to possible liability.

As a common practice nurses rely on orally expressed consents and on consents implied by patient's behaviors for the authorizing of the relatively low risk nursing activities such as the measuring of vital signs providing of skin care assisting with nutrition etc. The long standing customary requirement of explaining to the patient, the nature of the nursing care prior to commencing the nursing activity is required and endorsed by the nursing profession. The explanation has as its purpose, to give the patient sufficient information that the patient's consent may be obtained and his intelligent participation in the process encouraged. It is reasonable for nurses to support a patient's right to have adequate information for the purpose of his making free and informed decisions concerning care requirements, alternatives and preferences. This right is recognized in Nursing's Code of Professional Ethics. [11]

The Emergency Situation:

Consent may be *deemed* to be present by the courts, after the fact of the alleged assault. In the true emergency situation the court may justify the treating of the patient, on the basis of the artificial mechanism of concluding that the emergency situation implies consent, or by directly suspending the need for consent. This will only happen if the patient has not, in fact, expressed his non-consent. For example, if the surgeon is performing particular surgery to which the patient has consented and the patient suffers a cardiac arrest the court will endorse the life-saving cardio-pulmonary resuscitation of the patient should the patient object after the fact. As early as 1933 the Nova Scotia Supreme Court dealt with the emergency issue, in *Marshall v. Curry*:[12] The plaintiff alleged the defendant surgeon removed a diseased testicle, during surgery to repair an inguinal hernia. The plaintiff alleged that the defendant removed the testicle without his consent and that in doing so the surgeon committed assault. The plaintiff contended that he had "simply told him I wanted the hernia cured". The evidence indicated that during the surgery the physician discovered the testicle was severely diseased and could cause blood poisoning. As well, in order to repair the hernia properly the diseased testicle had to be removed. The Chief Justice of Nova Scotia Supreme Court suggested that justification for the surgery would have to be found either in consent implied by the circumstances or on a principle founded on humanitarian considerations. The judge noted that the defendant, after making the incision in the plaintiff's body, discovered conditions which no one had anticipated and the defendant could not reasonably have foreseen. The court stated:

> " I think it is better, instead of resorting to a fiction, to put consent altogether out of the case, where a great emergency which could not be anticipated arises, and to rule that it is the surgeon's duty to act in order to save the life or preserve the health of the patient; and that in the honest execution of the duty he should not be exposed to legal liability. "[13]

Marshall v. Curry was distinguished on the facts, from *Murray v. McMurchy*[14]. In the latter the circumstances did not involve the urgency or the immediate decision-making in an emergency situation that existed in the Marshall case.

The emergency situation however may not be recognized by the court as creating a privilege to treat in the presence of expressed non-consent. In *Mulloy v. Hop Sang*,[15] (1935), the Alberta court awarded damages to the patient. An action had been initiated by the physician claiming for professional fees for the amputation of the defendant's hand which had been badly injured. The patient, as a defendant, coun-

terclaimed for damages for battery. The court accepted his evidence that he had expressly asked the physician not to cut off his hand as he wanted to have it repaired when he returned to his home town. (The physician stated that he amputated the limb because he considered that delay would result in blood poisoning.)

The foregoing cases all involved adults concerned with consenting to care for their own benefit. There are different considerations when the matter of consent concerns a child. In the event that a parent or legal guardian expressly refuses consent for treatment of a child, application to the court may be necessary. This matter is discussed under the concept of minority later in the chapter.

In summary, the common law permits the rendering of health care to unconscious or mentally incompetent person in an emergency situation, and as long as the patient does not express his non-consent while conscious or while mentally competent. However the common law is not clear as to what extent the *family* of the unconscious person can prohibit the physician, for example from rendering emergency care in a life-threatening position. An example would be that of a woman who is unconscious, and who has not voiced her non-consent to treatment but whose husband is vehement that the couple are actively practising Jehovah Witnesses and emergency care is not to be rendered. Certainly, the husband's giving or withdrawing of consent will not interfere in his wife's right to sue in assault, or in negligence for defective care. Canadian authors on the topic have recommended that a model consent act should provide and permit the health care provider to render essential treatment in the life-threatening situation, where delay would place the patient's life, limbs or vital organs in danger, and where the patient is unconscious or otherwise mentally incompetent.

VII. Critical Elements Inherent in Legally Effective Consents:

There are six elements, the absence of

any one of which may, after the fact, cause the court adjudicating allegations of battery to conclude that such absence has created mere submission rather than consent. These elements are:

1. The consent must be genuine and voluntary
2. The procedure must not be an illegal procedure
3. The consent must authorize the particular treatment or care and authorize the particular performer of the treatment or care
4. The consentor must have legal capacity to consent
5. The consentor must have the necessary mental competency to consent
6. The consentor must be informed

1. The Consent Must be Genuine and Voluntary:

Authorization of the patient obtained by use of coercion, coaxing, use of deceit, tricks or fraudulent misrepresentation will likely be perceived by the court as a submission of the patient not amounting to true consent. The patient's authorization to care must be voluntary. The Study Paper prepared for the Law Reform Commission of Canada in 1979, and entitled "Consent to Medical Care" cites a definition of a "voluntary act" from an American source:

> " The act of a person who is so situated as to be able to exercise free power of choice without undue inducement or any element of force, fraud, deceit, duress or other form of constraint or coercion. " [16]

Voluntariness is affected by subtle pressures arising from the very nature of the illness itself, the presence of (its) pain, a natural desire to be free of the pain, anxiety about the outcome of the illness, and by the nature of the various family and other relationships upon which the patient depends. The more subtle and controllable pressures affecting the patient's exercise of free choice of options include: the presence of conflict between the needs of the patient and those of the family; the perception that the professional health care worker knows best; the need to have the good will of the personnel delivering the care; and the hesitancy to challenge the proposal of the physician or nurse, for fear that such a challenge will threaten the patient-worker relationship. In one instance, when a patient requested access to a second opinion, the physician responded by withdrawing from the case leaving a somewhat threatened and disconcerted patient in a risk situation. The patient is frequently vulnerable. If either physician or nurse has notice that the patient is not in a situation to exercise free choice, constructive action should be taken to correct the situation.

In *Beausoleil v. Soeurs de la Charite*[17] (1965) a patient in Quebec requested a general anesthetic for a surgical procedure. After the patient was sedated the physician persuaded her to have a spinal anesthetic. The patient was paralyzed as a result of the spinal procedure. The court held that the sedated patient had not given a voluntary consent. The questionable practice of obtaining consent from the patient following sedation should be prohibited except in the true emergency situation.

The nurse who prepares the patient for surgery should discretely test the patient's awareness of the planned surgery prior to administration of the pre-operative sedation, and to presenting of the consent form for the patient's signature. For example, a student nurse presented a surgical consent form to the patient and explained the purpose of the form. The young student then said: "Dr. D explained the surgery you are having done this morning Mrs. Jones?" To which the patient responded: "He is taking a cyst from my ovary". The actual surgery booked for the patient was a hysterectomy and removal of the ovaries. The nurse reported the matter to the nurse in charge of the unit, who then contacted the surgeon. He interviewed the patient, and explained the procedure. The patient was then presented with the consent form for signature prior to receiving the pre-operative sedation. The foregoing is an example of reasonable advocacy on the part of nursing personnel which served to protect the patient's right to consent, and prevented possible liability for the surgeon and the hospital.

In *Kelly v. Hazlett* (1976) 15 O.R. (2d) 290 the thirty-three year old married plaintiff had been treated by the defendant, an orthopedic surgeon, for approximately six months in 1971. She subsequently sued the physician for damages relating to two operative procedures which the defendant had carried out on her right arm, (an osteotomy of the right humerus, in July 1971 and a manipulation of the right elbow in November 1971.) The plaintiff based her action in battery, alleging that the surgical procedures were performed without her consent. Alternatively she alleged negligence in performing the surgery without her consent.

The plaintiff had been referred to the defendant for treatment of the effects of rheumatoid arthritis in her right arm. Due to this condition there was a numbness, a wasting of the muscle in the back of the arm, and an inability to straighten her arm resulting in a crooked elbow. The plaintiff's main concern was to have her arm straightened. The defendant was of the opinion that the plaintiff required an ulnar nerve transplant and a cleaning out of the elbow joint which procedures would remove the numbness and normalize the muscle but would not straighten the arm. In order to do the latter an osteotomy or breaking of the bone was necessary. The plaintiff was allegedly emotionally unstable and the defendant tried to discourage her from having the osteotomy since the latter would require prolonged wearing of a cast. The night before surgery the plaintiff signed a consent form for the performance of the ulnar transplant and joint clean-out.

On the day of the surgery, and while under sedation, the plaintiff again requested that her arm be straightened. The defendant again advised against it, but upon urging by the plaintiff, finally consented. He did not advise the plaintiff of the real risks of temporary or permanent stiffness in her arm which might result from the osteotomy. As a result of the osteotomy the plaintiff developed permanent stiffness in her right arm. The Ontario court ruled that the defendant surgeon had failed to inform the patient, which failure voided the consent. One of the problems alluded to by the court was the fact that the surgical plan was changed after discussion with the sedated patient outside the operating room. The court did not find a lack of voluntariness but did state that in such circumstances the defendant must prove affirmatively that sedation did not affect the patient's understanding of the surgical option being presented.

How such risks are to be resolved in a particular situation is determined, in part, by written policy struck after clear examination of the problem by the interdisciplinary group on the institution's risk management committee. The matter of consent rights and requirements affect the potential liability of a variety of health care workers in the institution as well as the liability of the corporate authority itself. At the front line, it is the physician who is primarily at risk. However, the nurse or any other worker engaged with and assisting the physician in carrying out of treatment and care would also be at risk.

It is reasonable and prudent for the policy making committee or group to confront the issue of consent in the context of common problems or risks created by the type of population being serviced at the facility, and the type of high risk care being provided. The policy, be it a conservative or liberal one, is an expression of the values deemed important in the delivery of care. It should balance interests such as the following:
— The importance of the patient's right to voluntarily engage in a true consenting process
— The concern for the financial loss incurred by delay of treatment
— The concern for potential liability arising from situations which negatively affect the voluntariness of the patient's decision making.

It is important that the policy be expressed in writing, published in policy manuals available on the patient care units, and communicated to the physicians and nurses and other personnel so that clear direction and guidance are available to them.

2. The Procedure Must Not be an Illegal Procedure:

The object of obtaining the patient's consent to care, is to protect the patient's right to body integrity. An equally important purpose is to reduce or prevent the risk of civil liability in an action taken by a disgruntled patient for damages for assault and battery. However the criminal liability dimension of care is also significant. There are certain limits drawn by the criminal law in relation to the inflicting of harm within the context of health care delivery.

Canada's criminal law is intended to protect the public interest in peace, order and good government. The criminal process may be activated when the act of one person, directed against another, threatens those community values expressed in the criminal law and codified in the Criminal Code of Canada.

All persons have a right to protection under the criminal law which right cannot be waived by the individual or by a third party such as a spouse, a parent, or a guardian of the individual. The criminal law will not recognize the consent of the individual or a third party to a criminal act as a defence to criminal prosecution. For example, although it is no longer a criminal offence to commit suicide it is a criminal offence for a third party to aid and abet suicide. The fact that consent is rendered by the would-be victim is irrelevant in prosecution of such an offence. Health care workers who participate in the procuring of abortions or assisting with the procedure outside the limits set by the criminal code, are at risk of prosecution. Again the patient's consent is irrelevant. Nor can parents or guardians effectively consent to the performance of medical or nursing acts on children or dependents, if such acts are contrary to law.

It is possible for health care workers, in the performance of their professional activities, to place themselves outside the limits of the criminal law. Since 1980 there have been a number of highly publicized incidents involving physicians and nurses in which the criminal process was activated. In 1983 in western Canada, a public enquiry

was held into the death of a new-born infant suffering from severe birth defects. The enquiry was held when the justice department was informed of the death subsequent to the administration of an abnormally large dose of sedation used to relieve severe convulsions. The medical order was allegedly carried out by a member of the nursing staff in the hospital concerned. (Subsequent to the enquiry, the nurse concerned was disciplined by her professional association.) In Ontario in 1983, an extended public enquiry was held into the deaths of thirty-six children on the cardiac unit of a pediatric hospital. Autopsies indicated unexplainable, abnormal levels of digoxin in the victims blood. The Royal Commission, chaired by Mr. Justice Samuel Grange of the Ontario Supreme Court, has been highly controversial. Also, in 1983, a medical-nursing team in an Ontario abortion clinic were charged with breach of the Criminal Code of Canada.

3. The Consent Must Authorize the Particular Treatment or Care and Authorize the Particular Performer of the Treatment or Care:

" The essence of consent is an agreement by the patient to accept the specific risks involved... "[18]

It would be difficult to prove (and it would be the defendant's burden to prove) that the patient knew the risks involved in a particular treatment when the procedure was in fact different in nature from what the patient expected — for example, a tubal ligation when the patient expected a caesarian section, or a spinal fusion when the patient expected a repair of his toe. It would be difficult for the defendant to show that the consent given by the patient was an unlimited or open ended consent to the health care worker to do whatever, he, in his discretion, considered reasonable, and that the patient knew the risks involved in the open-ended list of options.

Although the patient is limiting his consent to a specific procedure (appendectomy, caesarian section, repair of toe) it is assumed that he is also implying consent to the usual

Sample Surgical Consent Form

_____ Hospital

Town (City)_____

Province: _____

CONSENT TO OPERATE

1. I authorize the performance upon:
   of the following operation: _____
   to be performed by Doctor:_____
   and with the assistance of such members of the medical staff and employees as required.
2. I consent to the administration of such local, general, and or local anaesthesia as is considered necessary.
3. I consent to the performance of such procedures in addition to the above surgery which the above named physician may consider necessary in the course of the operation.
4. I hereby certify that I have read and fully understand the above consent, the reason the above named surgery is considered necessary, its advantages, and possible complications which have been explained to me by Dr:_____
5. I certify that no guarantee or assurance has been made as to the results that may be obtained.
6. I consent to the disposal of tissue and parts removed surgically, according to the customary practice of the institution. DATED:

SIGNATURE:

SIGNATURE OF WITNESS:

   I confirm that I have explained the nature and effects of the above named procedure to the person who signed the above consent. DATED:

SIGNATURE OF PHYSICIAN:

procedures that must be completed in preparation for such surgical procedure, and for its management postoperatively. For example, it would be implied that he is consenting to x-rays, blood tests, dressings and injections necessary for the management of the surgical situation. (This assumes, of course, that the patient has not expressed his non-consent to a particular procedure, or to its performance by a particular individual.) The courts have suggested that the surgical consent impliedly authorizes the surgeon to engage an anesthetist.[19] The courts have also suggested, however, that the patient should be given an opportunity to choose the method of anesthesia when such options are available.[20]

In the day to day function of hospitals, it is impossible, impractical and unnecessary to obtain written consent for each and every medical treatment or nursing procedure. In the absence of non-consent (or

emergency), consent of conscious, mentally competent adults is commonly given verbally or is implied from the circumstances and the patients behavior.

It is recommended that health care institutions have two types of written consent forms in place:

1. A consent form signed on admission expressing consent in writing to examination and to performance of diagnostic and treatment procedures and
2. A consent form designating the specific surgical or medical procedure which is considered to have certain risks, and designating the person who is to perform the procedure, and authorizing in general terms, medical and other personnel to assist in the necessary treatment and care. (Above is a sample surgical consent form);

Consent to the performer of medical and nursing acts is not a real problem when the performer is delivering the particular treatment or care to a conscious, mentally competent person. Consent assumes authorization of a specific performer and such consent is obtained verbally or by implication at the time. Potential difficulties exist when the treatment such as a surgical procedure is being performed on an unconscious patient. The patient has agreed to accept the risks of performance of the technique by the named surgeon. If the surgery is performed by someone other than the named surgeon, the patient may well have an argument for saying that he had not accepted the risk of performance of the surgery by an unknown surgeon. In teaching hospitals it is expected that medical interns and residents obtain surgical experience. Policies and surgical consent forms in teaching hospitals need to address this reality and decide how these risks are to be balanced. Certainly where the patient specifically designates a particular surgeon to perform the operation, it would be in breach of his duty to permit some other surgeon to stand in his place without the permission of the patient. When the patient specifically excludes a particular physician or student, such should be noted and complied with by the surgeon who is in ultimate care and control of the treatment situation.

4. The Consentor Must Have Legal Capacity to Consent

Consent must be authorized by a person, who, in law, has the authority or power to render the consent, i.e. authority to make decisions which are legally binding and recognized before the courts. At what point does one acquire legal capacity to consent to treatment and by what process may an individual lose his legal capacity? In the absence of legal capacity who may stand in the person's place?

(a) Adults:

At common law an adult possesses legal capacity. At common law an adult is a person above the age of majority, and is twenty-one years of age or older. (However, the various provinces have, by legislation, created statutory ages of majority. A person may be an adult at eighteen in one

province, at nineteen in another province, in the sense of having reached the particular age of majority specified in the statute of the province concerned.)

In the absence of removal of legal capacity, the adult directly concerned is the only one possessing the legal capacity to consent to being touched. Only the person himself can give, withhold, and withdraw consent for treatment and care. No other person, (spouse, parent, son, daughter, brother or sister) has the capacity to consent on behalf of the patient such that the patient would be prohibited from suing in assault. Such consentors cannot, in law, remove the patient's right to sue, unless by legal process the capacity was removed from the patient and transferred to the person executing the consent.

There are a variety of statutes which effectively remove a person's legal capacity to consent on his own behalf. The legislation varies in number and type from province to province. For example, a province's hospital act might provide a legal mechanism whereby substitute consentors may stand in the place of the patient declared to be incapable:

> " If a person in a hospital is found by declaration of capacity to be incapable of consenting to treatment then that person may be treated either upon obtaining the consent of the guardian of that person if he has one, or if he had not a guardian upon obtaining the consent of his spouse or next of kin and where the spouse or next of kin is not available or consent is unable to be obtained, upon obtaining the consent of the Public Trustee. "

The foregoing is section 46 (2) of Nova Scotia's Hospital's Act. In *Re Boudreau*[22] an application was made to the court by the Public Trustee for directions as to his power to act on an application by a psychiatric hospital for consent to treat a patient admitted to the hospital under a lieutenant governor's warrant. A declaration of capacity to consent to treatment had been completed confirming that the patient was incapable of consenting. (The patient suffered from a schizophrenic disorder with manic features and was in need of routine diagnostic tests and chemotherapy. The patient's brother had refused to consent to treatment.) The court held that it was correct for the Public Trustee to find that consent was unable to be obtained within the meaning of the act, and the Public Trustee's authority to consent was confirmed by the court.

All of the provinces have mental health legislation which provides mechanisms for certifying persons suffering from psychiatric illness. Newfoundland's *Mental Health Act* for example, provides that:

> " Any person, who in the opinion of a physician is suffering from mental disorder to such a degree that the person requires hospitalization and treatment in the interests of his own safety, safety to others or safety to property, may without his consent be admitted to, detained within, and treated at a treatment facility. "[23]

The parameters of rights and duties created or altered by mental health legislation may not be clear. The foregoing section, for example, does not expressly remove the patient's right to consent to non-psychiatric treatment. In the event that the patient, certified pursuant to this particular legislation, required surgery, or medical treatment for other than his psychiatric problem, such therapy could not be condoned in the absence of a legally effective consent (except in emergency circumstances).

In summary, adults retain their legal capacity to consent to the particular treatment until such legal capacity is removed by legal process.

(b) Minors:

Parents have, by common law, the right to consent to treatment and health care on behalf of and in place of their infant children. Parents also have the duty not to withhold consent to treatment necessary to the life and health of their children. From 1660 the Crown had the right as parens patriae, (sovereign guardian of persons under disability) to intervene in the parental custody of their children when such custody was in conflict with the children's welfare. In the absence of such intervention, parents have sole legal custody which permits the parents to control their children, to supervise their education and upbringing and includes legal capacity to consent to required medical treatment. (Divorce proceedings in which the court grants legal custody of named children to one parent may serve to shift the legal capacity to consent to the parent obtaining the legal custody by court order.)

There is a point in the life of the minor when he may acquire the legal capacity to consent to medical treatment for himself. When that point arises is not easily determined as it is not tied to a definite chronological age but to the factual presence of the capacity to understand the nature and risks of undergoing the treatment concerned. This has been recognized at common law, and in certain jurisdictions, efforts have been made to clarify the situation by statute.

Historically, minors (persons under the age of majority) have not had the legal capacity to sue or be sued, or to enter into commercial contracts. This contractual incapacity was imposed by the courts as a protection against the exploitation of children in general financial dealings. However, lack of contractual capacity did not affect the legal capacity of minors to marry, to vote, to qualify for a driver's licence or to consent to engage in contact sports and to submit themselves to possible negligent and assaultive behavior.

The common law age of majority (age twenty-one years) has been modified in the various provinces by legislation for certain purposes. This age of majority legislation promotes a minor to an adult at the age of 18 years in Alberta, Manitoba, Ontario and Quebec, and at the age of 19 years in British Columbia, Newfoundland, Nova Scotia and Saskatchewan. Regardless of whether the age of majority is set by common law or by statute, there is authority for the position that a person under the age of majority, may render a legally effective consent to treatment for himself. In *Booth v. Toronto General Hospital*[24], (1910) the physician operated on a nineteen year old boy without the parents' consent. The boy was subject to epileptic seizures and was not of high intelligence. The court held that the patient's consent was satisfactory. In *Johnston v. Wellesley Hospital*[25], a case heard by the

Ontario High Court in 1970, the facts were as follows: The plaintiff was twenty years old. (The age of majority in the province at the time was twenty-one years.) The plaintiff signed a consent form at the defendant hospital for treatment of acne by a dermatologist. The latter burned the patient with the carbon dioxide treatment which caused further scarring. The patient sued in negligence and assault. The court held the minor's consent to be legally effective to defeat the allegation of assault and pointed out that:

> " Although the common law imposes very strict limitations on the capacity of persons under twenty-one years of age to hold, or rather to divest themselves of, property, or to enter into contracts concerning matters other than necessities, it would be ridiculous in this day and age, where the voting age is being reduced generally to eighteen years, to state that a person of twenty years of age, who is obviously intelligent and as fully capable of understanding the possible consequences of a medical or surgical procedure as an adult, would at law, be incapable of consenting thereto. " [20]

The vagueness of the common law position has caused concern to health care workers delivering non-emergency care to persons under the statutory age of majority in the particular province. Despite the dirth of Canadian cases on point, there is concern for more certainty to be introduced by way of legislation. Although there is no common law rule which renders a minor incapable of giving effective consent to treatment, neither is there any authority expressly establishing that a minor of a particular minimum age can effectively consent.

Certain provinces have provided by way of legislation for minors to give consent to medical treatment. In British Columbia, a minor who has reached the age of sixteen may effect a consent. In Ontario, the Public Hospital Act permits married persons, and minors of sixteen years of age to effect a personal consent. Since the protection is within the hospital statute, it would not protect physicians and nurses employed in medical clinics and health units attached to universities and colleges. It is within these settings that physicians and nurses have a major role in care and counselling in matters of sexuality, birth control and control of diseases. Teenagers, sensitive to their needs for privacy, and to avoid parental disapproval of their conduct, frequently refuse to permit physicians and nurses to consult parents for the purpose of obtaining parental consent. Faced with a non-emergency health care need the professional health care worker may refuse to render care in the absence of parental consent. This effectively denies the teenager access to health care.

In default of legislation or where there is legislation but the minor is below the minimum age (Quebec for example, where a minor of fourteen years of age can consent to treatment by a physician or in a hospital) there is still potential confusion about whether the minor's consent will be legally effective, except where the legislation expressly prohibits consent of the minor below the specified age.[27] However, in the absence of prohibition by statute there is an argument that the minor who has the intellectual capacity to appreciate the nature and consequences of the medical procedure concerned has the legal capacity to give a valid consent.

The American concept of the emancipated minor, i.e. a minor who is self supporting and living on his or her own and who is socially emancipated even though still financially dependent on parents, receives support in articles written on the topic by Canadian authors.

Again it is important for the managers of health care agencies who provide therapeutic abortion service, birth control devices and medication and services with probable risks of injury, to express their policies in writing for the clear direction of the professional staff in their provision of services to adolescents. A key to a reasonable policy in light of the vagueness of the common law is to require as a minimum that the adolescent have the intellectual capacity to understand the care proposal and that a genuine, voluntary, informed and written consent be obtained from the patient himself, to the particular treatment.

If parents arbitrarily refuse consent to urgently needed care such will likely be perceived by the courts as neglect. When parents refuse, for religious or other reasons, the authority in the health care facility has access to the courts, usually under the child welfare legislation. When such treatment is required to save the life of the child the courts will proceed in the best interests of the child and order legal custody to be transferred from the parents or legal guardians to a person who then has the legal capacity to consent on behalf of the minor. In February, 1983, the Ontario Family Court approved an application to transfer custody of a twenty-two month old infant from the parents to the welfare agency for a period of four months. The purpose was to provide for the consenting to the treatment of severe burns to sixty percent of the infant's body. The treatment required included blood transfusions. The parents, Jehovah Witnesses, had refused consent on religious grounds.

In the event of an emergency of such proportions that time is unavailable to apply to the courts there should be clear authority to the professional personnel to proceed to treat, to document the events and actions clearly, and to consult with the solicitor retained to represent the interests of the institution.

At common law there is no legal capacity granted to a spouse to consent or refuse consent for treatment of his or her partner. There is, therefore, no basis in law for obtaining of spousal consent and the hospital or physician who requires such consent is attempting to confer a right on the spouse that does not exist at law and to thereby negatively affect the right of the patient. Spousal consent is not required at common law even if the therapy involved is that of an abortion or such therapeutic sterilization procedures as hysterectomy, tubal ligation or vasectomy. There is no Canadian or English authority for the proposition that a person deprived of the right to have children by a spouse could sue for damages.

Some Canadian jurisdictions have expressly protected spousal autonomy by legislation. Ontario's Family Law Reform Act, for example, provides that married persons shall have the same legal capacity as if they were unmarried. Quebec's Health Services and Social Services Act expressly protects the medical autonomy of the person by stating that the consent of the consort shall not be required for the provision of care.

It is, for practical reasons, however, desirable to obtain spousal consent, but the consent of the patient should be obtained first, and where there is a conflict, priority be given to the patient's position.

5. The Consentor Must Have the Necessary Mental Competency to Consent

Mental competency contemplates the present ability to understand the subject matter in respect of which consent is requested and to appreciate the risks and consequences of giving and withholding consent. To provide a legally effective consent the patient must be of sound mind (*compos mentis*). The patient may, in fact, lack the necessary mental competency because of a chronic disability such as mental retardation or a chronic mental illness, or senility. A patient may also lack mental competency on a temporary basis because of the influence of alcohol, abuse of drugs or due to the influence of anesthetics and sedation within the hospital or nursing home setting. Consent taken from persons lacking mental competency would likely be invalid. In an action for battery the burden is on the defendant physician, nurse or hospital to prove that the patient was mentally competent at the time of rendering the consent. Substitute consent provided by a third party on behalf of and in place of the mentally incompetent person is not valid unless the substitute consentor has been granted the legal capacity to so consent. As mentioned under the concept of legal capacity, there are legal mechanisms to provide for application to be made and appointment of legally effective consenters. Other writers have suggested that it is prudent to obtain the consent of relatives for a mentally incompetent person to prevent them from taking legal action for (any) infringement of any right the family members might have.

The primary intent of a reasonable consent policy and practice is to protect the rights of the clients being served, and to thereby, reduce the risks to the corporate authority, employees and agents, of unethical or unlawful invasion of the client's rights. Among its standard provisions it should, then, note that mentally competent persons are free to designate a particular individual to stand in his place and represent his interests in the event of mental incompetency occurring. It should also encourage staff workers to carefully explain to clients the particular procedure, treatment or care and to request the client to describe in his own words his understanding of it. Finally, policy and practice in facilities offering services to clients with potential and actual problems of mental incompetency should provide for a system of substitute consenters in accordance with the legal procedure available in the particular province or territory. In some jurisdictions, provision is made by statute, (for example, in Nova Scotia pursuant to their Hospital's Act) for a gradation of relatives empowered to provide a substitute consent. Where there is no relative available or willing to act as a substitute, a public trustee may be appointed. In jurisdictions having no substitute consenting system legislated, the client is dependent on an outmoded process requiring application to a court of competent jurisdiction, for an order appointing a legal guardian. The guardian may be a relative who is reluctant, disinterested, or in a conflict of interest. For a person residing in a nursing home or extended care unit, the appointed guardian may be the administrator of the facility. By virtue of his position he may not be able to represent the best interests of a client who requires medical and surgical therapies on an elective basis. Court orders of guardianship may sometimes erroneously label the dependant person as incompetent for all purposes. Although a person may be unable to appreciate the nature, consequences and risks of a particular medical or surgical therapy, he may still be able to manage his own personal and business affairs. What may be needed in the particular case is a guardianship for limited purposes with safeguards to ensure the guardian is acting in the best interests of the dependent person. Alberta's *Dependent Adults Act*, proclaimed in 1978, provides such a legal device. The responsibility of the guardian is to represent the best interests of the client and his areas of responsibility are determined by the needs and capabilities of the client. If the latter requires protection in specific areas of living, as for example, in consenting to therapy, a partial guardianship is authorized. If protection is needed in all areas of living (housing, employment, social life, health care and legal proceedings) a plenary guardian can be appointed. The guardianship appointment is reviewed on a regular basis.

In the absence of appropriate legislation, and consent policies and practices, a mentally incompetent person is vulnerable. By virtue of his disability he may not have the physical, mental, financial or political strength to assert a fundamental right of consent and non-consent. A guardian and advocate to speak for him and to represent his interests when such are in conflict with the wants of family, professional health care, personnel and agencies, is a reasonable expectation.

6. The Consentor Must be Informed

This final element in a legally effective consent is one which has received considerable attention from courts and writers in recent years. These sources indicate a clear shift toward support of a patient's right to be involved in decisions about treatment and care offerings. This right to be involved may, depending on the particular facts, be enforceable in actions of battery or negligence or both.

(a) Requirements in Defence of Battery:

An offended patient may succeed in this particular action if it is proven that the treatment or care performed was an unconsented invasion of the person for reasons such as the following:

— the particular treatment was different in nature and character than that which the patient had authorized. For example, if the patient consents to repair of his toe such consent would not authorize a spinal fusion

— the patient had not been informed about the *nature* of the particular treatment, its expected *effects* and special *risks*. For example, the adult male who is offered female hormonal therapy for treatment of cancer and is not told that an expected effect of the particular treatment is female changes in body organs and functions, it could not be said the patient had consented to such treatment

— the patient has not been informed about or has been misled as to the risks inherent in the treatment such as to amount to a description of the treatment that is misleading about its nature. In *Haulshka v. The University of Saskatchewan*,[28] a 1965 decision of the Supreme Court of Saskatchewan, the court concerned itself with the following fact situation: Two physicians in the defendant university advertised for participants in a testing of an experimental anesthetic agent. The plaintiff applied and, prior to the test, signed a consent form. He was told at that point, that the testing was a safe procedure and was not informed that the procedure required a catheter to be passed into one of the chambers of the heart. While the procedure was being carried out the plaintiff suffered a cardiac arrest and subsequent brain damage due to cerebral anoxia. The defendants were held liable in assault because of failure to provide the plaintiff with:

" a fair and reasonable explanation of the proposed treatment including the probable effect and any special or unusual risks. "[29]

In *Koehler v. Cook*,[30] a 1976 decision of the Supreme Court of British Columbia, the plaintiff inquired of the risks involved in surgery proposed to correct migraine headaches. The risks inherent in the surgery included the risk of temporary and permanent loss of the sense of smell. The defendant surgeon knew of these risks but assured the plaintiff there were no complications of importance. The plaintiff suffered permanent loss of the sense of smell

and the court held the defendant surgeon liable in trespass. In the previously mentioned Ontario case of the same year, *Kelly v. Hazlett*, the trial court stated that to have a successful defence to a battery action, the physician must have given the patient information concerning the basic nature and character of the treatment, and need not have informed the patient concerning "collateral risks" associated with the treatment, unless these risks were so integral to the treatment as to form part of its basic nature and character. The court went on to say that in an action in negligence, the physician has a duty to take reasonable steps to ensure that the patient is informed of the special risks of that treatment and the failure to do so is negligent conduct. In 1980, the Supreme Court of Canada reaffirmed the trial court's finding of battery and negligence in *Reibl v. Hughes*, and reaffirmed the trial court's finding of negligence for failure to inform in *Hopp v. Lepp*. In 1981 the trial court held the physician to be negligent for the same reason in *White v. Turner*, and in 1982 the British Columbia court made a similar finding in *Rawlings v. Lindsay*, all of which cases are reviewed under the concept of negligence in this chapter.

Reibl v. Hughes[31] involved a defendant surgeon who had operated on the plaintiff for removal of an occlusion in his left internal carotid artery. The surgery was done in a non-negligent manner but the plaintiff suffered a stroke following the surgery. The plaintiff had signed a consent form for the particular surgical procedure but he alleged that he had not given an informed consent. At trial the plaintiff succeeded in battery for the defendant's failure to obtain an informed consent, and succeeded in negligence on the basis that the defendant had failed to live up to his professional standard of care. The Supreme Court of Canada confirmed the decision of the trial court.

The trial court attempted to clarify the distinction between battery and negligence as two causes of action concerning consent. The court determined that to succeed in battery the plaintiff need only prove that what the physician did differed substantially from that to which the plaintiff gave consent. The onus rests on the defendant to show that an adequate explanation was given as to the essential nature and quality of the treatment, and explained in language which the patient could understand. Risks integral to the nature of the treatment had to be explained. Whether or not a particular risk was "integral to the nature" of the treatment was determined by such factors as the probability of the particular risk and the severity of the consequences of the risk if such risk materialized. A description of the procedure without clear explanation of the aspects of these risks would be misleading as to the nature and quality of the treatment.

In *Reibl v. Hughes*, the trial court found that, at the time the surgery was performed, the defendant surgeon knew that the patient was subject to a 14% risk of mortality and stroke as a result of the surgery and that disclosure of these risks formed an integral part of the surgery and failure to disclose the risks constituted battery.

(b) Requirements in Defence of Negligence:

The preponderance of recent cases concerning defective consents have been determined by the courts on the basis of negligence. The Supreme Court of Canada, in *Reibl v. Hughes*, limited liability in battery to those situations where there is no consent to the actual treatment performed or, in the absence of emergency, to treatment that went beyond that which the patient authorized, or where the patient has been mislead as to risks inherent in the basic nature of the treatment. The Chief Justice of the Supreme Court of Canada said as follows:

" actions of battery in respect of surgical or other medical treatment should be confined to cases where surgery or treatment has been performed or given to which there has been no consent at all, or where, emergency situations aside, surgery or treatment has been performed or given beyond that to which there was consent... This standard would comprehend cases where there has been misrepresentation of the surgery or treatment for which consent was elicited and

a different surgical procedure or treatment was carried out... Unless there has been misrepresentation or fraud to secure consent to the treatment, a failure to disclose attendant risks, however serious, should go to negligence rather than to battery. "[32]

The scope of the duty to inform and whether or not the duty has been breached are matters which must be decided in relation to the particular facts and circumstances of the case. The determination of the proper scope of the duty to inform in negligence, is often a matter of considerable difficulty. At a minimum it can be said that there is a duty to inform the patient of all *material risks*. This may be defined as those risks to which a reasonable person would be likely to attach significance in deciding whether or not to undergo the proposed treatment. It includes those risks which a reasonable physician would disclose in the circumstances as well as those risks which a reasonable patient would want to know.

In *Kelly v. Hazlett*, a 1976 Ontario case, the plaintiff sued in battery and negligence and succeeded in the latter. She alleged that the defendant had failed to properly inform her of the risks of an osteotomy. (The reader will recall that this case was described under the concept of genuine and voluntary consent.)

The plaintiff had been referred to the defendant surgeon for treatment of complications of rheumatoid arthritis of the arm. The defendant recommended a radial nerve transplant to relieve numbness. The plaintiff wanted her elbow straightened which could only be done by an osteotomy requiring a breaking of the bone and application of a cast. The surgeon advised her against this procedure. Following administration of her pre-operative medication the plaintiff again requested the defendant to perform the osteotomy. He agreed but did not advise her of the risk of temporary or permanent stiffness. Following the surgery the plaintiff's arm was permanently stiff. The court concluded:

" ... the risk of stiffness both temporary and permanent, was a definite risk of the proposed osteotomy in the circumstances of the plaintiff's condition. It was a "special" risk relating to the nature of the operation, as opposed to being a unusual risk incident to, or possible in, any operation... Indeed, on the evidence, it was the only risk of this kind of the operation, and in my view it was the defendant's duty to be satisfied that it had been brought home to the patient before he could reasonably regard her apparent consent as being valid "[33]

The court characterized the risk as a special collateral risk and concluded that the failure of the defendant to advise the patient of this special collateral risk was the cause of the injury in that had the patient been informed, she would not have consented to the surgery.

The foregoing case reflects the difficulty in distinguishing the two categories of risks *inherent in the nature* of certain treatments but *collateral to* other treatments. One type of risk, if undisclosed, will constitute battery, and the other, (collateral risks), if undisclosed, constitute negligence. The distinction is of legal significance with the burden being different and more difficult for the plaintiff if his cause of action is in negligence. In negligence, the plaintiff must show that the injury which he suffered was a definite risk of the particular procedure, that the particular defendant had a duty to disclose the risk, that he failed to do so and his failure to disclose was the direct and proximate cause of his injury. The plaintiff's case will be defeated if he is unable to prove *causation*, and most cases fail on this basis.

1. Risks: Basic, Probably and Possible:

It is not necessary to explain to the patient those basic risks which are inherent in all treatment such as morbidity or death due to infection, or negligence. Neither is it necessary to explain every possible risk however remote. However it is critical to explain *probable risks* and such *possible* risks, which if materialized, have *severe consequences*. It is also critical to answer questions posed by the patient inviting a response to possible risks. The fact that the patient asks the question is evidence that the risk is material to him. The health care worker has a responsibility to volunteer certain information, and an added responsibility to answer

the specific inquiries of the patient:

" Had there been a specific question of the kind alleged (and I assume, it would be sufficient if the question or questions asked could reasonably be construed as inviting a response to possible risks), it would have been the duty of the appellant to answer it. "[34]

Probable risks are material to the patient's decision. The Supreme Court of Canada, in *Hopp v. Lepp*, defined probable risks as

" ... those that, if he was informed about them, would reasonably be expected to affect the patient's decision to submit or not to submit to a proposed operation or treatment. "[35]

Probable risks must be disclosed to the patient, i.e. those special or unusual risks that have a probability of occurring in the particular treatment. Recall the facts of *Kelly v. Hazlett*: Temporary or permanent stiffness was a definite, special risk of osteotomy. In *Reibl v. Hughes*, a risk in surgery for removal of an occlusion of the internal carotid artery, was a 14% risk of stroke.

Certain possible risks must be disclosed. As stated by the Supreme Court of Canada in *Hopp v. Lepp*:

" If a certain risk is a mere possibility which ordinarily need not be disclosed, yet if its occurrence carries serious consequences ... it should be regarded as a material risk requiring disclosure. "[36]

The case, *Hopp v. Lepp*[37] was a decision of the Alberta Supreme Court confirmed by the Supreme Court of Canada in 1980. In this case, the plaintiff had suffered from a spinal condition requiring surgery. The defendant surgeon allegedly advised the plaintiff that there were no unusual risks attendant on the surgical procedure and that he, the surgeon, could carry out the procedure in the local hospital and that it was not necessary to have it done in the larger medical facilities located in Calgary. It was the first time the surgeon had performed the particular surgery since he had been certified. The plaintiff suffered permanent injury, and sued alleging that he had not given an informed consent as the surgeon had not told him that this was the first time he would be performing the surgery. The trial court held tht the defendant was under no obligation to tell the patient how many times he had performed the particular surgery, that such was not a matter contained within the sphere of information pertinent to the decision of the patient as to what procedures may be carried out.

Reibl v. Hughes incorporated certain *possible* risks as ones which must be disclosed if they are special or unusual with serious consequences but with respect to which the risk of their materializing is a mere possibility. In *White v. Turner*,[38] a 1981 decision of the Ontario High Court, the plaintiff had consented to breast reducing surgery for cosmetic and therapeutic reasons. The surgery resulted in misshapen breasts, with misplaced and scarred nipples. Further and major surgery partially corrected the condition but resulted in further scarring.

The plaintiff succeeded in negligence not only because the surgery was defectively performed, but also because the surgeon breached his duty to inform the patient of special or unusual (material) risks involved in the surgery. In determining what constituted material risks, the court applied "the reasonable patient standard", a subjective test rather than the objective, reasonable and prudent physician standard applicable in medical negligence cases. The court concluded that the predominant aim of the surgery was cosmetic. The defendant had not disclosed such possible risks affecting appearance such as undue scarring, boxlike appearance and poor positioning of the nipples. The court classified such possible risks as material risks and concluded that if the plaintiff had been given information of such risks she might reasonably have decided against the surgery.

The probability of benefit to a patient is a consideration examined by the courts in relationship to the probability of the risks. In 1982 the British Columbia Supreme Court, in *Rawlings v. Lindsay*[39] made a finding of liability following such a consideration. The plaintiff had suffered a permanent facial nerve damage following removal of wisdom teeth, and sued in negligence alleging breach of the duty to disclose the risk of facial nerve damage. Evidence indicated that the risk occurred in 10% of the particular jaw surgery cases. The defendant had mentioned *the possibility* but not the *likelihood* or the permanency of the complication. There was also a low probability that the surgery would improve the jaw condition. The court found liability.

2. Therapeutic Privilege and Patient Waivers:

There is a duty to disclose material risks. Once a court has determined that a risk was material and was undisclosed, the next question to be answered would be whether or not there was a lawful excuse for withholding information about the risk. Case reports and writings on the point indicate two possible excuses, therapeutic privilege, and, patient waiver of his right to know.

Therapeutic privilege recognizes that the right to autonomy, which mandates full disclosure and understanding by the patient before consent is given, may not always be compatible with the need to prevent undue anxiety when such information would be harmful to the physical or mental wellbeing of the patient. The law does permit use of discretion in the informing which is referred to as a therapeutic privilege. A physician is justified in exercising such a privilege for the therapeutic benefit of the patient and not for non-therapeutic or research benefits of the physician.

In 1932, The Ontario Court of Appeal, in *Kenny v. Lockwood*,[40] considered the situation where the patient suffered from Depuytrene's contracture. The defendant surgeon informed the patient that the recommended surgery was not serious. An obscure complication occurred postoperatively. The court held that the defendant physician had a duty to honestly inform the patient of the character, importance and probable consequences of the surgery but the duty did not extend to warning him of *possible* dangers which would likely distress or frighten him. (The court did not discuss material risks. The fact that the complication was an obscure one and characterized as a possible risk would suggest that the particular risk was a remote one.) In 1967, the Ontario Court of Appeal in *Male v. Hopmans*,[41] considered the complexity of the treatment and the subsequent difficulty of the patient's making an intelligent informed decision. The plaintiff was being treated for a staphyloccal infection of the knee (osteomyelitis). The physician ordered an antibiotic which had a 10-20% risk of causing deafness. The drug caused permanent deafness in the patient. The plaintiff alleged that he had not given an informed consent. At trial the court concluded that the final consideration in informing the patient is the adverse effect upon the plaintiff's morale that might result from a detailed explanation and that the defendant properly exercised his discretion in view of the uncertain nature of alternate modes of treatment. This uncertainty, said the court, would give the patient great difficulty in making an intelligent decision. The court applied the following considerations set out by the Court of Appeal of New Zealand in *Smith v. Auckland Hospital Board*:

> " To be taken into account should be the gravity of the condition to be treated, the importance of the benefits expected to flow from the treatment or procedure, the need to encourage him to accept it, the relative significance of the inherent risks, the intellectual and emotional capacity of the patient to accept the information without such distortion as to prevent any rational decision at all, and the extent to which the patient may seem to have placed himself in his doctor's hands with the invitation that the latter accept on his behalf the responsibility for intricate or technical decisions. "[42]

(The defendant, in *Male v. Hopmans*, was held liable in negligence on the basis of his failure to properly evaluate the patient's response to the therapy. The case is discussed further in the chapter entitled the Tort of Negligence and the Nursing Process, and the duty of care owed to assess the patient's response to the plan of care and to modify the plan on a timely basis.)

In *Reibl v. Hughes*, the Supreme Court of Canada indicated that where (because of his emotional state) the patient is unable to cope with certain information, the physician may be able to withhold certain facts or generalize the information which he would otherwise be required to describe in detail. In this situation, the extent to which the patient may seem to have placed himself in the physician's hands with an invitation to the physician to accept responsibility for the decision is relevant. Such a patient may be considered by the court to have waived his right to know the risks and to have been prepared to submit to the treatment without the necessary information.

3. Concept of Causation in the Negligent Failure to Inform:

When the alleged risk in a particular dispute has been determined by the court to be a material risk which had not been disclosed to the plaintiff, the court must then resolve the issue of causation. (This is to satisfy the requirements in actionable negligence.)

The causation test applied by the Supreme Court of Canada in *Reibl v. Hughes*, was the reasonable person in the patient's position test. What would a reasonable person, in the patient's position, have done if the particular risk that materialized, had been disclosed prior to the treatment? Would a reasonable person have refused the treatment? In *Reibl v. Hughes*, the plaintiff was under the mistaken impression that the surgery would cure his migraine headaches. Such was not the case. If the plaintiff had known that the surgery, which had a 14% mortality and morbidity risk factor, would not cure his headaches, what choice would he have made? The court concluded that a reasonable person in the patient's situation would, on a balance of probabilities, have refused the therapy offered.

In the 1980 decision of the British Columbia Supreme Court in *Dendaas (Tylor) v. Yackel*,[43] the plaintiff failed to prove battery, but succeeded in negligence because of the defendant's failure to inform her of the risk of pregnancy following tubal ligation and to point out that abdomenal sterilization was safer. Four months after surgery, the plaintiff became pregnant, required an abortion, and suffered subsequent depression. The court concluded that if the plaintiff had known of the relative risks involved and the safety of the option she would have opted for the abdomenal sterilization. The same court, in the previous year, in *Strachan v. Simpson*[44] found the surgeon to be liable in negligence for failure to inform the patient. The plaintiff had lost the use in his lower extremities. The defendant recommended surgery but did not inform the patient of the particular risk (paraplegia) associated with the surgery. The risk materialized for the particular plaintiff. In finding the defendant liable, the court stated it could not be said the plaintiff would have undergone the surgery had he known of the particular risk.

However, in the 1983 Ontario case, *Ferguson v. Hamilton Civic Hospital*,[45] the plaintiff's case failed on the basis of causation. The plaintiff had experienced difficulty with his vision and underwent a bilateral carotid arteriograph. The physician explained the procedure and informed the plaintiff of the risk of death but did not inform him there was a risk of stroke. Following the procedure the plaintiff was quadriplegic. The court determined that any reasonable person in the plaintiff's position would have elected to undergo the procedure and that therefore causation had not been established.

VIII. Summary of Basic Informing Principles and Practices:

It is recognized that the current status of the law makes it difficult to determine, in instances of defectively informed consents, whether the action lies in battery or negligence. However, in terms of day to day practice of professional health care workers, there are certain guidelines available to determine what constitutes a fair and reasonable explanation.
— Consider the gravity of the condition, the emotional and intellectual status of the patient, the nature of the proposed treatment, its expected benefits and natural consequences, the availability of alternate options, and the special and unusual risks of undergoing the treatment as compared to not having the treatment.
— Consider as material risks attendant upon the proposed treatment unusual or special risks that have a probability rather than just a mere possibility of occurring but inform of those possible risks which have serious consequences, and disclose all non-serious risks raised by questions posed by the patient or the legal guardian.
— Explain the nature of the treatment, expected consequences, and special and unusual risks, in language that the patient can understand and test the patient's understanding by having the patient respond to the disclosure in his own words.
— Consider as material those risks which the reasonable and prudent professional would disclose and those which a reasonable person in the patient's position would want to know in deciding whether or not to submit to the proposed elective treatment or care.
— Consider that the patient is entitled to have adequate time and environment to enable him to consider his position.
— *Consider who it is that has the duty to inform the patient* about the particular procedure or care. The person who intends to carry out the particular procedure or care has the duty to inform. This duty cannot, in law, be delegated to a third party sufficiently to insulate the performer from potential liability in the event of defective informing. (In a practical sense there are hazards in having a third party explain a proposed treatment. The information volunteered or offered in response to the patient's questions, may be inaccurate or incomplete and cause the patient to submit without a legally effective consent.) The physician informs of medical and surgical treatments. The nurse informs about nursing treatment and care.

IX. Sample Consent Policy:

A consent policy and practice of a particular health care facility should be researched

Sample Consent Policy

_____ HOSPITAL

TOWN (CITY): _____

PROVINCE: _____

AUTHORIZED BY: Board of Directors

EFFECTIVE DATES: May 19, 1980

Policy # **12 Page 1 of 3**

REVISION DATED: February 21, 1982, June 30, 1983

DEPARTMENTS PRIMARILY

AFFECTED: Admitting Department

                 Medical Staff

                 Nursing Units

SUBJECT: CONSENT

POLICY:

A surgical, or medical procedure, and administration of anaesthetics shall not be performed without a signed and witnessed consent from the patient or person authorized to consent on behalf of the patient.

POLICY PURPOSES:

1. To protect the patient's right to consent and withdraw consent to treatment.

2. To provide documentary evidence of consent.

3. To reduce risks to the hospital, and its staff.

and expressed in light of current statutory and case law applicable in the particular province or territory, the philosophy and goals of the agency, the type of patient population being serviced by the agency, and the probability of risks involved in the particular treatments and care offered. Reasonableness calls for systems of specific written consents for those treatments and procedures which carry known risks of severe consequences.

The following statement is a modified version of the method used by one health care facility to balance the rights of the patient and the risks of the corporate authority, employees and agents in a _particular jurisdiction and based on the statute and case law relevant in that province at that time:_[40]

PROCEDURE:

1. Time Period For Obtaining Consent:

For elective treatment an informed and written consent shall be obtained within twenty-four hours prior to the proposed surgery or medical procedure and prior to the administration of the preoperative sedation.

2. Responsibility for Informing:

— The attending physician is responsible for: informing the patient regarding his condition, the nature of the proposed treatment, its expected results, probable risks that are special and unusual, and such possible risks having severe consequences, and answering specific questions raised by the patient.

— The anesthetist is responsible for informing the patient of the anesthesia to be administered, its expected results, risks involved and alternate anesthesia reasonably available.

— The surgeon is responsible for informing the patient of the surgery to be performed, expected results, probable risks and those possible risks having severe consequences, and answering specific questions posed by the patient.

— The attending nurse is responsible for informing the patient of the nature of the nursing care being offered, the expected results, probable risks that are special and unusual, and such possible risks having severe consequences.

3. Responsibility for Witnessing Signatures:

I. *Consent for Treatment:*

The patient's or authorized person's signature on the consent form shall be witnessed by the admitting officer (in the absence of an emergency). In the event the signature is not obtainable on admission, responsibility for follow-up efforts is that of the admitting department, and nursing unit personnel shall assist in follow-up attempts.

II. *Consent for surgery, and particular risk treatment:*

The patient's signature on the surgical consent form shall be witnessed, preferably by the physician performing the proposed treatment. If he is unavailable, a registered nurse shall witness the signature of the patient after satisfying herself that the physician has informed the patient concerning the treatment.

4. Required Signatures:

(a) *Consent for Treatment:*

A patient must sign a consent form unless he is a minor excluded under this policy, is mentally incompetent, or legally incapacitated.

(b) *Emergency:*

In the event it is not possible to obtain the required signature authorizing emergency treatment of an adult or minor, and in the opinion of the physician, the emergency treatment is necessary, the physician shall, immediately following the emergency treatment, document the matter with an explanation of why the treatment was given without a written consent.

(c) *Consent for Treatment of Minors:*

Parental or guardian consent shall be obtained for persons _____ years old and younger. (Cite the particular provincial statute governing minority for purposes of treatment.)

EXCEPT THAT:

(I) Parental or guardian consent shall not be necessary for emergency treatment of a minor, providing documentation is completed by the attending physician.

(II) An emancipated minor (person under the age of _____ years) who is earning his own livelihood, or attending post-secondary education, and is mentally competent to appreciate the various elements of information included in "informed consent" shall consent.

(III) Any minor may consent to medical diagnosis and treatment of venereal disease.

(IV) Any minor parent may consent to medical and surgical treatment of his or her child and a married minor may consent to his own care.

(V) Where the minor is a ward of the court, (in a foster home) the representative authorized by legislation shall sign. (Set out the particular section of the child welfare legislation applicable in the jurisdiction.)

(VI) If parents are deceased, the legal guardian shall sign.

(VII) If parents are divorced the parent having legal custody shall sign.

(VIII) If parents are living separate and apart, the parent responsible for the care of the child shall sign, and if possible, consent of both parents will be obtained.

(d) *Substitute Consent for Persons Lacking Mental Competency:*

(1) For emergency care signed consent shall not be required

(2) The person previously authorized by the patient, in writing, to substitute consent, shall execute the written consent

(3) (Set out the procedure for substitute consent as determined by the particular legislation governing same in the province or territory concerned.)

5. Validity of Consent:

The persons signing the formal consent form shall:

(1) Be of sound mind.

(2) Be informed of the nature of the treatment, other available treatment options, expected results, and consequences, and probable risks, and possible risks with severe consequences, and those special risks indicated by the questions posed by the patient.

(3) Be provided with an environment and sufficient time to execute a voluntary consent.

(4) Be directed to read the consent form, or shall have the consent form read to him, prior to signaturing.

6. Consents Obtained From Substitute Consentors by Telephone:

Such consent may be obtained by use of extension telephones by two witnesses to the conversation, who shall sign a statement setting out the consent. The person giving the consent shall be requested to forward a telegram confirming the consent, or shall sign the consent form within a reasonable time period.

APPROVAL:_____ BOARD CHAIRMAN
SIGNATURE   TITLE

June 30, 1983

X. Endnotes:

1. Reference to (1976) 1 C.C.L.T. p. 2-3 in annotation of Lewis N. Klar
2. Supra n. 1 referring to article of L. Rozovsky at (1973) 11 Osgoode Hall Law Journal at 103
3. Murray v. McMurchy [1949] 2 D.L.R. 442 (B.C.S.C.)
4. Schweizer v. Central Hospital (1974) 6 O.R. (2d) 606, 53 D.L.R. (3d) 494
5. Allan v. New Mount Sinai Hospital et al. (1980), 109 D.L.R. (3d) 654, reversed in part 125 D.L.R. (3d) 276, (Ont. C.A.)
6. Reference to Fleming J.G. The Law of Torts (Law Book Company Limited 6th ed. 1983) Chapter 5
7. Ibid supra n. 6 p. 77-78
8. Beale v. Beale (1982) 52 N.S.R. (2d) 550
9. Black H.C. Black's Law Dictionary (St. Paul Minn. West Pub. 1979) at p. 276
10. Supra n. 9 at p. 276
11. Canadian Nurses Association: Code of Ethics: An Ethical Basis for Nursing in Canada approved by Board of Directors February 1980. Part Three was suspended following 1980 annual meeting of membership. See also draft code published Canadian Nurse, February 1984, Vol. 80, #2.
12. Marshall v. Curry [1933] 3 D.L.R. 198 (N.S.S.C.)
13. Supra n. 12 at p. 275
14. Supra n. 3
15. Mulloy v. Hop Sang [1935] 1 W.W.R. 714 (Alberta C.A.)
16. Law Reform Commission of Canada: Consent to Medical Care, Protection of Life Series, Study Paper prepared for the Law Reform Commission of Canada by Margaret A. Somerville, 1979 p. 46
17. Beausoleil v. Soeurs de la Charite (1966) 53 D.L.R. 2d 65 (Que. C.A.)
18. Kelly v. Hazlett (1976) 15 O.R. (2d) 290, 75
19. Picard E.I. Legal Liability of Doctors and Hospitals in Canada, (Carswell Pub 1984) at p. 66
20. Villeneuve v. Sisters of St. Joseph Hospital [1971] 2 O.R. 593, 18 D.L.R. (3d) 537 (reversed, in part, on other grounds), (1972) 2 O.R. 11, 25 D.L.R. (3d) 35 [1975] S.C.R. 285
21. Kangas v. Parker [1976] 5 W.W.R. 25 (Sask. Q.B.)
22. Re. Boudreau 43 N.S.R. (2d) 212
23. Mental Health Act 1971 (Nfld.) No. 71 sec 6
24. Booth v. Toronto G. Hospital (1910) 17 O.W.R. 118
25. Johnston v. Wellesley Hospital [1970] 17 D.L.R. (3d) 139 (Ont. H.C.)
26. Supra n. 25 at p. 144
27. Supra n. 16 at p. 72
28. Halushka v. University of Sask. (1965) 52 W.W.R. 608, (Sask. C.A.)
29. Supra n. 28 at p. 616
30. Koehler v. Cook (1975) 65 D.L.R. (3d) 766 (B.C.S.C.)
31. Reibl v. Hughes [1980], 114 D.L.R. (3d), 1, 33 N.R. 361 (S.C.C.) revg 89 D.L.R. (3d) 112, (C.A.), 78 D.L.R. (3d) 35
32. Supra n. 31, [1980] 114 D.L.R. (3d) at p. 10-11
33. Supra n. 18 (1976) 1 C.C.L.T. at p. 34
34. Hopp v. Lepp [1980], 112 D.L.R. (3d) 67 at p. 72
35. Supra n. 34, at p. 80
36. Supra n. 34, at p. 80-81
37. Supra n. 34
38. White v. Turner (1981) 31 O.R. (2d) 773 (Ont. H.C.)
39. Rawlings v. Lindsay (1982) 20 C.C.L.T. 301 (B.C.S.C.)
40. Kenny v. Lockwood [1932] O.R. 141, [1932] 1 D.L.R. 507 revg. [1931] O.R. 438, [1931] 4 D.L.R. 906 (Ont. C.A.)
41. Male v. Hopmans [1966] 1 O.R. 647, 54 D.L.R. (2d) 592 varied [1967] 2 O.R. 457, 64 D.L.R. (2d) 105 (Ont. C.A.)
42. Supra n. 41 citing Smith v. Auckland Hospital Board [1965] N.Z.L.R. 191 (C.A.)
43. Dendaas (Tylor) v. Yackel 1980, 109 D.L.R. (3d) 455 (B.C.S.C.)
44. Strachan v. Simpson [1979] 5 W.W.R. 315 (B.C.S.C.)
45. Ferguson v. Hamilton Civic Hospital et al [1983] 144 D.L.R. (3d) 214
46. Sample policy only, and adapted in part, from Sir Thomas Roddick Hospital policy manual, Stephenville, Nfld.

Chapter Four:

Tort of Negligence and the Nursing Process:

1. Concept Objectives:

This chapter will:
— identify common risks which may arise in the nursing care of patients
— identify the legal duties of care which the nurse undertakes in the carrying out of the nursing process
— emphasize the basic knowledge, skill, care and the honest exercise of intelligent judgment inherent in the concept of a reasonable nursing process
— emphasize the importance of effective communication skills in the carrying out of the required dependent and independent nursing functions involved in the nursing process
— focus on the value of prevention of risk and the promotion of safety through a commitment to the use of a reasonable nursing process.

II. Introduction:

The intent, in this chapter, is to examine the tort of negligence within the framework of the nursing process for the purpose of emphasizing the importance of this relatively new artificial construct for nursing care. Although the Canadian courts have not yet expressly referred to that which the professional nurse does, as a "nursing process", the cases analyzed in this chapter indicate that the courts do identify and value the essentials of the nursing process in their consideration of the presence or absence of nursing negligence.

The reader will recall in the chapter entitled Tort of Negligence: An Overview, a very early definition of negligence was transposed to define nursing negligence as follows:

" Nursing negligence is the "omission to do something which a reasonable [nurse], guided upon those considerations which ordinarily regulate the conduct of [nursing] affairs, would do, or doing something which a prudent and reasonable [nurse] would not do. " [1]

What it is that the reasonable and prudent nurse would do or not do is suggested in publications of nursing practice standards by the provincial, territorial association and Canadian Nurses Associations, and in writings by nursing authors concerning customary and approved nursing practice. These sources indicate that the registered nurse is the authority on nursing care just as the physician is the expert in medical matters, and that each within his field is selling a professional service. The person who enters the nursing field undertakes to bring to nursing practice, the exercise of a reasonable degree of care and nursing skill. She represents herself as understanding the subject and qualified to practice nursing. She is expected to have both nursing skill and nursing judgment, and the ability to prepare plans and specifications for nursing care and to implement that care safely.

The concept of negligence assumes the notion of foreseeable risk of harm and the notions of undertaking and reliance. In the nurse-patient relationship there is a definite reliance by the patient on the nurse's knowledge and expertise to protect him from foreseeable harm. Certain nursing care situations are fraught with risk because of the stage of development of the patient, his physical handicaps, the physical structure of the nursing unit, the disease condition of the patient, or the complexity of care being offered to the patient. The more probable the risk the higher is the duty owed by those who can be said to have undertaken the care and control in the nursing situation.

1. Nursing Process (defined):

Central to the considerations which ordinarily regulate nursing are particular types of plans and specifications known as the *nursing process*. Specifically this constitutes the approved approach to delivering nursing care for the very purpose of controlling foreseeable harm to the patient. The nursing process is a systematic approach to the identification of the patient's nursing care problems. It is a design for nursing intervention directed to the resolution or control of nursing problems in order of their priority, i.e. in order of their urgency and life and health threatening features.

2. The Nursing Process and Minimum Standards of Practice:

As indicated in chapter one, the process involves a series of separate but closely interrelated phases analogous to the phases inherent in medical care:
— assessing and obtaining a history for the purpose of making an accurate diagnosis
— designing a plan of care expressed in written orders
— implementing the plan of care
— evaluating the patient's response to the care and modifying the plan as necessary.

The "plans and specifications" used by the physician include documents such as history sheets, medical order sheets, laboratory reports of diagnostic tests, and progress notes. It is through the contents of these documents and others that the patient's medical problems, the physician's plan of action to deal with the problems and the patient's response to the plan, are to be found. The "plans and specifications" used by the nurse include documents such as the nursing history, nursing care plans that identify the nursing diagnosis and the nursing orders, and nurses notes which record the patient's responses to the medical care and to the nursing care.

The nursing process is a cyclical process characterized by a very deliberate methodology based on problem solving techniques. It is not a trial and error approach. It is not a "nursing routine" approach. The plan is directed to the needs of a particular patient and by its very nature would be inappropriate for any other patient in the nursing unit. The process may involve all of the nursing functions identified in chapter one of this text:
— independent nursing functions
— dependent nursing functions
— interdependent nursing functions
— advocacy functions.

The nursing plan of care is one that is tailored to the individual needs concerned. The registered nurse engages in such a process in order:
— to determine the patient's nursing needs in the order of their urgency and threat to life and health
— to eliminate irrelevant and dangerous

nursing activity
— to prevent foreseeable harm to patients
— to secure maximum safety, health and comfort for the patient.

Current nursing publications suggest that the organized nursing profession in Canada (the territorial and provincial nursing associations and the Canadian Nurses Association) expect the nurse to carry out a reasonable nursing process. For example, in July of 1982, the College of Nurses of Ontario published its revised statement of the *Minimum Standards and Criteria for the Assessment of the Practice of the Registered Nurse and Registered Nursing Assistants*.[2] The first of the published minimum standards stated:

Standard 1: *The registered nurse effectively uses the nursing process.*[3]

In 1980 the Canadian Nurses Association published (in the Canadian Nurse Journal)[4] the *draft report on standards for nursing practice*. The report contains five standards labelled *standards related to the nursing process*. The five standards concern the phases of the nursing process:
— collection of data
— analysis of data
— planning of the intervention
— implementation of the intervention
— evaluation.

There is some common ground between the standards described by the organized nursing profession in Canada and the *reasonable* and *prudent nurse standard* applied by the courts in those few nursing negligence cases which have been reported in Canada. It is therefore, reasonable to conclude that the registered nurse, on entry into the profession, holds herself out as qualified: to carry out systematic investigations of patient's problems, to design and implement appropriate nursing intervention, to assess the effectiveness of nursing interventions and to revise the care plan where necessary.

III. Phases of the Nursing Process as Legal Duties: An Overview:

The nursing process has been variously described to include four phases:

— a nursing assessment including the completion of a *nursing history*, a physical examination of the patient, a review of the physician's findings and clinical tests, for the purpose of making a tentative or confirmed *nursing diagnosis*

— a design of a written nursing care plan based on a current nursing assessment, and directed to resolution or control of nursing problems in the order of urgency as identified in the nursing diagnosis. The design includes the *nursing orders* which the registered nurse is expected to implement

— implementation of the nursing care plan

— evaluation of the patient's response to the nursing plan of care and the revision or modification of the plan to accommodate the patient's changing status of health or illness.

In the examination of the tort of negligence and the nursing process the argument is made that the registered nurse has an *overall legal duty* to execute a reasonable nursing process, including the following specific duties:

— to conduct a nursing assessment that is reasonable in the circumstances, i.e. one that is timely and of a frequency and depth called for by the foreseeable risks

— to design a written nursing care plan based on a current and adequate nursing assessment

— to implement a plan of care on a timely basis and to use knowledge, skill and care in its implementation

— to conduct an evaluation of the patient's response to care and to modify the plan as necessary and on a timely basis in order to avoid foreseeable injury.

The cases suggest that to meet the duty of care required by tort law, the nurse must render the quality and quantity of care that the reasonable and prudent nurse would render in the circumstances. As a general rule, the registered nurse who adheres to reasonable and approved customary practice in the various phases of the nursing process will not likely be found negligent by the courts. If, in the process, the nursing diagnosis is wrong, or the nursing intervention is detrimental rather than beneficial, there will not be a finding of liability where the appropriate standard of care was met.

The nurse is an independent practitioner in the administration of basic nursing care; she may delegate many procedures and duties but she cannot delegate her professional or legal responsibility for planning, supervision and assessment of nursing care. The employer, the attending physician and the patient all have a right to rely on the nurse carrying out her responsibilities in a reasonable manner. For example, in the 1974 Ontario medical and nursing negligence suit *Kolesar v. Jeffries et al*,[5] the family of the deceased succeeded in an action against the hospital for the negligence of its nurses. The physician's only defence was that he had relied on the nurses to carry out reasonable nursing care and that he had a right to so rely on them. The court agreed and dismissed the action against the physician and entered judgment against the hospital on the basis of vicarious liability. There had been a failure to carry out a reasonable, or indeed, any nursing process during the night tour of duty. (The particular case is analyzed in some detail later in this chapter.)

IV. Comparative Study of the Nursing and Medical Process:

As mentioned earlier the phases of the plan of care managed by the physician compare with the phases of the nursing process and some of the principles and standards of care identified by the courts in medical negligence suits are equally applicable to the nursing process. For this reason both medical and nursing negligence cases are analyzed here in the process of examining the standard of care applicable in the nursing process.

V. The Nursing Process and Nursing Negligence: A Case Analysis of the Duties of Care:

Using the following comparison of the medical and the nursing process, each phase of the latter is examined below in the light of relevant case law for the purpose of reaffirming some basic first principles.

MEDICAL PROCESS	NURSING PROCESS
STAGE 1: MEDICAL ASSESSMENT: — medical history — physical examination — clinical testing Purpose of assessment: To obtain an accurate medical diagnosis	**STAGE 1: NURSING ASSESSMENT:** — nursing history — physical examination — review of medical finding and results of clinical testing. Purpose of assessment: To obtain an accurate nursing diagnosis
STAGE II: DESIGN OF A REASONABLE PLAN OF MEDICAL CARE: Purpose: To manage, control or eliminate presenting, or probable medical problems, and in their order of urgency or threat to life and health. Expressed in the form of written **MEDICAL ORDERS**	**STAGE II: DESIGN OF A REASONABLE PLAN OF NURSING CARE:** Purpose: To manage, control or eliminate presenting, or probable nursing problems in order of their urgency or threat to life and health. Expressed in the form of written **NURSING ORDERS**
STAGE III: IMPLEMENTATION OF THE MEDICAL PLAN OF CARE: Includes combinations of conservative therapies such as diet, rest, exercise, drugs; radical therapies such as surgery, and use of psychosocial therapies directed to resolution of the problems identified in or associated with the *medical Diagnosis*: May include rehabilitation as well as curative measures.	**STAGE III: IMPLEMENTATIONS OF NURSING PLAN OF CARE:** Involves carrying into effect medical orders and nursing orders and includes activities directed to assisting the patient to accommodate his needs for nutrition, rest, exercise, drug therapy as determined in part by the *medical diagnosis* and *the nursing diagnosis*: May include caring, rehabilitative and educational activities.
STAGE IV: EVALUATION OF THE PATIENT'S RESPONSE TO THE PLAN OF MEDICAL CARE: Purpose: To intervene on a timely basis to prevent or control negative and idiosyncratic patient responses to therapy and to modify the therapy in accordance with the patient's needs.	**STAGE IV: EVALUATION OF THE PATIENT'S RESPONSE TO THE PLAN OF NURSING CARE:** Purpose: To intervene on a timely basis to prevent or control negative and idiosyncratic responses to nursing care, or in the instances of negative responses to medical therapies, for the purpose of communicating the findings to the physician for timely medical intervention.

1. The duty to conduct a nursing assessment that is reasonable in the circumstances: i.e. one that is timely and of a frequency and comprehensiveness called for by the foreseeable risks: (Phase 1 of the Nursing Process)

(a) Introduction: Purpose of the Assessment

The minimum standards of nursing practice direct that *the health needs of the patient and his ability to meet these needs are assessed by a registered nurse.* It has been implied in case law, that the reasonable and prudent registered nurse would not implement nursing care (emergency excepted) without first having in place a current nursing assessment.

The first phase of the nursing process, assessment, is clearly an independent function for which the nurse does not necessarily require a physician's order. In the absence of a medical order, the frequency and comprehensiveness of the patient review is within the registered nurse's discretion, and the physician has the right to rely on the nurse carrying out such a review as frequently and as comprehensively as the situation reasonably demands. Indeed, the courts have confirmed that the physician may so rely.[6]

The safety and relevancy of nursing care can only be assured if the information collected about the patient is accurate, complete, properly interpreted and if it accurately reflects the patient's current situation. To that end one requires a systematic framework within which to collect patient information. The traditional framework for information gathering in nursing assessments has been the "head to toe" approach based somewhat on the medical model for assessment. However more recent constructs may include a hierarchy of human needs approach or one based on a functional abilities structure.

The nursing assessment is the ultimate responsibility of the registered nurse. She causes the assessment to be done immediately on admission of the patient to the nursing unit and arranges for the assessment to be continued at a frequency dictated by the foreseeable risks identified in her findings i.e., by the nature of the patient's illness, his stage of growth and development and the complexity and risk involved in the therapies offered to the patient.

The immediate purpose of obtaining a nursing assessment is to arrive at an accurate nursing diagnosis just as the purpose of obtaining a medical assessment is to arrive at an accurate medical diagnosis. It would be unreasonable and dangerous for the physician to treat the patient without having completed a medical assessment (emergency excepted) because in the absence of a medical assessment, the diagnosis has a high probability of being wrong. When the diagnosis is wrong the treatment will in all likelihood be not only inappropriate but detrimental to the patient. Likewise, nursing care carried out in the absence of a current nursing assessment will likely result in inappropriate and possibly, detrimental care.

In 1978, the Ontario High Court heard *Wade v. Nayernouri*[7], a negligence action against the physician by the estate of the deceased. The physician diagnosed the patient as having migraine headaches although the patient had no previous history of migraines. Two weeks following the misdiagnosis the patient died as a result of a subarachoid hemorrhage. The court held the physician liable for:
— failure to take a proper medical history
— failure to conduct adequate neurological testing, and
— failure to employ the usual diagnostic aids.

(b) Defective Assessments:

In *Wade v. Nayernouri*, the Ontario High Court said the following about the duties in the assessment phase of the medical process. The assessment principle applies equally well to nursing:

> " In my opinion the cases have established that an erroneous diagnosis does not alone determine the physician's liability. But if the physician, as an aid to diagnosis, does not avail himself of the scientific means and facilities open to him for the collection of the best factual data upon which to arrive at his diagnosis, does not accurately obtain the patient's history, does not avail himself in this particular case of the need for referral to a neurologist, does not perform the stiff neck tests and the lumbar puncture tests, the net result is not an error in judgment but constitutes negligence. "

In 1978, the Supreme Court of Canada heard an appeal from the Quebec Court: *Hopital Notre Dame De L'Esperance v. Laurent*[8]. The case involved a female patient who had fallen while curling. The defendant surgeon examined her, but did not order an x-ray despite the patient's accident history and physical signs. He diagnosed the problem as a simple contusion and ordered medication for pain. One week later he renewed the medication following a discussion by phone, and without re-examining her. Three months later another physician examined her, ordered an x-ray and correctly diagnosed a fracture of the head of the femur. The liability of the physician was upheld on appeal.

The purpose of a medical assessment is to ensure, as far as is reasonable, that the diagnosis is accurate. In the absence of an emergency, the reasonable and prudent physician would not design a treatment plan without a current and adequate medical assessment in light of the patient's history and symptoms. The foregoing does not mean that the physician warrants that his medical diagnosis will necessarily be accurate, but only that it is reasonable in the circumstances, and that the diagnosis is in keeping with the presenting signs and symptoms and history of the particular patient. The courts acknowledge that "diagnosing" is not a scientifically precise process.

(c) The Nursing Diagnosis: Its Nature and Purpose:

A *nursing diagnosis* is quite distinct from a *medical diagnosis*; it tends to be related to a specific sign or symptom while a medical diagnosis tends to be a grouping of signs and symptoms under a disease label. The object of a *nursing diagnosis* is to identify those

---

SAMPLE MEDICAL DIAGNOSIS

— Myocardial infarct
— Viral pneumonic
— Appendicitis
— Osteomyelitis
— Cerebral Aneurysm
— Depressed fracture of skull
— Diabetes Mellitus
— Peptic Ulcer
— Pulmonary embolism
— Ventricular septal defect
— Hiatus hernia
— Peritonitis
— Acute cholecystitis
— Renal calculus
— Polycystic renal disease
— Rheumatoid arthritis

SAMPLE NURSING DIAGNOSIS

— respiratory distress (such as dyspnea)
— elevated temperature
— hypothermia
— hypotension
— Altered levels of consciousness or orientation (including drowsiness, lethargy, confusion, unconsciousness)
— Dehydration, edema
— Disturbances in appetite or digestion, (including nausea, vomiting, lack of appetite)
— Disturbances in bowel function (including diarrhea, constipation)
— Urinary disturbances (including urinary retention, dysuria, glycosuria, polyuria, urinary frequency)
— Pain, bleeding, inflammation
— Abdominal distention
— Disturbance in rest, sleep and, or exercise patterns
— Impaired verbal communication
— Sensory impairment including deafness, blindness, or other visual disturbance
— Limitation of movement or disturbed coordination
— Fear, anxiety, depression, grief, loss and loneliness

problems that require nursing attention. It excludes those problems that are treated by the physician's intervention, through use of diet, surgery, or prescription drugs and nuclear medicine etc. Such are within the domain of the practice of medicine. Persons with different medical diagnosis, quite commonly have similar nursing diagnosis. Consider the foregoing sample list of Medical Diagnosis and Nursing Diagnosis.

A reasonable nursing assessment includes several features:
— systematic observation of the patient
— physical examination
— incorporation of relevant findings from the physician's history, and from the clinical testing ordered by the physician.

(d) The Nursing History: Its Purpose:
A nursing assessment also includes the taking of a *nursing history* from the patient and or his family. This nursing history is a written record of information concerning the patient and his family, preceding his present illness, injury or condition. The history includes concise and organized units of information about the patient's previous experiences with illness, his present illness and health problems, presence of allergies, summary of medications, activities of daily living including food preferences, sleep and activity patterns, elimination routines, usual health practices and usual religious practices.

Meyer v. Gordon & The Defective Nursing History:
The nursing history is a summary of critically important information which can dictate the success and safety of subsequent nursing care. This was demonstrated in the following case. *Meyer v. Gordon et al*, (1981) a decision of the British Columbia Supreme Court (which considered a number of first principles discussed throughout this text). In terms of the value of the nursing history the case evolved as follows:[9] The plaintiff was admitted to the defendant hospital for the birth of her second child. The infant suffered serious brain injury when the plaintiff gave birth to the child in the labour room of the defendant hospital prior to the arrival of her family physician. There was no nurse or physician in attendance in the labour room when the infant's head presented shortly before 12:32 p.m. on March 21, 1977.

The plaintiff's prenatal history of the birth of her previous first child included a labour process of four hours and fifty-five minutes, a much shorter labour than the average for a nullipara mother (woman who has not produced a viable offspring). This rapid first labour indicated that the plaintiff's second delivery would probably proceed rapidly. At approximately 9:30 a.m. on March 21, 1977, the plaintiff's membranes broke while she was at home. She notified the physician. Her husband transferred her to the defendant hospital. She was admitted to the labour room at 11:30 a.m. Nurse W conducted a vaginal examination shortly after admission and concluded that the patient was in early labour. Nurse W testified that she was unaware Mrs. M's first labour was a rapid first labour. The trial judge stated:

 " It is my finding on the evidence that Nurse W was aware that Mrs. M was experiencing her second labour but that she did not ascertain that the first labour had gone rapidly. "[10]

The court, in reference to the standard of care provided by the nursing staff stated:

 " When Nurse W conducted her examination of Mrs. M shortly after eleven thirty she omitted to ascertain Mrs. M's obstetrical history and that her first labour and delivery had been a rapid one. Nurse W agreed on cross-examination that if she had taken the history of the rapid first labour she would have realized that she must watch Mrs. M more closely then she did. "[11]

The Court also drew attention to the evidence of Nurse W to the effect that:

 " a record of the previous birth history was routinely taken by the admitting nurse whether or not the prenatal form was available. Even if I assume that the prenatal form was not available to the hospital at the time of Mrs. M's admission, I am unable to conclude that its absence was a reasonable justification for the nursing staff failing to be aware of the previous birth history . . . "[12]

The nursing history is a tool to promote safe care and is as important to the patient's situation as the medical history. Each of these professionals is expected to have a patient history in place within a reasonable time after commencing the professional-patient relationship and to take that history into consideration in planning the required intervention. (In time, with the computerization of hospital records, it is likely that there will be one common history record on which is identified the pre-admission events of significance to physicians, nurses and other members of the health team.)

The evidence in the *Meyer v. Gordon* case indicated that from 12:05 p.m. that day until the infant was born (at approximately 12:32 p.m.), Mrs. M had been left unattended, and lying in an inappropriate, unsafe position. At 12:15 p.m. when the plaintiff's husband sought attention for his wife, he claimed Nurse W brushed him off as a nervous husband. Shortly after, when Mr. M checked on his wife, the baby's head was emerging. The infant girl was born in severe distress, flaccid, limp and coated with excessive meconium. The infant survived but as a result of the intrauterine distress and asphyxia, (due to the meconium) hypoxia resulted, with consequent brain damage, cerebral palsy and permanent mental retardation.

The court stated it had no difficulty in finding that the defendant hospital and its nursing staff failed to provide a reasonable standard of care:

> " Indeed, at the most critical time, from shortly after twelve noon until Nurse T rushed to the labour room, as the head of the child was delivering, at about twelve thirty-two, Mrs. M received no nursing care apart from the injection of demerol and gravol at twelve o-five. " [13]

In terms of nursing assessment, the Meyer case points out that the omission of Nurse W to obtain a nursing history, set the scene for the subsequent injury to the infant. (The failure to keep proper records of the progress of delivery compounded the situation.) The case indicates that in certain circumstances the importance of the nursing history may far outstretch that of the

medical history. The Meyer case reaffirms the principle that the higher the risk, the greater is the duty to conduct timely and frequent reviews of the patient's condition. The lack of a current nursing assessment makes it difficult, if not impossible, to obtain a correct nursing diagnosis. Without a correct nursing diagnosis, the plan of care will likely be inappropriate for the particular patient. Following are two more cases which highlight the importance of timely nursing assessments.

(e) Case Analysis of Defective Nursing Assessments:

In *Laidlaw et al v. Lions Gate Hospital et al*[14] (1969), the courts concerned themselves with nursing negligence for failure to carry out a reasonable nursing assessment. The plaintiff school teacher was married with two children, aged six and seven years. On April 21, 1966 at the age of forty-four years, the plaintiff was admitted to the defendant hospital for a cholecystectomy (surgical removal of the gallbladder). On the evening prior to surgery she was examined by the anesthetist who determined that the plaintiff was in good physical health. The following day the surgery was completed. While still anesthetized, the plaintiff was transferred to the care of the nursing staff in the post-operative recovery room. While in their care she suffered hypoxia resulting in permanent brain damage. Consequently she was reduced to the infantile state and required permanent confinement to hospital. She was unable to walk without assistance and her vision and hearing were impaired.

> " [She] will require for the remainder of her life to be fed, dressed and put on a commode. She is unaware of her own existence. " [15]

At trial, evidence was provided by three physicians, the director of nursing, supervisor and the two nurses involved in the incident. Three physicians were called as expert witnesses regarding the required standard of nursing care. (This was as inappropriate as it would be to call nurses as expert witnesses on the standard of medical care.)

Evidence indicated that the plaintiff had

been admitted to the recovery room at approximately ten thirty a.m. Twenty minutes prior to her arrival the second nurse in the recovery room left for her coffee break. This left one nurse in the recovery room. (The nurse in charge). The recovery room had six patient care units and was used to service five operating rooms. Each of the operating rooms was booked on that particular morning.

The charge nurse testified that on admission of the plaintiff she proceeded to carry out a nursing assessment. She determined the patient's respiration and pulse. However, before she was able to measure the blood pressure another patient was admitted, accompanied by a physician. The latter ordered an injection for his patient. (By this time there were five patients in the post-operative recovery room.) The nurse interrupted the assessment of Mrs. Laidlaw and proceeded to prepare the injection for the other patient. At trial, the nurse's claim that she was away from Mrs. Laidlaw for approximately three to four minutes was rejected. Instead, the court accepted the evidence of the anesthetist who indicated that the gap from the time of the plaintiff's admission to the unit to the time when the patient experienced breathing difficulty was approximately twenty minutes. The court concluded that the plaintiff had not been assessed in that period, and should have been assessed every two to three minutes. The latter was the standard required:

" Respiratory arrest is not an uncommon occurrence in the recovery room and, therefore, the personnel in this room must be watchful and alert at all times in order to protect the patients in this liable and vulnerable stage. The nurses in this room are there for the purpose of promptly recognizing any respiratory problem, cardiovascular problem or hemorrhaging. They are expected to take corrective action and or to summon help promptly. Many doctors gave evidence at this trial. No one challenged the principle that the patient is more prone to crisis after the operation than while in the operating room where the respiration is being controlled . . . This known hazard carries with it, in my opinion, a high degree of duty owed by the hospital to the patient. As the dangers or risks are ever-present, there should be no relaxing of vigilance if one is to comply with the standard of care required. " [16]

The charge nurse was held to be negligent in failing to provide the required observation, and as the nurse in charge, in permitting the other staff nurse to leave the unit for coffee at a time when she expected, or should have expected, the arrival of other patients from the operating room. (The court determined that the staff nurse was also negligent in leaving the unit without concern for the patients present at that time, or for the anticipated arrivals).

" The staff nurse was experienced enough to know that a respiratory obstruction could occur easily and go undetected if patients were not checked frequently. Armed with the knowledge she, nevertheless, nonchalantly went for her coffee. " [17]

The court concluded that the nurses' omissions constituted more than mere errors in judgment:

" I am mindful that the standard demanded by law is not that of perfection, but an anesthetized person is entitled to expect a high degree of performance, diligence, and observation . . . . because of the great risk of an obstruction or other trouble developing. "

" These negligent breaches of duty on the part of the nurses brought about the injury suffered by Mrs. L, and the injury could have been prevented by adequate and skillful nursing care. " [18]

In *Krujelis et al v. Esdale et al*[19] (1972) the background of nursing negligence was as follows:

The twelve year old boy was admitted to the defendant hospital in July of 1967 for cosmetic ear surgery. Prior to the operation he was a normal, healthy and intelligent boy and the only child of Latvian immigrant parents. Subsequent to the surgery the child suffered a cardiac arrest in the recovery room. (He died following the trial.) The parents sued the hospital and two of the physicians. (The court dismissed the action against the physicians.)

The allegations of negligence directed

against the nursing staff included the following:

— that the head nurse and one staff nurse negligently failed to check the boy's condition with sufficient frequency of care
— that the same two nurses negligently failed to observe visually what was discernibly happening to the patient
— that three of the five nurses in the unit were absent for coffee leaving the recovery room inadequately staffed
— that the head nurse was negligent in permitting three nurses to be absent from the unit at the same time.

The court found as a fact that the patient had been transferred to the recovery room between 9:40 a.m. and 9:45 a.m. and had been examined by the head nurse on admission and his condition was satisfactory at that time. The boy was placed in the unit still draped to the neck, and was positioned in the Trendelenburg position on his right side. At that time there were six other patients in the recovery room.

Nurse W and Nurse B had taken a coffee break and returned to the unit at which point the three remaining nurses left for coffee. When Nurse B returned she examined the patient. He was cyanotic and the vital signs were absent. She immediately called Nurse W who sounded the general alarm. The court stated that the precise time of sounding the alarm was highly important, and found that the time was between 10:10 and 10:13 a.m. The court concluded that the patient had not been assessed for a twenty to twenty-eight minute interval, and that the tragic event which occurred in this interval was the result of inadequate observation of the patient. They further determined that the inadequacy of the nursing assessment arose from the absence of three of the five nurses from the unit during that period which is ordinarily the busiest time of the day.

The court applied the standard of care which had been set out in the previously cited *Laidlaw v. Lions Gate Hospital* Case. The court concluded that the negligence was not that any omission or commission caused the patient to go into cardiac arrest, but rather that the negligence was in their fail-ure to observe the condition after it happened:

" ... The nurses in this room are there for the purpose of promptly recognizing any respiratory problem, cardiovascular problem, or hemorrhaging. They are expected to take corrective action and or to summon help promptly. "[20]

The court in the *Krujelis case* also addressed the problem of the "draping" on the patient which apparently had obstructed the nurse's observation.

The court's view on the point is consonant with the nursing profession's belief about the responsibility to arrange for examination, observation and assessment generally:

" The nursing staff, all specially trained for their exacting task, have complete jurisdiction, without consulting with anyone, to change the draping of a patient, if they consider such to be desirable ... "[21]

In the *Krujelis case* the child had potential, and then actual problems of respiratory difficulty, cyanosis and abnormal vital signs. In the circumstances of the case (the recovery room situation), there was a very high and foreseeable risk of problems occurring. The nurses therefore, owed a very high duty of care to that patient. Their duty was to carry out nursing assessments of such frequency that would permit prompt recognition of the respiratory and cardiovascular problems, and timely intervention.

2. The duty to design a written plan of care that is reasonable in the circumstances, i.e. one that is based on a current and adequate nursing assessment, and calling for the use of reasonable nursing measures:

(Phase 2 of the Nursing Process)

(a) Introduction: Purpose of the Design:

Within the nursing profession the standards of nursing care require that:

" There is a written plan of care, developed under the direction of a registered nurse, based on the assessed nursing needs of the individual, family and his needs as a person. "[22]

The idea of designing care assumes a

decision-making exercise involving analysis of the collected data. Within the context of a true medical process, designing is the determination of a course of medical action according to some rationale and, to be reasonable, must not be a trial and error or haphazard design unrelated to the patient's history and physical findings of the physician. Similarly, within the context of the nursing process, designing is the determination of a course of nursing action according to some rationale and for the purpose of fulfilling certain goals. To be reasonable, it must not be a trial and error or haphazard design unrelated to the patient's nursing history and findings from a nursing assessment. Analysis of medical and nursing negligence cases suggests that the professional may have completed a current and reasonable assessment, and accurately determined the medical or nursing diagnosis as the case may be, but the patient can still suffer an injury from the defective design of the plan. A *defectively designed* medical or nursing care plan is a distinctly different management and prevention problem from that of a safely designed plan that has been *implemented defectively*. Defective designs may include:

— use of obsolete procedures of high risk
— use of experimental procedures of high risk
— failure to coordinate the medical and the nursing plan of care
— failure to adequately inform the patient in advance in order to secure a legally effective consent
— failure to build in adequate consultation on a timely basis
— failure to commit the design to writing in a clear and accurate manner causing errors to be made in carrying the plan into effect.

This second phase of the nursing process is clearly an independent nursing function but one that depends in part for its safety, on its coordination with the medical plan of care.

The reasonable and prudent physician designs a realistic plan of care and does so in a timely fashion. His "design" may call for any of the conservative and radical therapies in various combinations and including: nutritional and drug therapy, use of combinations of rest and exercise, or surgical intervention involving the removal of body parts, insertion of body parts from matched doners or from an artificial supply. Alternatively, or as an adjunct, the medical plan of care may include psychiatric therapy using specific treatment modalities, for the purpose of relieving primary psychic stress or stress that is secondary to some other physical or psychosomatic illness. The medical plan of care is set out on the patient's record referred to as the doctor's order sheet, or the medical order sheet. The design focuses on cure of illness, prevention of complications and rehabilitation of the patient. The objective of the design is to manage, control, eliminate or prevent certain diseases, trauma and complications. In probable risk situations it is imprudent and unreasonable for the physician to neglect to design a plan of care on a timely basis, when the patient's medical diagnosis calls for one. Alternatively, it would not be prudent for the physician to design one so defectively that it is foreseeable the patient will be injured if subjected to the treatment set out in the plan.

(b) Case Analysis of Defective Designs:

Following are four cases concerning defective care plans. In *R v. Rogers*[23] the British Columbia courts held that the physician was guilty of criminal negligence in the treating of a child. He had diagnosed the child's condition as exfoliative dermatitis. He prescribed a low protein diet and the child died of malnutrition. (This case concerns a criminal conviction and is not a civil action in damages for negligence.) In *McCormick v. Marcotte*[24] the plaintiff suffered a fracture of the thigh and was treated by the defendant plysician. On the request of the plaintiff the physician consulted an orthopedic surgeon. The latter recommended skin traction followed by the insertion of an intramedullary nail. The defendant physician performed an open reduction and used instead, the obsolete method of a metal plate and screw and then applied a cast. The surgery was unsuccessful. The screws on the one side of the fracture tore away from the bone. The plaintiff suffered a permanent disability. The trial court held the physician to be negligent. This decision was upheld by the Supreme Court of Canada in 1972. In 1975 the Supreme Court of Canada reviewed the Nova Scotia Court of Appeal decision in *Eady v. Tenderenda*.[25] In this case the surgeon was found to be negligent when the plaintiff suffered a partial facial paralysis. The physician had used the obsolete method of chisel and hammer during mastoid surgery instead of the modern microscope and drill method. Bone chips from the mastoid became imbedded in the facial nerve causing the paralysis. (The physician had failed to remove the bone chips during the surgery.)

In 1983 a judicial enquiry was held into the death of a man whose autopsy showed death due to a combination of alcohol and barbiturate overdose. The deceased had a known alcohol addiction problem. The physician allegedly prescribed a large quantity of tuinol, a drug that was considered by medical experts to be inappropriate for use with persons with alcohol addiction because of the drug's addictive qualities. The evidence also indicated that the drug order was excessive in amount, potentially lethal and no longer recommended for use. Purportedly the drug was ordered by telephone by the physician without examination of the deceased.[27]

The timeliness of the care plan is of important consideration. It may well be that the assessment was reasonable, the medical diagnosis accurate and the design (medical orders) absolutely appropriate, but the delay in carrying out the orders may be related to the damage suffered. For example, in *Wine v. Kenohan et al*[27] the plaintiff suffered a serious infection while on a fishing trip. The physicians at the nearby hospital failed to operate promptly and the plaintiff suffered additional pain, scarring, and required further treatment which the court concluded, could have been avoided by prompt and correct treatment.

(c) Nursing Orders: Their Purpose:

The nursing care plan is a prescription expressed in *nursing orders* setting out specific nursing actions. The specific nursing actions are directed to the nursing problems identified in the assessment, in their order of priority in terms of their life or health threatening character. The prescription for nursing action is revised as often as necessary according to the changing needs of the patient. It is unreasonable for the nurse not to have a management plan in place for the patient presenting such nursing problems as:

— pain from a diagnosed or undiagnosed cause
— fever
— unstable vital signs
— abdominal distention
— urinary retention
— anorexia
— nausea and vomiting
— bleeding

The foregoing nursing diagnoses are but a few of the problems whose presence or potential existence dictate that nursing orders be prescribed on a timely basis and provide for appropriate nursing intervention.

A reasonable nursing care plan is not an inflexible and unchanging prescription for action. It is revised as often as necessary and according to the needed reordering of priorities as indicated by the current status of the patient.[28]

The nursing orders are committed to writing. It is critical that the plan be in writing to ensure that the information is available to all the nursing personnel caring for the patient. The recording of the information increases the precision and accuracy in the continuous care. Depending on the type of records kept by the institution, the nursing orders may be recorded on a document called a nursing care plan. The focus of the plan is care rather than cure, and includes activities to prevent problems and complications. As well, it includes activities directed to rehabilitation and education of the patient and his family for self management where possible. Although the design of the care plan is an independent nursing function it is determined in a large way by the medical care plan. The plan is directed to supporting the medical care plan. Specifically, it is directed to assisting the patient regarding his needs for nutrition, rest, exercise, proper ventilation and elimination.

The challenge is to keep the nursing care plan current, relevant and clearly communicated to the nurses responsible for implementation. This tool is the central source of the particular nursing needs of the particular patient.

An author in the text *The Nursing Process: A Scientific Approach to Nursing Care*, sets out a master nursing care plan covering the fundamentals of patient care which include:[29]

— nursing plans related to the physician's orders
— nursing plans related to hygienic care
— nursing plans related to environmental adjustments
— nursing plans related to the assistance needed by the patient
— nursing plans related to safety precautions
— nursing plans related to the prevention of complications
— nursing plans related to problems of elimination
— nursing plans related to rehabilitation
— nursing plans related to patient and family teaching
— nursing plans related to psychological support
— nursing plans related to spiritual care
— nursing plans related to referrals

Under each of the foregoing twelve categories is a listing of fundamental care needs. For example under the fifth heading, nursing plans related to safety precautions, are included such fundamentals as:

— assessment of levels of consciousness and degree of mental responsibility
— warning about sensory and bodily defects
— provision for call bells or lights
— safe bedside unit, equipment in working order, with bedrails in place when necessary
— constant attendance, and safety belts on stretcher and wheel chair during transportation
— safe administration of heat, cold and flammable gases.

Under the sixth heading, nursing plans related to the prevention of complications are included:
— maintenance of a patent airway, by positioning, intubation suctioning
— provision for good body alignment, by positioning, the use of supportive devices, such as pillows, bed board, foot board, appropriate mattress, bed
— prevention of contractures, decubitus ulcers, circulatory disturbances, hypostatic pneumonia, by arrangements for moving and turning patient
— prevention of respiratory complications by deep breathing and coughing exercises
— avoidance of circulatory constriction due to mechanical appliances
— warning against massage of extremities
— prevention of fluid and electrolyte imbalance, by estimating food consumption and measuring fluid intake and output
— responsibility for observing administration of parenteral fluids to avoid infiltration into tissues
— prevention and detection of clogging in drainage tubes
— prevention of cross infections
— degree of isolation necessary
— protection from excessive irradiation
— prompt relief of pain to avoid deleterious physiological reactions to pain

Under the seventh category, nursing plans related to problems of elimination, are included:
— responsibility for observing abdominal distention when the patient is incontinent of urine or feces, and when he is suffering from urinary frequency, diarrhea, or constipation
— provision for offering the bedpan frequently whenever diuretics are administered
— appropriate fluids and diet

With respect to nursing orders included in the nursing care plan (the prescribed nursing actions) Marriner makes the important point that the prescribed nursing actions must be specific:

" What direction does "force fluids" give a nurse? How much of which kind of fluids? When? How? What is allowed on the patient's diet? What are his likes and dislikes? When does he prefer which type of fluids? ''[30]

Thora Kron in the fifth edition of *The Management of Patient Care*[31] makes another critical point concerning nursing orders:

" The nursing staff must understand that when a specific nursing action is written on the care plan, other personnel cannot change the order just because they do not agree with it. Nor can they ignore a nursing order any more than they can ignore the physician's order. However, if a change in the patient's condition occurs, then a change in the nursing orders will probably be necessary, so someone must always be responsible for maintaining the care plan for the entire twenty four hours. If two nurses disagree about the way of meeting the patient's needs, they must, just as physician's do, discuss their different opinions in order to arrive at a mutually acceptable method. ''[32]

Kron also makes the point that the possible need for the physician's approval of the proposed nursing solution is determined, in part, by whether the proposed intervention is merely a modification of hospital policy or procedure, or whether it involves some aspect of the physician's treatment plan. It is also determined by the degree of rapport existing between the two professional health care workers.

(d) Analysis of: MacDonald v. York C. Hospital et al; and Badger v. Surkan

The critical importance of the second phase of the nursing process, that of designing a reasonable plan of care is indicated in the following case, *MacDonald v. York County Hospital*[33], a case to be examined in terms of the adequacy of the plan designed by the nurses concerned. (The appeal court reaffirmed finding of negligence on the part of the physician, but found that "such negligence as there may have been on the part of the nurses or other members of the hospital staff" was not a contributory cause to the patient's loss.) However the adequacy of the nursing care plan is set out for review in the excerpt from the nursing notes set out in the following paragraphs:

The case concerned an eighteen year old man who had suffered a severe commin-

uted fracture and dislocation of the left ankle in a motorcycle accident on March 19, 1969, some seven years before the case was reviewed by the Supreme Court of Canada. The senior staff surgeon performed a closed reduction and then placed the plaintiff's leg in an unpadded cast reaching from the base of his toes to his groin. No written or oral orders were provided the nursing staff except a written order for demerol for pain.

The nursing record for the critical thirty hour period following the application of the cast was as follows:

March

19th	23:00	Appears satisfactory
19th	24:00-02:00	Sleeping—Awoke—complaining of severe pain—toes warm, colour good, movement sufficient of all toes but little one, which is stuck to cast.
20th	02:15	Demerol 75 mgms.
20th	06:45	Demerol 75 mgms. for pain. Toes good colour, warm. Patient able to feel any touch on toes.
20th	07:30-15:30	Bed bath given—complains of pain—left foot
20th	10:30 a.m.	Demerol 75 mgms. for pain in leg, toes warm to touch but no *apparent feeling in them*, taking fluids well.
20th	11:00	*Dr. M visits—notified re. condition of toes*
20th	12:00	Complains of pain
20th	13:00	Toes still numb—complains of a great deal of pain
20th	14:10	Dr. V visited
20th	14:30	Phenophen No. 2 Complains of nausea.
20th	15:30	Resting quietly
20th	18:00	Having lots of pain—Phenophen No. 2 Toes on left foot dark and cold has no sensation in them.
20th	21:00	Demerol 100 mgms.
20th	23:30	Patient's toes very cold and colour is purple and numb—sleeping.
21st	03:45	Demerol 100 mgms. Slept

		at intervals — toes on left foot cold, discoloured, no sensation.
21st	08:00	Demeral 100 mgms. for pain — toes very cold and blue, no feeling or movement in them. *Dr. V notified by phone re leg.*
21st	08:45	Cast bivalved by Dr. V.[34]

In the time period circulation to the limb was so impaired that gangrene set in and the limb had to be amputated. The trial court made a finding of negligence on the part of the physician. The court identified three specific failures on the part of the physician said to constitute negligence:

— the physician's failure to attend the patient for some eighteen hours during which the patient's condition continued to deteriorate

— his failure to prescribe anticoagulant drugs at an earlier stage in the treatment, and

— his failure to consult with a cardiovascular specialist when he found himself unable to diagnose the serious symptoms which had developed and which dictated his decision to amputate the plaintiff's foot.

The documentary and oral evidence indicated that from the time of the defendant physician's visit at 2:10 p.m. on March 20th (when there was already clear evidence of circulatory impairment), until 8:00 a.m. the following morning when the physician was notified by telephone, there was a gradual and unmistakable deterioration of the plaintiff's foot. There was no evidence of any action taken by the nurses except to record the changes and administer pain killers as prescribed. From 6:00 p.m. on March 20th, three of the classic signs of circulatory impairment were noted by the nurses. The court concluded that in the absence of any medical evidence to the contrary, and having regard to what were the ultimate consequences of the symptoms, serious and radical changes were taking place over the period and that no physician had been contacted:

" Since there is no entry for the critical period of some eighteen hours, I find as a fact, that no doctor was contacted and since no explanation of any kind was offered as to why no doctor was contacted, or as to any attempt being made I find as a fact that no attempt was made to contact one. "[35]

The nurses' notes indicated a five and a half hour gap between the nursing assessment at 18:00 hours on March 20th when the toes were first shown as being dark, and the next assessment at 23:30 hours when the toes were purple. Another four hours lapsed before the next assessment and a further four hours before an assessment a 8 o'clock on March 21st when the defendant physician was alerted.

The trial court found that the nurses were negligent in failing to inspect the patient's condition at frequent intervals when the classic symptoms of circulatory impairment appeared. On appeal, the Ontario Court of Appeal overturned the finding of liability against the nurses based on the evidence of the defendant physician given in cross-examination. (The appeal court agreed with the trial judge that the symptoms observed were those of serious change. However the defendant physician, when questioned as to his probable course of conduct had he been notified of the change, stated that he would have attended at the hospital and examined the plaintiff but that he doubted that he would have taken any action at that time.) (Refer back to the concept of causation in actionable negligence set out in Chapter Two).

While it may be that the nurses were remiss in not calling the physician, and therefore negligent, said the court of appeal, there was, in view of the physician's evidence, no reason for the court to believe that the nursing negligence was a contributory cause of the patient's loss. The court made the observation that any person who has even the most elementary knowledge of first aid, or of the human anatomy, including even a school child of fairly tender years who has been taught the basic elements of first aid, knows that circulatory impairment is a very serious matter and that time is of the essence in relieving the impairment. In practice, knowledge of the risks involved in the application of casts is basic knowledge in undergraduate nursing curriculum.

The nursing care design in *MacDonald v. York County Hospital*, was not based on the nursing problems that were probable and actual in the situation. If the design had been so based it would have called for immediate consultation between the nursing and medical personnel for the purpose of modifying the plan of care and intervening to relieve the circulatory impairment caused by the restricting cast.

Badger v. Surkan et al[36], a 1972 decision of the Saskatchewan Court of Appeal dealt with a fact situation similar to the foregoing case. In the latter the hospital was sued together with the defendant physician, but the trial court dismissed the action against the hospital. The case involved a thirty-eight year old plaintiff treaty Indian who was married and had four children, the eldest of whom was seven years old. On April 26, 1968, the plaintiff was run over by a tractor. He was admitted to the defendant hospital at midnight and was seen immediately by a physician who referred him to the defendant Dr. S. Dr. S examined the plaintiff between 12:15 and 12:30 on April 27th and noted comminuted fractures of the tibia and fibula of the right and left legs. He performed a closed reduction of the four fractures, and applied a cast from the hip to toe of both legs. Treatment was completed at 1:55 a.m. At 8:00 a.m. the toes were pale and cold and the plaintiff required morphine. Dr. S visited the patient at 12:45 p.m. and considered the plaintiff's condition satisfactory. However later in the afternoon the nursing assessment revealed the toes to be cyanotic, swollen and cold. (This was reported to a Dr. T who then completed a medical assessment and had the cast on the right foot trimmed back to give the toes greater freedom.) At 4:00 p.m. on that day, an assessment by a nursing assistant revealed the toes to be cold, bluish and swollen and the plaintiff was complaining that the casts were too tight. The night nurse assessed the patient hourly from midnight and noted that the toes had become numb and had lost the power of movement. At 8:00 a.m. on April 28th, the

nurse again noted the foregoing signs and Dr. T again assessed the plaintiff at 10:30 a.m., when he found marked cyanosis and loss of movement. He instructed the nurse to contact Dr. S immediately, which she did. Dr. S saw the plaintiff at 11:00 a.m. and learned for the first time that the swelling and cyanosis had appeared. (He testified at trial that he marked the casts along the sides and ordered the nurse to have the casts univalved. However, the nurses' notes stated only that: "11:00 a.m. Dr. S visited and marked casts" and the nurse testified that Dr. S directed only to mark the cast. The trial judge resolved the conflict in evidence by accepting the nurse's interpretation of the events.) Again at 2:00 p.m. Dr. T saw the plaintiff and again noted the abnormal signs and at that point cut the casts on the inside of the legs. Dr. S visited at 4:30 p.m. and ordered morphine for the patient. At midnight on April 29th, a nurse assessed the plaintiff and considered that his condition had worsened, yet it wasn't until the day shift that the nurses contacted Dr. S again. At that point he instructed that the cast on the other foot be cut and that a physician be called for consultation. At this stage however, the left leg was irreversibly damaged. Four days later the left leg was amputated. Three weeks later the right leg was amputated.

At trial medical experts gave the opinion that:

> " Coldness, blueness, numbness, tingling and lack of movement are signs of impaired circulation, and, perhaps nerve damage. If any of these things occurred, the cast should be bivalved immediately. " [37]

The evidence in *Badger v. Surkan* indicated that the foregoing symptoms were present as early as the beginning of the day shift on April 27th. Yet it wasn't until 11:00 a.m. on April 28th that the defendant Dr. S, saw the patient for the first time following application of the cast. The court had no hesitation in finding the defendant negligent for failure to carry out an adequate examination after the casts had been applied.[38]

This case makes the point that the patient's injury was not due to the original disease or injury. The injury resulted from a defective medical plan of care and failure to modify the plan of care to prevent the foreseeable damage which in fact occurred. Unlike the situation in *MacDonald v. York Hospital et al*, in which the nurses did not report their findings, the Badger case resulted from the physician's failure to intervene after he was given the nursing findings. The two cases raise the issue of the sometimes difficult situation which arises in the immediate post-cast period. Newly applied casts shrink in the drying process. Newly injured limbs may become swollen. Casts applied to injured limbs may act as tourniquets which at a certain stage can cause impairment of circulation. The nurse owes a duty of care to the particular patient to carry out accurate and frequent nursing assessments of the patient following the application of a cast. This data must be recorded accurately on the nursing records and communicated to the attending physician if signals of possible impairment begin to present. It is the nurse's responsibility to ensure that her actions are reasonable and prudent in the circumstances and directed to prevention of the probable risks which accompany cast application. What would the reasonable and prudent nurse have done in a fact situation similar to the *MacDonald* and the *Badger* cases? There is a very definite hierarchial structure within the nursing department and the medical staff organization. The reasonable nurse would use the formal communication system to report her findings to the physician. In the event that the physician does not attend to examine the patient, the nurse is expected to consult with her immediate supervisor on the matter who may need to again communicate with the physician. Further communication with the chief of the surgical service, or medical service concerned, may be required if the patient's condition remains unassessed by the attending physician. As the courts in the *MacDonald* and the *Badger* cases suggest, a person with the most elementary knowledge of anatomy or first aid knows the seriousness of circulatory impairment and that time is of the essence.

3. The duty to implement a nursing care plan on a timely basis using reasonable knowledge, skill, care and an honest exercise of judgment.

(Phase 3 of the Nursing Process)

(a) Introduction:

Implementation focuses on the quality and quantity of nursing care actually being delivered and calls for the use of a well written plan of care to guide both the nurse assigned to a particular patient and the registered nurse in charge of the unit. In phase three the role of each of these two categories of personnel will be studied. First, a detailed analysis will be made of the previously mentioned *Kolesar v. Jeffries et al* for the purpose of demonstrating the interrelatedness of nursing assessment, design and implementation, when the assigned nurse is delivering "hands on" nursing care. Secondly, a brief study will be made of the role of the charge nurse required to ensure a safe implementation of care by persons under her supervision. In this regard brief references will be made to the previously studied cases *Laidlaw v. Lions Gate Hospital*, *Krujelis v. Esdale*, *Meyer v. Gordon* and other cases.

(b) Analysis of Kolesar v. Jeffries et al

Kolesar v. Jeffries et al (1974), was an Ontario case which concerned nursing negligence arising subsequent to the death of a patient in the immediate post-operative period. Mr. Kolesar had been injured in a motor vehicle accident on January 26, 1969. On December 26, 1969 he was admitted to the defendant hospital for surgical repair of his injuries. A discogram revealed herniation of the L5-S1 disc. Surgery was performed on December 30th in which the defendant Dr. B removed bone from the iliac crest and grafted it to the spinal area where the diseased disc had been removed. Following the surgery and while still in the operating room the patient was placed on a stryker frame, transferred to the post-operative recovery room and from there to the surgical unit at approximately 12:10 p.m. on December 30th, 1969.

Between six and eight p.m. that evening the patient was visited by his wife. At trial she recalled that on that visit her husband was very pale, complaining of severe pain in his head, neck and back, and complained as well, of a heavy feeling in his stomach. There were no recordings made on the patient's chart from 10:00 p.m. that evening until he was discovered dead at 5 a.m. the next morning.

An autopsy report revealed gastric juice in the deceased's lungs and a grossly distended bladder. The pathologist had concluded that death was due to pulmonary edema and hemorrhage, which appeared to be secondary to the aspiration of the gastric juice, and which aspiration probably occurred three or more hours prior to death.

An action was brought by the widow, in negligence against the surgeon, the hospital and the nurse employees who had the management of the care of the deceased. The action was also brought against the motorist. He had admitted liability for the injury to the deceased in the motor vehicle accident the year prior to the hospital admission. The motorist joined the plaintiff in pursuing Dr. B and the other defendants for reimbursement of any damages and costs he might be required to pay the plaintiff because of the fatality. (See the concept of Joint Tortfeasors in Chapter Two.) The defendant physician did not make specific allegations of negligence against the hospital or the nurses, but successfully pleaded the following:

> " . . . that he was entitled to and did rely on the nursing care and supervision performed by the employees of the defendant hospital and was at no time notified of any change in the condition of William Kolesar until approximately 5:30 a.m. on December 31st 1969 at which time he was advised that the patient had expired. "[30]

The defendant hospital and nurses denied fault but made no allegations of negligence against the surgeon.

At trial, a stryker frame was introduced as an exhibit. This is a narrow bed with an apparatus that enables it to be turned 180 degrees on its longitudinal axis so that the supine patient is then lying face downwards on the frame and is strapped into the frame so that his spine remains in a fixed position while the healing process continues. The court noted that use of the frame presented special problems to the nursing management of the patient and that from the outset there were grave risks of regurgitation. These risks were heightened by the following realities:

— the patient was reacting to an anesthetic and to the onslaught of the various drugs he had received for relief of pain
— there was a danger of the bladder becoming distended and pressing on the bowel and stomach and causing difficulty of breathing
— there was shock to the bowels following spinal surgery. Such shock could cause a paralytic ileus, a condition which interferes with peristalsis. (These are rhythmic wavelike contractions of the muscle of the bowel in successive circles by which the bowel contents are propelled along.) The stomach could become easily overloaded and for this reason it was critical that great care be taken not to give the patient too much fluid by mouth, and to ensure that the stomach contents were not allowed to rise to a point where the patient could regurgitate. (Regurgitation can take place in a number of ways. It can be massive and be projected through the esophagus into the throat and quickly smother the patient. Regurgitation could, alternatively, be minimal and occur over a period of time, so that the patient has increasing difficulty in oxygenating his blood.)
— when the bladder is full the capacity of the lung could be impaired through pressure exerted by the overdistended bladder against the organs above it. The cumulative effect of the drugs depressed the central nervous system causing drowsiness, changes in mood, mental clouding, depression of respiration and cough reflex, decrease in motility of the stomach and intestinal and urinary retention.

Required Standard of Nursing Care:
The court examined the standard of nursing care which Mr. Kolesar was entitled

to expect in light of his medical diagnosis, and surgical treatment, position on the stryker frame and the fact that he was within the first twenty four hours following surgery (the acute post-operative phase). The required standard of nursing care was described by two nursing experts, a member of a school of nursing faculty who taught orthopedic nursing, and a director of nursing from an orthopedic hospital. Their evidence was summarized as follows:

— that a post-operative patient is usually very disturbed and sleeps only from hour to hour. If the particular patient slept peacefully all night, that in itself was a danger signal. The patient should have been roused hourly and compelled to breathe deeply and cough. If fluid was in the throat, or tubes were present, a suction device should have been brought in

— physiotherapy in the form of movement of the arms should have been given when the patient was awakened

— the large quantity of fluids ought not to have been given to the patient. On learning of the fluids which had been given prior to midnight, (together with the constant flow of intravenous fluid) the nurses should have realized that the body's system was overloaded. The patient should have been watched carefully because of the danger of regurgitation, his stomach palpated and his bladder catheterized

— the vital signs should have been taken and recorded at regular intervals.

Standard of Nursing Care Allegedly Received:

The court compared the nursing care actually received by Mr. Kolesar during his first post-operative night with the standard of care identified in the evidence of the nursing experts. The court noted that: At midnight two nurses and one nursing assistant made a tour of the unit together. Armed with flashlights they looked into the various rooms and if all seemed well the patients were left alone. The patients were not roused to ascertain their condition. The nursing practice was to permit the patients to wake up on their own and then answer their calls. Mr. Kolesar was not awakened, or given any nursing care.

The court concluded that when the defendant hospital admitted the deceased it assumed a non-delegable duty to ensure that Mr. Kolesar received careful and competent treatment at the hands of the nursing staff. The court found that the patient's death was caused by the negligence of the defendant nurses, in their allowing the patient large quantities of fluid, in not rousing him at regular intervals through the night and in their failure to take and record the patient's vital signs on a regular basis. The court believed that Mr. Kolesar died slowly over a period of hours, that he was in a weakened state due to the effect of the drugs and the accompanying anoxia and the position on the stryker frame, and that he was limited in his struggle to call for help:

> **"** I have not the slightest doubt that had he been given adequate nursing care, his condition would not have occurred, or would have been detected timely. **"** [40]

In exonerating the attending physician, the court concluded that he was entitled to rely on the nursing staff in the management of the post-operative care of the patient. At one point in the trial the court questioned whether the physician had a responsibility to leave specific orders for deep breathing exercises every hour. Later the court determined that it was the physician's routine to expect the nurses to carry out such activities for the first twenty-four hours or even longer. The court decided that the physician had a right to expect and to rely on such activity being done. (This accords with approved customary and independent nursing practice considered to be within the discretion of the registered nurse.) This case was appealed to the Ontario Court of Appeal which overturned the judgment of the trial court. On further appeal to the Supreme Court of Canada, the judgment of the trial judge was reinstated and the appeal of the hospital and the nurse in charge was dismissed.

In the Kolesar case there was no nursing

care plan designed to meet the needs of the patient. Instead the nurses followed "routines" which caused all the patients on the nursing unit to be cared for in a similar manner, regardless of their diagnosis, and treatment and probability of risk. The burden was placed on the patient to request nursing intervention. Yet, the duty was on the assigned nurse to determine needed nursing care based on a current nursing assessment, identification of nursing diagnosis and in accordance with prescribed nursing orders. Because there was no current assessment, the nursing problems were not identified and consequently needed nursing care was not carried out. What little care was given was in fact, lethal: too much fluid intake, insufficient fluid output, too much sedation and insufficient deep breathing exercises. Such sub-standard care was not excusable in law.

(c) Staffing Patterns and Assignment:

In the Kolesar case, the court compared the nursing care actually received by the deceased on that particular night shift, with the standard of nursing care set out by the nursing experts. The court noted that the plaintiff had been placed on a surgical ward with a night staff of two registered nurses and one registered nursing assistant. There were thirty-four patients on the unit of which eleven had had surgery that day and three were scheduled for surgery the morning of the deceased's death. The court noted that the nurses had extra duties such as making up the medications, checking ward stock, completing the census sheet and checking the pharmacy. The court questioned how such a small number of nursing staff could look after so many patients. (The case raises questions of the staffing obligations and staffing rationale of a hospital authority. In this case however, the personal duty of the corporation in the provision of numbers of persons was not placed in issue by the parties.)

The foregoing points out as well, the unique responsibilities of the nurse in charge of the nursing unit. It requires that she know the nursing needs of the various patients in the unit and that she organize

for their care based on some reasonable rationale. It requires that she assess needs on an ongoing basis, determine whether approved staffing ratios are sufficient, confirm that sufficient approved staff are available and make choices for the allocation of staff in accordance with the most urgent needs of patients.

Traditionally, staffing patterns were determined on the basis of bed occupancy rates and average patient-stay days. However, such a model does not take into consideration such factors as the diagnosed condition and treatment needs of the particular patient, physical layout of the nursing unit, type of functions delegated to nurses from management and from the physician, the type of assignment methods (team nursing, unit assignment etc.) or the philosophy of care in the particular unit. There are now more effective models available for determining appropriate staffing patterns. For example, there is a model that directs attention to the assessment of desirable levels of nursing care in the actual unit. It identifies the numbers and type of professional and non-professional workers required to meet the nursing care level identified as desirable. This tends to be more accurate than a staffing pattern based on occupancy rates and average length of patient stay days.

Appropriate staffing also requires that the nurse in charge of the unit know the limits and capabilities of the various members of the nursing staff assigned to the unit. Nursing labels such as registered nurse, student nurse, or certified nursing assistant do not necessarily guarantee the degree of safety of knowledge, skill and judgment of a particular worker assigned to carry out nursing care. A system should be in place for performance evaluation of staff on a regular basis, and where the charge nurse is put on notice that a particular staff member is unsafe, she has a duty to take corrective action to ensure that the unsafe situation is remedied.

When a particular patient is placed at risk, the cause of the problem is not necessarily lack of numbers of nurses. Rather, the problem may be due to lack of nursing care on a timely basis. For example, in the previously mentioned Laidlaw case, the court noted that the staffing pattern in place on the particular day was in compliance with the recommended quota. The problem arose because the nurse in charge allegedly permitted the nurses to go to coffee break without requesting temporary replacements in accordance with hospital policy. The manner in which the charge nurse scheduled the available staff contributed to the absence of adequate nursing care for Mrs. Laidlaw on her admission to the post-operative recovery room. The court was satisfied that the charge nurse breached her duty of care to the patient and that the particular breach caused or contributed to the patient's injury.

When a patient is injured the causes may include a mix of inadequate staffing quotas and defective assignment patterns for allocating particular nurses to particular patients. For example, in the previously mentioned *Meyer v. Gordon* case, the British Columbia trial judge noted the following:

> " It is my conclusion that Mrs. Meyer was left unattended because there were heavy demands on the hospital staff on the labour floor from 11:30 until after 12:30. During the last critical half hour of this period Mrs. Meyer appears to have been no particular nurse's patient or responsibility. Nurse W said that she did not conduct a vaginal examination prior to administering the demerol because she did not consider that Mrs. Meyer was her patient at that time. The side of the labour floor where Mrs. Meyer was located was assigned to a Nurse K until Nurse K went to lunch at 12:15. Yet there were no entries on Mrs. Meyer's chart by Nurse K. It is clear that neither Nurse W nor Nurse M felt that Mrs. Meyer was her patient although Nurse W stated that Nurse K had told her to "watch her patients" before she, Nurse K, went to lunch. "

> " Nurse M agreed that the reason she did not check the fetal heart rate after 12:00 noon was because she thought Nurse W was in charge of Mrs. Meyer . . . "[41]

The evidence in the critical incident report prepared by Nurse W at the time of the injury stated:

> " . . . As I was admitting nurse that day Mrs. Meyer was not my patient, but I did go back to her at about 12:15 to check on her and found that she was coping well with her strong contractions. "[42]

The trial judge concluded:

> " Although I have had difficulty in understanding why Nurse W did not check the fetal heart rather than Nurse M, I have concluded that this occurred due to breakdown in communication between Nurse M (head nurse) and Nurse W. "[43]

The court held the hospital liable for the inadequate nursing care prior to the birth, concluding that:

> " It is clear from the evidence that fetal distress is not uncommon. It is a risk which the hospital recognized in its procedural manual (ex. 15) and which all of its obstetrical procedures were designed to prevent or lessen. It as a risk of which all of its nursing staff were aware or ought to have been aware. "[44]

(d) The Role of the Charge Nurse and the Nurse Assigned to Patient Care:

The nurse in charge has a responsibility to communicate accurately that which the assigned nurse is to do. Errors in the giving of care may occur when the charge nurse's direction does not clearly indicate who is to perform the care and carry out the medical and nursing orders involved. One of the traditional means of communicating within the nursing staff is through the use of the *nursing report*. This is the name given to a conference held at the beginning of shift in which nurses from the previous shift orient the oncoming staff about the current status of the patients on the unit and the medical and nursing orders in effect. The object of the exercise is to inform and to pass over care and control of the unit at the end of shift to oncoming staff. Other communication tools include the patient's chart, the written nursing care plan, the policy and procedural manual, and written job descriptions. Such references, to be safe and effective, need to be current.

The role and responsibility of the nurse in charge is a pivotal one and it is possible, in law, that failure to carry out charge nurse duties in a reasonable manner, could constitute nursing negligence. For example, in *Smith v. Brighton and Lewes Hospital*[45], a 1982 English case, the courts focused on the duties of the nurse in charge and made a finding of liability in negligence. The physician had ordered thirty injections of streptomycin at eight hour intervals. The plaintiff actually received four extra doses of the drug and suffered damage to the eighth cranial nerve causing permanent loss of his sense of balance. The nurse in charge of the unit was found by the court to be solely liable for the injury by her failure to keep an accurate system of written communication that would indicate the time at which the prescribed number of doses had been completed. (The court also noted that the charge nurse subsequently concealed the fact of the extra doses from the attending physician, "an ugly and unfortunate feature ... which deprived the patient of the protection of the doctor's trained mind.")

The individual nurse is expected to comply with the reasonable and prudent nurse standard in the implementation phase. The reasonable and prudent nurse would ensure that her knowledge and skills were current and adequate, would not attempt a trial and error approach to new procedures, would function within the limits of assigned authority and would know the policies of the hospital. Written policies are intended to guide and limit practice. When such policies are "published" in manuals on the various units, the employees concerned are deemed to know their contents. Such policies may for example, provide guidelines concerning safety precautions in use of restraints and siderails, the consent requirements in the performance of procedures, or setting out the certification process for the performance of medical-nursing functions. The reasonable and prudent nurse is expected to carry out medical orders and nursing orders using knowledge, skill, care and an honest exercise of judgment.

Following are a series of cases involving physician negligence and others involving nursing negligence in the implementation of the care plan. The defective care in each instance resulted from one or more of the following:
— lack of reasonable knowledge on the part of the performer of the treatment or nursing care
— lack of skill in manipulating equipment, or supplies, or
— lack of care in the sense that the health care professional was "careless" in the particular instance.

Nyberg v. Provost Municipal Hospital Board[46], reviewed by the Supreme Court of Canada in 1927, reaffirmed the presence of nursing negligence. Two hot water bottles had been placed in the patient's bed following surgery to counteract surgical shock. The next day it was determined that the patient's left leg had been severely burned while he was unconscious. The court concluded that the nurse's failure to ensure that the hot water bottle was not a source of danger to the patient was inexcusable and constituted negligence. In *Harkies v. Lord Dufferin Hospital*[47], a 1931 decision of the Ontario courts, the hospital was held liable for the negligence of a student nurse. The student set up a steam inhalation for a three year old patient suffering from pneumonia. The set up was defective and the child was severely burned. The court concluded that the student failed to exercise proper care and such failure constituted personal negligence on the part of the student for which the hospital was held vicariously liable. In *Beatty v. Sisters of Misericorde of Alberta*[48] (1935), the Alberta Supreme Court held the hospital vicariously liable for the failure of a student nurse to adequately supervise the patient in the immediate post-operative phase, and for the negligence of the night supervisor in the reinsertion of a rectal tube. The post-operative patient had been given an injection of morphine and a sedative. The supervisor instructed the student to stay with the patient until the sedation took effect. The student left the room and the patient fell out of bed. The fall caused a catheter to be pulled out of the surgical site and the patient developed a fistula and required further surgery. During the second surgery the surgeon inserted a rectal tube. Following the surgery the tube slipped out. The night supervisor reinserted the tube and in the process damaged the surgical site and the patient developed a fistula between the vagina and rectum. In an action in negligence the court reviewed statistics regarding the percentage of patients who had fallen out of bed in the defendant institution in the previous three years. Of nineteen cases, eleven of the patients had fallen out of bed shortly after the administration of sedation. Such statistics indicated to the court the importance of supervision of sedated patients. (The court also determined that in the circumstances the supervisor was negligent in reinserting the rectal tube.)

In *Farrell v. Regina*[49] (1949), a decision of the Saskatchewan King's Bench, a student nurse was weighing an active infant, and the infant rolled off the scale unto a steam radiator, causing second degree burns. The court held that because of the activity of the child and the proximity of the radiator, a very high degree of care was required in the circumstances and the student nurse failed to meet the duty of care.

In the decision of the Supreme Court of Canada in 1952 the defendant hospital was held liable for the negligence of an intern in *Fraser v. Vancouver General Hospital*.[50] The intern examined the patient who had injured his neck in a motor vehicle accident. The intern misread the x-rays. Without consulting the radiologist on call, he concluded there was no injury and the patient was discharged. In fact the patient had a fractured neck and subsequently died. The court held that the intern was negligent in misreading the x-ray, in failing to consult the radiologist and in failing to give an accurate report to the attending physician thereby causing the plaintiff to be discharged without treatment. In 1964 the Ontario High Court held the defendant hospital liable for the negligence of an intern in *Murphy v. St. Catharines General Hospital*,[51] the intern used an intracath for the patient and in the process severed the intracath and lost nine inches of the catheter in the patient's basilic vein. The intern had not read the directions for the use of the intracath and he had not received instructions in the use of the relatively new procedure.

The foregoing cases point out that the physician and the nurse owe a definite duty of care to the patient to implement medical care or nursing care as the case may be, with adequate knowledge, skill and care.

(e) Duty to Inform and Warn: Patient Education:

There is a well recognized legal right by the patient to be informed about the plan of care to be implemented. The basic principles involved in the concept of "informed consent" have been set out in chapter three, which considered the matter within the context of battery and negligence. The particular chapter points out that the patient's right to information is a critical aspect of reasonable and prudent health care service. It is a right that has been translated by the courts into a duty on the part of health care workers, a duty recognized in the torts of battery and negligence.

In general, the defence to the touching of a patient by a physician, nurse, lab technician or radiologist as the case may, is the presence of the patient's consent. In order for consent to be said to be present in law, the patient must have very definite information on which to make choices about whether to accept or reject the touching involved in a particular treatment or care. The necessary informing requires that the patient have knowledge of the nature of the particular treatment, its expected results, and an awareness of the risks peculiar to the particular treatment.

It is important to appreciate that a health care worker may be quite knowledgeable, skillful and careful in the technical aspects of treatment, yet the court may make a finding of negligence against the worker for failure to properly inform the patient concerning risks. The court may conclude that, not having been informed of the risks, the patient had not consented to accept the risks involved. The court may find, on the particular facts, that if the patient had had the information of the risks involved in the treatment, he would have decided not to accept the treatment and thereby avoid the risk now being complained about. The courts in such an instance are saying that the health care worker's duty to inform had been breached and the breach of duty caused the patient's injury. (The reader is referred to Chapter Three for a review of the critical elements in informed consent.)

It is the registered nurse's duty to inform the patient to whom she is delivering care, about the nature of the planned nursing care and treatments about to be administered by the nurse. The purpose of so explaining is to obtain the patient's agreement with the plan of action and to the particular person who is to administer the care. (It is not the nurse's duty to explain to the patient the particulars of the surgical or medical therapies to be administered by the physician.)

An equally important purpose of informing the patient is to encourage his participation in his own care with intelligence and safety. It is important in health care practice and in law, to warn the patient of particular hazards associated with the treatment. In 1972 the Ontario Court of Appeal reviewed the decision in *Crichton v. Hastings*[52]: The defendant orthopedic surgeon prescribed an anticoagulant drug following surgery. The patient hemorrhaged. In an action in negligence she alleged that the physician breached his duty to warn her of the possible side effects of the drug. The court held that the defendant was liable. There was, said the court, a duty on the part of the physician to:

— warn his patient about the dangerous side effects of the drug, and

— to instruct the patient as to the importance of immediately reporting the appearance of any side effects, to the physician.

The court stated it was not a defence that immediately after surgery the physician had relinquished the care of his patients to others. The court stated that it was incumbent on the physician to foresee the possible dangerous side effects of the drug and to arrange for adequate instructions. The physician should have foreseen the possibility that the patient would be leaving the hospital with a continuation of the drug by self administration.

In the 1930 case, *Antoniuk v. Smith*,[53] the court raised the matter of the nurse's duty to warn. The nurse employee had been directed by the physician employer to operate an x-ray machine in the treatment of skin problems. In performing the treatment on the plaintiff the latter suffered electric shock and burns. He sued in negligence. At trial, the court determined that the nurse was personally negligent in failing to warn the patient. However, on appeal, the action was dismissed.

The case is of interest only in the fact that it suggests that nurses too, have a duty to inform their patients. Where aspects of patient management are customarily delegated to other members of the health team such as nurses, the latter may well be held accountable for any personal negligence in the carrying out of care and including the duty to inform. In areas that are not commonly delegated, the physician may be perceived by the court as having a personal duty to do the informing, a duty which, in the particular instance, cannot be delegated in a way to effectively insulate the physician himself from liability.

Patient education is a well recognized responsibility of nurses. Consider for example, the nursing care planning required prior to discharge of a patient with diabetes mellitus. The patient, in order to manage his condition safely at home, may need to have skill in testing his urine for sugar and acetone, skill in the manipulation of an insulin syringe, and knowledge about the protection and use of insulin. He may need information about his special nutritional needs, the manner of preventing skin breakdown, and an understanding of the illness itself. Are there probable risks involved if the patient is uninformed in self management in such an instance? Within the profession it is recognized that discharge planning, including patient teaching, is a basic part of each patient's plan of care considerations. If the patient is being discharged from the health care institution with a medical order for continuation of certain treatments or medications, it is in the best interests of the patient, the physician and the nurse to have a clear understanding about which person or persons shall carry out the teaching. A method is needed for determining that the patient does understand the required information and has the required self-management skills. Today, for example, it is becoming increasingly common to discharge patients suffering from respiratory problems, with orders for self-administration of drugs, oxygen and use of ventilators. It is also common to discharge patients suffering from kidney disease and requiring renal dialysis, with orders for family management of the process within the home. Consultation between the physician(s) concerned and the nurses planning for discharge, is important. The ability of the patient and his family to manage care is assessed. It may be that the patient will require referral to one or other of the community agencies for home care. A record, known as a referral record, is completed requesting the continuation of care from the agency concerned.

4. The duty to conduct an evaluation of the patient's response to care and to modify the plan of nursing care on a timely basis:
(Phase 4 of the Nursing Process):

The standard articulated by one of the provincial nursing associations reads as follows:

> " The registered nurse participates systematically and continuously evaluates the extent to which the individual's health needs are being met. "

> " On the basis of the evaluation, the registered nurse modifies the nursing care plan as required. " [54]

(a) Purpose of Evaluation:
The purpose of evaluation, in the context of the medical and the nursing care process, is to determine how the patient is responding to the plans of care, so that appropriate action may be taken should the therapy or nursing care require modification or complete change. This fourth phase is as important as the previous phases of the process. Despite accurate and timely medical and nursing diagnoses, despite well designed medical and nursing care plans, implemented in accordance with the appropriate

standard, it is possible that the patient may not respond to care in the pattern predicted and required. The failure to do so may be due to a number of factors some of which may be foreseeable and controllable:

> " It is thus apparent that the negligence which caused the damage suffered by the patient is not limited to the original error. It also includes the doctor's failure to concern himself enough about the patient's condition to appreciate the need to see her again and to obtain the x-ray film which would have immediately revealed the need for surgery. As time went on without the pain disappearing, the need for a more thorough examination became increasingly evident . . . " [55]

There are instances where the cure and the care can be worse than the disease. Indeed the cure and, or the care, may become, in law, and in fact, the cause of a patient injury. For example, it is possible that the patient could have an unexpected allergy or untoward reaction to certain drug therapy, bleeding as a result of certain surgery, inflammation or infection, impaired circulation following application of a cast, or an intolerance to a particular therapeutic diet or components of it.

(b) Defective Follow-Up Evaluation:
In this phase of the process, the physician is highly dependent on the nursing team's monitoring system in the detection of the patient's responses. The nurse, in the supervision of the patient, is expected to make timely observations, to record her findings accurately and to report the findings on a timely basis so that appropriate intervention may be taken to prevent or limit potential damage from the therapy or nursing care. There are no cases on point within the nursing process. However it is appropriate to include cases decided within the context of the physician's responsibility. In *Bergstrom v. G*[56] (1967 Quebec) the physician applied a plaster of paris cast to the plaintiff's foot. The following day the plaintiff experienced pain but was unable to contact the physician or his temporary replacement. Seven days elapsed before the physician examined the patient at which time it was discovered that gangrene of the

limb had set in. It was necessary to amputate the patient's leg above the knee because of the complication. The physician was held to be liable for the patient's loss, because of the failure to evaluate the situation in that period of time. In *Male v. Hopmans*[57] the physician prescribed enomycin, an antibiotic, to treat a staphlococcal infection. The drug cured the infection but caused permanent deafness and kidney damage. The Ontario court concluded that the physician was negligent in his failure to carry out urinalyses and hearing tests during the course of therapy in order to detect the patient's responses. In the 1979 decision of Manitoba's Queen's Bench, in *Rietze v. Bruser*[58], the court concluded that the physician was negligent in his surgical treatment of the patient's Paget's Disease. Subsequent to the surgery and the application of a cast to the patient's diseased arm, clawing of the hand and loss of use of the fingers occurred. The court determined that the physician should have been alert to these complications and taken further steps to determine the cause of the patient's pain and swelling, including removing certain of the sutures and examining the surgical site.

It is important to note that what is reasonable and prudent in terms of the frequency of the evaluation and the components of the evaluation, is dictated by the known risks associated with the patient's stage of development, the disease, and the known risks associated with the physician's intervention. The physician is not expected to guarantee that each and every untoward reaction shall be detected at the moment of appearance. Nor is he expected to prevent any and all complications. There is only the expectation within the profession and the law that reasonable monitoring take place. In *Wilson v. Swanson*,[59] (1956) the Supreme Court of Canada noted that "negligence" may consist of a failure to apply the proper remedy upon a correct determination of the patient's condition, or it may result from a failure to properly inform oneself of these conditions. If the latter, then it must appear that the physician had a reasonable opportunity for examination and that the true physical condition was so apparent, that it

could have been ascertained by the exercise of the required degree of care and skill. It is also acknowledged by the courts that true emergencies may call for immediate intervention in the presence of unexpected, unpredicted demands and appropriate staffing, equipment or supplies may not be available. Where life threatening crisis calls for intervention without time for complete assessments to be done prior to intervention, injuries which may arise could well be assigned by the court to misadventures and not negligence.

There are no Canadian cases expressly finding nursing negligence for failure to conduct a timely assessment of the patient's response to nursing care intervention. (The reader will recall however, that the courts in *MacDonald v. York County Hospital* and in *Badger v. Surkan* did direct their attention to nursing's responsibility in assessing the patient's response to medical treatment in the nature of cast application.) Although there are no cases on point it is reasonable to assume that the first principles applicable to the physician's duty are applicable to the nurse's duty. It must appear that the nurse had a reasonable opportunity for evaluation and that the true physical conditions were so apparent that they could have been ascertained by the exercise of the required degree of nursing care and skill.

In summary, the nursing process is a system which values the use of problem-solving methods and avoidance of trial and error approach to patient care. Ultimately it is a process designed to promote better communications between health care professionals and the patient for better risk management in the delivery of safe, effective and humane patient care.

VI. Endnotes:

1. Blyth v. Birmingham Waterworks Co. (1856) 11 Exch. 781 at p. 784
2. *Standards of Nursing Practice For Registered Nurses and Registered Nursing Assistants*; (July 1982)
3. Supra n. 2 at p. 7
4. Canadian Nurses Association: *A Definition of Nursing Practice on Standards for Nursing Practice*, (June 1980)
5. Kolesar v. Jeffries (1974) 9 O.R. (2d) 41, at

p. 43 and p. 50

6. Supra n. 5 at p. 43 and p. 50
7. Wade v. Nayernouri (1978) 2. L.M.Q. 67 (Ont. High Court) p. 1
8. Hopital Notre Dame de L'Esperance v. Laurent [1978] 1 S.C.R. 605, 17 N.R. 593, 3 C.C.L.T. 109; affirming (1974) C.A. 543
9. Meyer v. Gordon 17 C.C.L.T. 1
10. Supra n. 9 at p. 7 and p. 43
11. Supra n. 9 at p. 11
12. Supra n. 9 at p. 45
13. Supra n. 9 at p. 11
14. Laidlaw v. Lions Gate Hospital (1969) 70 W.W.R. 727, (B.C.S.C.)
15. Supra n. 14 at p. 729-730
16. Supra n. 14 at p. 735
17. Supra n. 14 at p. 736-737
18. Supra n. 14 at p. 736-737
19. Krujelis v. Esdale [1972] 2 W.W.R. 495, 25 D.L.R. (3d) 557 (B.C.S.C.)
20. Supra n. 19 at p. 561
21. Supra n. 19 at p. 560
22. This statement of nursing standard is extrapolated from a publication of the Registered Nurses Association of Nova Scotia entitled: Framework For Practice of Nursing in Nova Scotia: Guidelines and Standards, at p. 9. The reference notes that the Standards of Nursing Care on that page are based on Guidelines for Developing Standards for Nursing Care, Canadian Nurses Association, Ottawa, 1972 p. 3; See also the 1983 Standards For Nursing Practice, the current reference for nurses in Nova Scotia.
23. R. v. Rogers [1969] 65 W.W.R. 193, 4 C.C.C. 278 (B.C.C.A.)
24. McCormick v. Marcott [1972] S.C.R. 18, 20 D.L.R. (3d) 345
25. Eady v. Tenderenda [1975] 2 S.C.R. 599, 9 N.S.R. (2d) 444, 3 N.R. 26, 51 D.L.R. (3d) 79 reversing 41 D.L.R. (3d) 706
26. In unreported magisterial inquiry
27. Wine v. Kenohan et al (1978) 2 L.M.Q. 129
28. See Miller B.F. and Keane C: *Encyclopedia and Dictionary of Medicine, Nursing, and Allied Health*, (Toronto, W.B. Saunders, 1983) p. 791.
29. See Marriner A. *The Nursing Process: A Scientific Approach to Nursing Care.* (St. Louis, C.V. Mosby, 1983), article by Nancy C. Kelly, p. 149-150
30. Supra n. 29 at p. 87
31. Kron T: *The Management of Patient Care: Putting Leadership Skills to Work* (5th edition Toronto; W.B. Saunders 1981) p. 151
32. Supra n. 31 at p. 125

33. MacDonald v. York County Hospital [1973] 1 O.R. (2d) 653; affirmed (sub nom. Vail v. MacDonald [1976] 2 S.C.R. 825; 8 N.R. 155 at 163 (S.C.C.)
34. Supra n. 33 p. (This excerpt from the nursing notes is also set out in Chapter Five: Hospital Records, Evidence, Access and Confidentiality)
35. Supra n. 33 3 [1972] O.R. at 495
36. Badger v. Surkan [1973] 1. W.W.R. 302, 32 D.L.R. (3d) 216 affirming 16 D.L.R. (3d) 146 (Sask C.A.)
37. Supra n. 36 at p. 216 and at p. 224
38. Supra n. 36 at p. 216 and at p. 225
39. Supra n. 5 at p. 43
40. Supra n. 5 at p. 50
41. Supra n. 9 at p. 14
42. Supra n. 9 at p. 17
43. Supra n. 9 at p. 20
44. Supra n. 9 at p. 37
45. Smith v. Brighton and Lewes Hospital unreported but summarized in the Times June 1982
46. Nyberg v. Provost Municipal Hospital Board [1927] S.C.R. 226, [1927] 1 D.L.R. 969
47. Harkies v. Lord Dufferin Hospital 66 O.L.R. 572 [1931] 2 D.L.R. 440
48. Beatty v. Sisters of Misericorde of Alberta [1935] 1. W.W.R. 651 [1935] 2 D.L.R. 804 (Alberta C.A.)
49. Farrell v. Regina [1949] 1 W.W.R. 429 (Sask K.B.)
50. Fraser v. Vancouver General Hospital [1952] 2 S.C.R. 36, [1952], 3 D.L.R. 785
51. Murphy v. St. Catherines General Hospital [1964] 1 O.R. 239, 41 D.L.R. (2d) 697
52. Crichton v. Hastings et al [1972] 3 O.R. 859, 29 D.L.R. (3d) 692 (Ont. C.A.)
53. Anotoniuk v. Smith [1930] 2 W.W.R. 721 (Alberta C.A.)
54. Supra n. 3 at p. 9—Standard I, D (2)
55. Supra n. 8 at p. 126
56. Bergstrom v. G [1967] C.S. 513 (Que S.C.)
57. Male v. Hopmans [1966] 1 O.R. 647, 54 D.L.R. (2d) 592; varied [1967] 2 O.R. 457, 64 D.L.R. (2d) 105 (Ont. C.A.)
58. Rietze v. Bruser (#2) [1979], 1 W.W.R. 31, (Manitoba Q.B.)
59. Wilson v. Swanson [1956] 5 D.L.R. (2d) 113 (S.C.C.)

Chapter Five: Nursing Records, Evidence, Access and Confidentiality

VII. Problem Oriented Records:
1. *Data Base*
2. *Problem List*
3. *Nursing Care Plan*
4. *Flow Charts*
5. *Progress Notes*
6. *Discharge Plan*

VIII. Reasonable and Prudent Nursing Recording Policies, Practices and Systems

IX. Use of Incident Reporting Systems:
1. *Purposes*
2. *Policy Considerations*
3. *Suggested Content of Critical Incident Record*
4. *Critical Incident Reports as Evidence: Confidentiality and Privilege*

X. The Hospital Records: Confidentiality and Access to Health Information:
1. *Ownership*
2. *Sources of Legal Duty to Maintain Confidentiality*
3. *Exceptions to the Duty to Maintain Confidentiality:*
   (a) Patient's Consent
   (b) Statutory Duty
   (c) Court Order
4. *Right of Access to Information*
5. *Storage and Disposal of Hospital Records*

XI. Endnotes

I. Concept Objectives:

The intent in this chapter is to:
— describe the trial process and the role of witnesses and hospital records as a source of evidence for the trial
— examine nursing notes as evidence of compliance or non-compliance with the standard of care required by law
— examine ways and means of preparing nursing notes so that they may be more effective both as health care tools and as evidentiary tools
— increase the nurse's awareness of nursing recording practices, policies and systems, which make nursing notes more effective health care tools and proof of reasonable and prudent nursing practice
— examine the patient's right to confidentiality of health information
— examine the rights of patients and third parties to information from the patient's record
— identify options in policies and practices that balance one's right to information with the patient's right to privacy.

II. Introduction:

The focus in the previous four chapters of this text has been primarily on the content of and the legal and professional rationale for, nursing standards and the nursing process. Chapter five, however, will have a significantly different approach. It will examine the *record* of the nursing process as *evidence*, i.e. the hospital record, and in particular nursing notes. The change in format is undertaken because, in order to understand the evidentiary purpose of hospital records, it is necessary for the reader to envision a courtroom with a trial in progress. The nurse may be at a civil trial as the plaintiff, or the defendant, or as an expert or ordinary witness for the plaintiff or defendant. In a criminal trial she may appear as the accused, or as a witness for the crown or for the accused. In this chapter the reader will be referred back to cases examined in some detail in previous chapters, such as *Dowey v. Rothwell, MacDonald V. York County Hospital, Kolesar v. Jeffries et al,*

Laidlaw v. Lions Gate Hospital and *Meyer v. Gordon*. These cases, previously considered for their relevance to negligence or battery issues within the context of the nursing process, will now be reviewed for the evidentiary aspects of the hospital records used in the trials concerned. These cases will be examined in terms of the nursing notes and their effectiveness in demonstrating that the nurse concerned adhered to the legal standard of care called for in the situation.

The second part of this chapter will focus on the hospital record as property and information and will examine the shifting balance between rights to confidentiality and rights of access to information. Such shifting requires a regular review and possible revision of policies and practices of health care institutions and professional personnel in the protection of such rights.

Hospital records (also commonly referred to as the patient's record, or the chart) generally have the following components in the permanent record that is filed in the medical records department of the institution following discharge of the patient:
— admission record
— medical history
— nursing history*
— physician's orders
— medical progress notes
— nursing notes
— laboratory reports
— nursing care plans*
— radiology reports
— operative records**
— anesthetic records**
— post-operative recovery room record**
— pathology reports
— autopsy reports
— discharge summary

Hospital records serve a number of purposes. The main and most important purpose is to ensure continuity, coordination and safety of patient care. Such a purpose

(*may form part of the permanent record depending on hospital policy;
**the presence of such records is of course determined by whether the particular patient is being treated conservatively or surgically.)

requires that the record reveal in clear terms, the particular health problems and their immediate priority or urgency; that it reveal in clear terms the nature and type of health service planned to deal with the problems; that it reveal in clear terms, the type and time of care actually delivered together with an evaluation of the patient's response to the care. Safe patient care also requires that the record reveal any actual amendment made to the care plan needed to prevent, reduce or eliminate any negative responses to care by the patient. Secondary purposes of the hospital record are to provide data for statistical, research and education use. And last but not least, the record has definite legal uses at trial to demonstrate that the standard of care provided was, in the circumstances, a reasonable one.

III. Evidence, Proof and Trial Process:

The outcome of a trial is determined by whether the information which a party wishes to put before the court, is *admissible*, and if admitted, the weight that will be assigned to it by the court. The outcome of the dispute is also determined by the arguments of counsel for the parties and the acceptance or rejection of the legal precedents cited as authority for the case.

Not all that is said, or written, qualifies as proof. Through the centuries, courts have created common law rules of evidence and legislatures have created evidentiary statutes. These by their very nature continue in a state of flux, adjusting over time through judge made law and by statutory amendments, to meet changing problems and needs. The reader will sense the evolutionary quality of the rules of evidence law later in the chapter in the analysis of *Ares v. Venner*[1]. This decision of the Supreme Court of Canada changed the evidentiary rules of the game with respect to the admissibility of nurses notes as an exception to the *hearsay rule*. (This rule is examined in some detail later in this chapter.) The reader will also appreciate the impact on admissibility of the various evidence statutes. (For example,

whether or not a particular federal, provincial or territorial evidence statute expressly provides for admission of *medical records* in addition to *business records* as an exception to hearsay evidence, will determine how heavy a burden the party will have in proving his case and how time consuming and costly the process will be.)

The fact that something is in written form does not mean it will necessarily constitute admissible evidence. The fact that a person says something as a witness does not mean it will necessarily constitute admissible evidence. If it is not admissible the judge will not permit it to form part of the record on which he will base his decision. One or the other of the parties may have a particular witness or document that is absolutely crucial to the success of the case. If the court rules that the particular evidence is inadmissible, the party's entire case may be defeated.

For a clearer understanding of the role of evidence and its impact on the success or failure of the particular dispute being litigated the reader will need an overview of the typical civil trial process which is as follows:

A trial is the process of examining the issues in a dispute which issues are set out in the "pleadings" of each of the parties to the dispute: The statement of claim of the plaintiff, the statement of defence of the defendant, and reply and joinder of issue of the plaintiff.

The trial begins with opening statements by each of the counsel for the parties. Counsel for the party who initiates the proceedings (usually the plaintiff) begins by setting out for the court the issues, and the intended proving of the claim. When he is finished, counsel for the opposing party makes his opening statement.

When opening statements are completed, and any preliminary motions are disposed of, the following sequence of events will usually take place:

1. Examination in Chief:

Counsel for the party who initiated the proceeding (the plaintiff) will call his first witness. The witness "is sworn" and counsel will examine him. This is also referred to as the "direct examination". Counsel will ask a series of questions to which the witness is expected to provide factual replies, and not opinion (unless the witness is sworn as an expert witness). Counsel is not permitted to ask leading questions (questions which suggest the answer). The kinds of questions permitted to be asked are more limited than those permitted by opposing counsel in the cross-examination phase. The purpose of the examination in chief is to reveal all of the facts within the knowledge of the witness.

2. Cross-Examination:

The second phase involves questioning of the witness by counsel for the opposing side. The objective is to attempt to attack the truth of what the witness had to say and to cast doubt on the credibility of the witness. The range of questions allowed at cross-examination is wide and leading questions may be allowed.

3. Re-Direct Examination:

Involves a requestioning of one's own witness upon those matters arising during the cross-examination phase. It is for the purpose of correcting, counteracting or minimizing the negative effects created by the cross-examination. Counsel is restricted by the questions asked in the cross-examination and is not permitted to introduce new matters at this stage. (At the end of phases two and three above the judge may ask questions for clarification.)

When all of the witnesses have been called for the plaintiff, counsel for the defendant will then present his witnesses. Counsel for the plaintiff will cross-examine and the defendant's counsel will re-direct as before. On completion both counsel will present closing arguments.

4. Closing Arguments:

These include a summary of the evidence and arguments on the law appropriate to the issues in dispute. If the judge is sitting without a jury, he may deliver his judgment from the bench, or reserve judgment, publishing it at a later date.

The trial process essentially concerns itself with the hearing of evidence, determining what evidence will be admitted and for what purposes and what weight will be assigned to the evidence in the final determination of the dispute before the court.

5. Evidence (defined):

Evidence is defined as the means by which a fact is proved or disproved at trial, and *proof* is defined as the end result or effect of the evidence. The outcome of the trial turns on the matter of *burden of proof*: Which party has the obligation to adduce evidence of particular facts? Has the party bearing the obligation discharged the burden of proof? The party who begins first (usually the plaintiff) has the burden of offering sufficient evidence to establish a *prima facie case* i.e., the evidence in his favour is sufficient for the opposing party to be called on to refute it. If there is no case to answer the plaintiff's case will fail. If there is a case to answer and the defendant is unable to bring sufficient evidence to disprove the prima facie facts, the court faced with cogent, uncontradicted evidence will accept the facts as true and make a finding in favour of that particular party.

What does the party have to prove? It depends on the cause of action. For example in a negligence action the plaintiff has the burden of proving the following critical elements:
— that the particular defendant had a duty of care to the particular plaintiff
— that the defendant breached his duty of care to the plaintiff
— that the plaintiff suffered a material injury
— that the breach of the duty "caused" the injury i.e., was the direct and proximate cause of that injury.

If the plaintiff sues in assault, the obligation on the plaintiff is to prove only that he was touched without his consent. The obligation then moves to the defendant to prove that the plaintiff did, in fact, consent to the touching.

The trial strategy revolves around how the facts are to be presented to prove the critical elements, in what sequence and by what means i.e. through use of ordinary witnesses, use of expert witnesses, and, or use of documentary evidence such as hospital records. The rules of evidence will dictate what, of what a witness says, or a record records, shall be admitted as proof. Of the facts that are admitted the court will determine what weight should be assigned in their quest to determine whether the party has made out a prima facie case, and if so, whether the opposing party has counteracted the case. Credibility of the various witnesses is an important determinant.

IV. Means of Proof and Establishing Facts:

Facts (and limited opinion) may be presented at trial by the following five means:
— oral evidence of witnesses (viva voce evidence)
— documentary evidence (including affidavit evidence)
— demonstrative or real evidence
— admissions by the parties
— judicial notice of certain facts

1. Oral Evidence:

This is the most common method of proving the required facts at trial and is provided by a *witness*. If a particular person is required to give evidence at trial, counsel may invite the witness to appear voluntarily, but more commonly the witness is *subpoenaed*. The latter is a written court document compelling the witness to appear and give oral testimony (*subpoena ad testificandum*) at a certain date and time in the court named and for the party named (the plaintiff or the defendant). Should the witness fail to appear he or she will be found in contempt of court and will be summonsed to the court and penalized. Subpoenas have the legal effect of a court order. If the witness is also commanded to bring certain documents or records the subpoena is referred to as *subpoena duces tecum*, commanding the witness to bring those records in his possession or control for production at trial.

Witnesses are sworn before they proceed to give evidence, i.e. they take an oath "to tell the truth, the whole truth, so help me God". Failure to tell the truth is *perjury*. This criminal offence results when the person, willfully and knowingly states as true that which he knows to be false. When the witness is sworn, he may refer to notes to refresh his memory. However the documents used must have been made by the witness or adopted by him as the correct account of the alleged facts and must have been made at or about the time the alleged facts or incident occurred.

(a) Direct Evidence:

Generally the witness is permitted to give only *direct evidence* (evidence which he observed through his own senses, of *fact* and not *opinion*). If the facts are *material* they go to prove the fact in issue. If they are relevant to the fact in issue, i.e., some surrounding fact such would qualify as *circumstantial evidence*. (They are facts which show the existence of circumstances from which the court may infer a material fact.) For example, in a criminal trial, if the accused had been charged with theft of particular goods and the witness for the prosecution states that he personally saw the accused take the particular goods and remove them such would be *direct evidence*. If however the witness can only testify that what he observed, was the door to the room concerned was broken and open and the goods were no longer there, such would be *circumstantial evidence*.

(b) Hearsay Evidence:

Evidence of a statement made by a particular witness may or may not be *hearsay evidence*. It is *hearsay evidence* and, (subject to certain exceptions to the hearsay rule) *inadmissible* if the purpose of such evidence is to establish the truth of what is contained in the statement. The evidence is not *hearsay* and is *admissible*, when the use to which evidence is to be put, is not to prove truth, but only to prove the fact that the statement was made.

The hearsay rule starts from the premise that out of court assertions of persons who are not called as witnesses, offered as proof of the truth of the matters contained in the statement, are not admissible. The basic objection to hearsay is that the court cannot be assured that the third party statement in fact was made, and if it was made, that the repetition is an accurate recounting of it. Third party assertions are unable to be subjected to the truth testing process of cross-examination, (a potent tool in the assessment of evidence). Not only is a third party not available for cross-examination, but is not under oath to tell the truth under threat of perjury, and is not in full view of the court for a first hand view of his credibility and demeanour. A physician, who has physically examined a patient prior to surgery, could be called to give oral evidence as to his findings found on examination. If that same physician ordered a consultation with a specialist, the former is not permitted to give evidence on the findings of the consultant. The latter would have to be called to speak to his own findings.

(c) Use of Expert Evidence:

Oral evidence provided by *expert witnesses* is unlike that given by ordinary witnesses. The latter recounts facts of which he has personal knowledge but he does not give *opinion evidence*. One who has been declared an expert witness testifies beyond what he has perceived or observed personally (directly). He can give evidence of scientific, medical or nursing issues and standards, including his opinion and conclusion about causes and effects in the particular situation. For example, in a nursing negligence action, a nursing expert may be called on behalf of the plaintiff to set out for the court the standard of nursing care to which the defendant was required to adhere in the care of the party who claims to have been injured. In the previously discussed *Dowey v. Rothwell*,[2] a 1974 decision of the Alberta Supreme Court, the plaintiff, a patient of the physician defendant, sued him for injuries suffered in his office while under the supervision of a registered nurse. The plaintiff, with a history of epilepsy, had, weeks prior to the incident taken herself off her anti-epileptic drugs. On the day in question she felt an "aura", went to the doctor's office and was interviewed by the registered nurse. She recounted the foregoing facts to the nurse who then took her into the examining room and placed her on an examining table. Some time later the nurse walked away from the patient. The latter seizured, fell from the table and suffered an extensive fracture of her arm. In the judgment, the court referred to the assistance provided to the court by a nursing instructress called as an expert:

" ... to assist the court in knowing the expected standard of nursing care and the minimal standards which the public would have a right to expect from any person with nursing qualifications. She states firstly that if an adult says that she is an epileptic and says she is going to have a seizure any alert nurse should believe this and should put her into a room (usually on the floor) and should move the furniture beyond arm or leg length and stay until the aura of seizure has passed. In that intervening time the nurse should get some kind of history of the aura of seizure and ascertain what pattern it follows. When specifically asked, she stated that if a person had not been taking the prescribed drugs she would expect a dandy—a grand mal seizure and that she would stay to make sure there was no stoppage of respiration. She indicated that the presence of a nurse was important because a nurse could prevent injury and while the presence of a nurse could not guarantee safety this would tend to minimize the possibility of injury. In answer to questions she stated (and it was almost unnecessary to so state) that when a doctor employs a nurse, the nurse must meet minimal nursing standards and that both the doctor and the public have a right to expect a reasonable standard under all circumstances. "[3]

The court, compared the evidence of the nursing actions of the defendant to the standard set out by the nursing expert. The court concluded that the nurse had breached the duty of care to the patient and that the breach caused the plaintiff's injury. The defendant has, in the instance, the right to cross-examine the witness. It is critical, if the defendant nurse is to be relieved in the foregoing fact situation, that she counter with evidence that she adhered to approved nursing practice. Where there is uncontradicted expert evidence, as mentioned earlier, the court will find the defendant liable. (The reader is referred to the case analysed in Chapter Two: "Tort of Negligence: An Overview" and Chapter Four: "Tort of Negligence and the Nursing Process", to appreciate the important role of the expert witness, and proof of compliance with approved practice.

2. Documentary Evidence:

This is the term used for a written statement adduced during trial either to prove the truth of its contents for admission into the trial record or for some other use. Such evidence can be crucial to a case, its admissibility determining the success or failure of the trial for the party tendering the evidence or objecting to it. Whether or not part or all of a particular record is permitted to be admitted into evidence is determined by: the presense of consent from the opposing party, or by the current state of the common law and the particular evidence statute. To be admissible, such documents must either comply with the criteria set in the particular evidence act of the province or ordinance of the territory, or be otherwise admissible at common law as one of the exceptions to the so called *hearsay rule*. For example, documentary evidence played a significant role in the outcome of the previously mentioned *Meyer v. Gordon* case, both in identifying the required standard of care and in evaluating the nursing care actually received by the patient during the time the patient's new-born infant was injured. Three types of documents were reviewed at trial:
— nurses notes
— hospital procedure manual
— hospital's critical incident report compiled about the event and injury.

The nurses notes were flawed because of omissions, inaccurate descriptions of nursing assessment results, and alterations of the record after the event. The hospital procedure manual outlined the hospital's statement of the care required to prevent fetal distress in the high risk labour period (the end of the first stage of labour and the beginning of the second stage). The written statement called for a monitoring and assessment of the fetal heart sounds every

fifteen minutes. This standard was in startling contrast with evidence that the nurses had failed to check the plaintiff's fetal heart for some thirty-two minutes immediately prior to the birth of the infant. When the court examined the critical incident report completed following the birth of the infant, it noted there was conflict between its contents and the content of the nursing notes and both records contained meaningless description which destroyed the nurse's credibility. (This case is discussed in considerable detail later in the Chapter.)

3. Demonstrative Evidence:

This is also known as "real evidence" and is physical in nature and evaluated by inspection by the court. Examples of demonstrative evidence include fingerprints, weapons, and equipment. For example, in *Kolesar v. Jeffries et al*, the reader will recall that nursing care of a patient on a Stryker frame was analyzed. Included in evidence placed before the court was a Stryker frame which was used to demonstrate the particular risks unique to any patient confined to such a frame.

4. Judicial Admissions:

This is a term which refers to admissions made by counsel for the plaintiff and or defendant prior to trial in such pleadings as the plaintiff's statement of claim, or the defendant's statement of defence or in subsequent documents filed with the court in preparation for trial of the matter. Admissions may be made by either side during the pre-trial examination for discovery, or at the trial itself. The effect of admissions is to reduce the time and cost of proving the facts which would be otherwise required.

5. Judicial Notice:

This is a term which refers to the prerogative of the judge at trial to acknowledge the existence of certain universal and public facts without requiring the production of evidence of such facts. The judge may take judicial notice of certain statutes, common law precedents, historical events, customs, certain geographical facts, and facts in certain textbooks and dictionaries. (The reader will note in the final chapter, Regulation of the Nursing Profession in Canada, that disciplinary tribunals in certain of the cases took judicial notice of facts set out in approved nursing texts.) The reason the courts have made use of judicial notice is that certain common knowledge is within the court's own ascertainable knowledge, as for example, the days of the week, meaning of certain words, or rules of Parliament. The effect of judicial notice is to reduce the number of facts that have to be proven in the process of trial.

V. Admissibility of Hospital Records at Common Law and Pursuant to Statute:

A basic common law rule against hearsay evidence generally prohibits the introduction in court, of written statements (or oral statements) made by third parties who are not before the court, as proof of the truth alleged. For example, witness Jane Doe R.N. states under oath that Mary Brown, a patient, told her that she, Mary Brown, saw Jane Smith, the patient, fall out of bed. Such second hand information is not admissible as proof of the truth that Mrs. Smith fell from the bed. Witness Mary Brown would have to be called to the stand and state the facts of what she saw. However since 1870 certain exceptions to the hearsay rule were justified on the basis of *necessity*. Authors Sopinka and Lederman, in their text *The Law of Evidence in Civil Cases* outlined the necessity basis as follows:

> " An exception was justified for this class of hearsay statement on the basis of necessity, the declarant no longer being available to give evidence. Moreover, the statement was said to possess a circumstantial guarantee of truth arising from the fear of the declarant of censure and dismissal should an employer discover an inaccuracy in the statement and from the fact that *constant routine* and *habit* in making entries provide some likelihood of accuracy. The traditional rule can be enunciated as follows:
>
> Statements made by a *deceased declarant under a duty* to another person to do an act and *record* it in the ordinary practice of the declarant's

business or calling are admissible in evidence provided they were *made contemporaneously* with the fact stated and without motive or interest to misrepresent the facts. "[4]

At common law, those business records containing objective facts and meeting the foregoing criteria could be admitted to prove the truth of the contents of the documents.

1. *Admissibility of Hospital Records as Exception to Hearsay at Common Law:*

In 1970 the Supreme Court of Canada opened the way for admissibility of nurses notes in *Ares v. Venner*[5], a medical negligence case in which a twenty-one year old arts student sued the physician for negligent treatment received after he (the student) fell while skiing. The accident occurred on February 21, 1965 at approximately 4:00 p.m. That evening the defendant physician (a specialist in internal medicine) surgically reduced the severe comminuted fracture of the right tibia and fibula. He then placed a plaster cast on the injured leg from the toes to the upper thigh. The procedure was completed at approximately six p.m. Within the next three days the plaintiff suffered increasing signs of circulatory impairment, which signs were recorded in the nurses notes. However, the defendant physician did not completely bi-valve the cast until the evening of the third day by which time the circulatory impairment was irreversible. Two months later, in April of 1965 the plaintiff's right leg was amputated below the knee. He subsequently sued the physician and the hospital. At trial the judge permitted the admission of the nurses notes as prima facie evidence of the truth of what was recorded in the notes. Counsel for the defendant physician objected to the admission of the nurses notes without the plaintiff's counsel calling the recorders of the notes to the stand so that the defence counsel could cross-examine them. The trial judge made the crucial finding that the classic signs or symptoms of circulatory impairment manifested themselves clearly and early. He based his findings on the nursing notes so that the accuracy of these records were extremely crucial to the outcome of the case. The trial judge dismissed the action against the hospital, found the physician liable and awarded damages of $29,407.13. The physician appealed and the main issue of the appeal was whether or not the nursing notes should have been admitted. The Alberta Court of Appeal upheld the dismissal of the action against the hospital but disagreed with the trial court's decision to admit the nursing notes and allowed the defendant's appeal. The appeal court made the following evaluation of the records in dispute:

> " These records, far from being a simple record in instrument readings or medical dosages, are the nurses' assessment of phenomena. They involve the nurses' ability to observe, and equally important, to record their observations accurately. Having inscribed their findings, there would still remain the degree to which an observed condition was present when such words as "blue", "bluishpink", "cool" and "cold" were used. All of these could be fruitful areas for cross-examination. Untested by cross-examination, it cannot be said that the evidence meets the test of "Circumstantial Probability of Trustworthiness" and should have not been admitted without the nurses being called to verify it and be available for cross-examination . . . "[6]

However, when the plaintiff appealed the case to the Supreme Court of Canada new law was made. The Court held the now frequently cited principle, setting out the conditions under which nurses' notes are now admissible as an exception to the hearsay rule:

> " Hospital records, including nurses notes made *contemporaneously* by someone having a *personal knowledge* of the matters then being recorded and *under a duty to make the entry* or record should be received in evidence as prima facie proof of the facts stated therein. This should, in no way preclude a party wishing to challenge the accuracy of the records or entries from doing so . . . "[7]

The Court stated there was a need to restate the hearsay rule to meet modern conditions and that such a need should be met by the court. The practical effect of the Ares rule is that now it is no longer neces-

sary to call each and every person who recorded in the hospital record. This eliminates the inconvenience arising from potential subpoena of multitudes of nurses and physicians from the hospital, a procedure which would be highly disruptive to the business of the health care institution. It also reduces the costs to the plaintiff by way of issuing and serving of subpoenas and providing of conduct money, and reduces the cost to the taxpayer of an otherwise extended trial time.[8]

Sopinka and Lederman make further arguments for the admissibility of nursing notes:

> " . . . it can be taken for granted that nurses will make every effort to keep accurate notes. The nurses have no interest, apart from their duty, in keeping the notes and therefore, in all likelihood, it is an impartial and trustworthy record of the patients' condition. Furthermore, nothing is to be gained by calling the nurses themselves. In all probability they will have no independent memory apart from the notes that they made, and therefore, the notes as evidence are superior to the testimony of the nurses. All of these factors give rise to a "circumstantial guarantee of trustworthiness" which justifies the reception of the document without the necessity of calling the declarants. "[9]

However the same authors point out two aspects of the hearsay dangers:[10]
— the inherent subjectivity of certain nursing observations
— the loss of the truth testing process of cross-examination.

The old hearsay rule permitted admission of objective, measured data as hearsay. The new rule permits admission of subjective and unmeasured data collected by the nurse pursuant to her nursing observations. The content of this subjective data is directly determined by: what the nurse observes from the actual data presented, what she selects as important and what choice of words she uses to describe the data. (For example, in *Meyer v. Gordon*, one nurse recorded in the nurses notes that labour was "good". The critical incident report described the patient's labour as "hard". When the nurse was cross-examined at trial she stated that the patient was in "active labour"). Subjective data is subject to degrees of variation and error.

Under the *Ares v. Venner* rule the party who wishes to benefit from the qualifying record may admit it as prima facie evidence of its truth without calling the recorder. The opposing counsel thereby loses access to the powerful tool of cross-examination and indeed that tool becomes the weapon of the party who introduced the record. What is stated in the nursing notes becomes the evidence of the party submitting it. If opposing counsel wishes to refute the truth, the burden is upon him to bring the recorder of the document into court as his witness. This limits him to going through an examination in chief which is much more restrictive in scope than the cross-examination process. Whereas cross-examination can, in the foregoing example, be used by the counsel who submitted the record, should he desire to do so.

In 1972 the Supreme Court of Canada heard an appeal of a medical negligence action with a fact situation similar to that of *Ares v. Venner*. The case, *MacDonald v. York County Hospital Corporation and Vail*[11] (discussed also in Chapter Four) concerned an eighteen year old man who had suffered a severe comminuted fracture and dislocation of the left ankle in a motorcycle accident on March 19, 1969. The senior surgeon at the hospital, a man of fifteen years' experience as a general surgeon, performed a closed reduction and placed the man's leg in an unpadded cast from the base of the toes to the groin. For thirty hours following the application of the cast the plaintiff suffered increasing and classical signs of circulatory impairment. As in the *Ares v. Venner* case the cast was not bi-valved until the irreversible damage occurred. The result was that the plaintiff underwent amputation of his toes, subsequent amputation of the foot and finally, a further amputation which was necessary to fit him for a prosthesis. The nurses' notes for the critical thirty hours from March 19th to the 21st were entered into evidence. When the defendant surgeon later took the stand, he admitted under cross-examination that the notations made by the nurses from

six p.m. on March 20th, 1969 to the following morning were classic signs or symptoms of impaired circulation. The recordings were as follows:[12]

TIME		
March		
19th	23:30	— appears satisfactory
19th	24:00–02:00	— sleeping — Awoke — complaining of severe pain — toes warm, colour good, movement sufficient of all toes but little one, which is stuck to cast.
20th	02:15	— demerol 75 mgms.
20th	06:45	— demerol 75 mgms. for pain. Toes good colour, warm. Patient able to feel any touch on toes.
20th	07:30–15:30	— bed bath given — complains of pain — left foot.
20th	10:30	— demerol 75 mgms. for pain in leg, toes warm to touch but no apparent feeling in them, taking fluids well.
20th	11:00	— Dr. M. visits — notified re condition of toes.
20th	12:00	— complains of pain.
20th	13:00	— toes still numb — complains of a great deal of pain.
20th	14:10	— Dr. V visited.
20th	14:30	— phenophen No. 2 Complains of nausea
20th	15:30	— resting quietly
20th	18:00	— having lots of pain — Phenophen No. 2. Toes on left foot dark and cold has no sensation in them
20th	21:00	— demerol 100 mgms.
20th	23:30	— patient's toes very cold and colour is purple and numb — sleeping
21st	03:45	— demerol 100 mgms. Slept at intervals — toes on left foot, cold, discoloured, no sensation.

21st 08:00 — demerol 100 mgms. for pain — toes very cold and blue, no feeling or movement in them.

21st 08:45 — Dr. V notified by phone re leg. Cast bi-valved by Dr. V.

The nurses' notes served as potent evidence of negligence. The record showed that five and a half hours lapsed from the inspection at 18:00 hours on the 20th and the next inspection when colour was noted to be purple and the toes very cold. There was no indication that the nurses took any appropriate intervention based on their assessment and the data collected. Another four hours lapsed before another inspection was done, followed by another four and a half hour lapse. The court found that the nurses were negligent in failing to assess the patient's condition at more frequent intervals and for failure to advise the physician of the changes that had been noted. $34,000.00 damages were awarded at trial. The judgment against the physician was maintained on appeal to the Ontario Court of Appeal. When the case was appealed in the Supreme Court of Canada, some seven years after the injury, the court upheld the finding of negligence against the physician but held that, although the nurses may have been negligent in not reporting the initial changes, their negligence did not contribute to the loss.

The *Ares v. Venner* principle states:

" Hospital records, including nurses' notes made contemporaneously by someone having a personal knowledge of the matters then being recorded and under a duty to make the entry or record should be received in evidence as prima facie proof of the facts stated therein. "

It has been followed in a number of cases since 1970, including *Duff et al v. Brocklehurst* (1978).[13] This decision of the Prince Edward Island court permitted the admission of a hospital report of a blood alcohol analysis into evidence in a motor vehicle negligence action. It was permitted to be admitted on the evidence of a witness from the hospital's medical record department and the casualty officer on duty at the time the test was taken. The record was admitted as prima facie proof of the facts stated in the record (that the blood alcohol level was 176 milligrams per millimeters at the time the test was taken). The person who made the report was not called as a witness.

The *Ares v. Venner* principle was also applied in Re. *Griffin's Estate* (1979)[14] permitting the admission of nursing notes. A widow's application for probate of her deceased husband's will was contested by the son alleging the deceased did not have testamentary capacity at the time he made the will. (The will had been drawn a short time following his admission to hospital for treatment of heart and liver problems.) The nursing notes, admitted as prima facie proof of the facts in the notes, recorded that the testator had been "confused", "very confused"…"agitated"…"depressed"… and "crying". The recorder of the notes was not called as a witness and therefore the applicant (widow) did not have access to cross-examination. The court denied the widow's application for probate because she had failed to prove that the deceased had had testamentary capacity at the time of drawing the will. The decision was upheld on appeal.

(The foregoing points out that the content of nursing observations and the use of words in describing the selected observations may have far reaching evidentiary repercussions.)

2. *Admissibility of Hospital Records Pursuant to Statutory Authority:*

Whether or not a particular hospital record is admissible as an exception to the hearsay rule depends on the status of the common law in the particular province, unless the evidence act of the province expressly provides for its admission. The Canada Evidence Act and most provincial evidence statutes provide for admission of those records that comply with the definition of "business records" in the particular statute. Whether or not nursing notes, nursing histories and nursing diagnosis records are admissible is determined by the particular wording of the act and fit within the meaning of a "business record". Hospital business likely fits within the usual definition of business as "every kind of business, profession, occupation, calling, operation or activity, whether carried on for profit or otherwise". "Record" has been statutorily defined in some jurisdictions as "a statement of fact" and in other jurisdictions as any writing of "any act, transaction, occurrence or event". Consider how many of the nursing recordings could come within such a definition. In *Aynsley v. Toronto General Hospital* (1968),[15] an Ontario case (which was finally appealed to the Supreme Court of Canada) confirmed that this definition of "record" could include routine entries in the hospital record such as:

— date of the patient's admission
— name of the attending physician
— routine medical orders such as those for drug administration
— nursing notations such as records of vital signs.

All of the foregoing were "acts, transactions or occurrences which take place routinely and which are recorded routinely", within the meaning of the statute.

Adderly v. Bremner (1968), was an Ontario case in which the plaintiff sued the physician in negligence after the plaintiff developed septicemia from an innoculation. He successfully alleged that the physician, in innoculating thirty-eight patients used the same needle for every two patients, an improper and unsafe procedure. However, the court refused to admit those hospital records containing the plaintiff's *medical history* and the *medical diagnosis* as exceptions to the hearsay rule. The court defined history as a "reported chronology of events which preceded the patient's admission to the hospital" and concluded that the Ontario Legislature did not intend in Ontario's *Evidence Act* to include "history" as one of the records that could be admissible as prima facie proof of the truth of the matters contained in the report. In order to use the history for such a purpose the recorder of the history would have to be called as a witness and be subject to cross-examination by opposing counsel. With respect to medical diagnosis, the court stated:

" . . . the making of a medical diagnosis is basic to the business of a hospital and it is made in the usual and ordinary course of that business. However diagnosis is a professional opinion, and in my view it is not an act, transaction, occurrence or event within the meaning of the words of this section. "[17]

The court in *Adderly v. Bremner* held that the hospital record was not admissible for the purpose of proving statements of opinion, diagnosis or impression. By extension of the court's ruling on medical history and medical diagnosis one can conclude that under such a statutory provision neither nursing histories nor nursing diagnoses would be admissible as exceptions to the hearsay rule. However the admission of an item of hospital records as exceptions to the hearsay rule is determined in light of the particular wording of the evidence act of the province and pleaded in the particular dispute. Statutes which expressly provide for admission of "medical records" in addition to "business records" will provide greater leaway for admission of such items as the medical history, medical diagnosis, etiology and prognosis of illness and the medical progress notes. Whether the particular statutory section concerning admissibility of medical records would extend to such nursing items as nursing notes, nursing history and nursing diagnosis is doubtful and would depend on the express wording of the particular statutory section. Those provinces which have provided specifically for *admissibility* of certain *medical records* by amendment to the evidence act, have provided flexibility and savings in time and expense and in the number of witnesses required at trial. On the other hand, the admissibility of medical records under *business records provisions* of an evidence act is much more restrictive. In *Kolesar v. Jeffries et al*, the case of *Adderly v. Bremner* was cited in the Ontario Court of Appeal's refusal to admit the autopsy report pursuant to the business section of Ontario's Evidence Act. The court concluded that such a report was an "opinion or diagnosis" rather than "act, transaction, occurrence or event" within the meaning of the statute. The reader may recall that in the Kolesar case the cause of death was a central issue and results of the autopsy as reported in the pathology reported was extremely important evidence. Whether or not the party wishing to enter an autopsy report is required to call the recorder of the report to the stand, could be crucial. Opposing counsel who do not have access to cross-examination of such a witness could be at a considerable disadvantage.

VI. Nursing Notes as Evidence:

" . . . a nurse's notes, like the physician's records, can be used to support her position or to show that she has, in some respect failed in her medico-legal duty. This is as it should be. A professional is one who has received clearly defined training, has shown evidence of competence, can assume extensive responsibility and can perform her duties in a highly skilled and competent manner. As a nurse, you work in the knowledge that your notes may be used against you, the doctor, or the hospital. This is one of the responsibilities of a true professional . . . "[20]

In the context of a nursing negligence suit, the registered nurse, as a defendant or as a witness for the defendant hospital, will likely need to rely heavily on her nursing records as evidence that her nursing process was reasonable and prudent and therefore not the cause of the patient's injury within the meaning of the tort of negligence. She may want the record itself to be admitted as prima facie evidence of the truth of its contents pursuant to the Supreme Court of Canada ruling in *Ares v. Venner*. Alternatively, she may want to use the notes to refresh her memory during her testimony. Nursing notes constitute a chronological diary of the various events involving the particular patient from the time of admission to hospital to the time of discharge. At trial, the nursing notes are commonly used to reconstruct the various events and the time of their occurrence and to resolve conflicts in testimony. (The latter sometimes tends to be subjective and distorted by memory lapse.)

There are a number of factors which determine whether the nursing record is admissible and, if admissible, the weight that will be assigned to it in the determination of the facts of the case. In order to be admissible as a prima facie proof of the truth of its contents, the record must be made *contemporaneously* by the person who had personal knowledge of the event recorded and who had *a duty to record* the event. However, whether or not the record will be accorded sufficient weight by the court in support or rejection of the plaintiff's or defendant's position, will be determined by such additional factors as the presence of entries at regular intervals, the accuracy of the times and events recorded, the absence of suspicious alterations and additions to the record after the fact. Following is a brief review of these factors within the context of the nursing negligence cases analyzed in chapter four, The Tort of Negligence and The Nursing Process. These cases are now referred to in terms of the evidentiary aspects of nursing notes.

1. *Contemporaneous Recording:*

This term refers to recording that exists or occurs at the same time as the event recorded. Undue delay between the occurring of the actual event and the notation of it may result in the court's refusal to admit the record as the prima facie truth about the event. The closer the proximity in time between recording and event, the greater is its potential for accuracy and thus greater is the weight that may be attached to it as evidence. For example, in the previously reviewed case, *Kolesar v. Jeffries et al* the patient died at the defendant hospital within twenty-four hours following spinal surgery. There were no nursing notations made for some eight hours preceding the patient's death. The court had a number of observations to make in its scathing attack on the recording practices of the nurses involved:[21]

" Finally there is the matter of nursing records. None worthy of the term were really kept. The nurses say it was their habit during the night shift to jot down on pieces of paper they were carrying, a note or two, and then at five or six a.m. they would get together, assisting each other to recall and record the events of the evening. "

The Supreme Court of Canada noted that the trial judge found most unsatisfactory the practice of not making notes on the charts contemporaneously with the performance of the service or observation but later in a joint conference. Consequently, concluded the Supreme Court of Canada, the notes represented the memory of the different persons who had been attending the patient.

" An examination of all the records of the patients show little or nothing. I find it remarkable. Perhaps even more remarkable is what happened following Kolesar's death. On hearing of it, the assistant director of nursing...examined the medical record and noted the absence of any entry from 10:00 p.m. on December 30th until 5:00 a.m. on the 31st. She asked Nurse M to write up a record...One is always suspicious of records made after the event, and if any credence is to be attached to ex. 29, it shows that at all times the patient was quite pale, very pale, and was allowed to sleep to his death. "

There is often long delay between the happening of the injury and the time when the dispute comes to trial. For example it wasn't until seven years after Mr. Kolesar's death that the particular trial took place. There were subsequent appeals to the Ontario Court of Appeal and the Supreme Court of Canada. Such long delay requires the witness to depend on the available records to assist in an accurate reconstruction of events. In *Kolesar v. Jeffries et al*, for example, the defence called the nursing assistant on duty on the particular night to testify, which evidence she gave from memory. The court discounted her evidence entirely:

" It was almost five years after the death and she spoke from memory. She purported to state with extraordinary emphasis that she had attended the late Kolesar at midnight, at 2:30 a.m. at 3:30 a.m. at 4:00 a.m. and that at 3:30 a.m. she had taken the patient's blood pressure for practice purposes only and thereafter confirmed her findings with Nurse B...Nurse B...swore that she did not know of anyone taking the blood pressure. Nursing Assistant S said she thought there was a blood pressure appara-tus on the patient's night table. There was none. The apparatus was on a cart kept in the nursing station. When asked about all the other patients she attended that night she could remember none, but admits to entering on the charts of 13 to 15 patients at 5:30 a.m., that they had slept well and these were the only entries that appeared on the charts for that shift...in cross-examination she admitted these were not her observations but rather they represented the recollection of herself and the other two nurses as they sat at the nurses' station in the early hours of the morning. On being further pressed to explain her total inability to recall any other patient that night, she replied that she recalled Kolesar because he was the only one to die. But she admitted her observations were made at a time when Kolesar was just like all the other patients and was not expected to die. I cannot accept the evidence of this witness. She impressed me as coming to court prepared to swear positively to one thing from a foggy memory confused by imagination. " [22]

The court did not expressly prohibit the admission of the nurses' notes in the Kolesar case. However, the tenor of the court's language points out the importance of recording at the time of the event if one wishes to rely on the records either to refresh one's memory of events, or for admission of the record itself as proof of the truth of the events on the date and time in question. Any tendency by the nurse to delay recording her observations and care of high risk patients to the end of shift should be strongly discouraged. Not only is such an unsafe practice fraught with communication errors and distortions, but also, such practices may well defeat the evidentiary value of the record for litigation purposes. (This does not ignore the fact that contemporaneous charting is often difficult when the nursing demands at a particular time during the shift are all-consuming, and it is in recognition of this difficulty that, later in this chapter, there is a summary of recording principles and practices addressed to the problem of how to maintain contemporaneous charting. There is also an outline of the problem oriented charting method, together with a sample flow chart as one option in more effectively meeting the evidentiary requirement to record at the time of the event.)

2. Recording From Personal Knowledge by the Person Who Has a Duty to Record:

Statutory criteria for "business records" and the common law require that the record be made by the person having personal knowledge of the event being recorded, if the party at trial wishes to succeed in having the record admitted as prima facie evidence. Use of third party recording will also destroy the accuracy of the record and the credibility of the witness who wishes to rely on the record. This is indicated in the previously analyzed case *Laidlaw v. Lions Gate Hospital et al* in which the oral evidence of the nurse was discounted because certain notes of treatment she had performed, were recorded by a nurse who was not present at the time the treatment was carried out. The record was damaging as well because of the inaccuracy of the times recorded in the nursing notes. The forty-four year old Mrs. Laidlaw was taken to the operating room at the defendant hospital on April 22, 1966 for removal of her gallbladder. The court made a finding of fact that Mrs. Laidlaw, while still unconscious and under anesthetic in the post-anesthesia recovery room, suffered a lack of oxygen to the brain for such a length of time that it caused permanent brain damage, which reduced the woman to an infantile state. The court held the hospital vicariously liable for the negligence of the head nurse and a staff nurse in the unit.

Evidence of the sequence of events and the exact time of their occurrence, from the time Mrs. Laidlaw was moved from the operating room until she suffered cardiac arrest, was crucial. The court fixed the time of Mrs. Laidlaw's admission into the recovery room at 10:30 a.m. (and the time that Nurse M had left the unit for coffee break at 10:25 a.m.). At trial there was a conflict between the evidence given by Dr. C (the anesthetist who responded to the emergency call from the recovery room), and the evidence of Nurse S. Dr. C contended that he was in the operating room and received a call and immediately came to the recovery room. He fixed this time as 10:50 a.m. and testified that his training in his work deals with watching the clock at all times in order to know how long a patient has been under anesthesia. Nurse S put the time that the patient stopped breathing at 10:35 a.m. (The reader will recall from the analysis of this case in Chapter Four, that the court concluded that the patient had not been assessed by the nurses for some twenty minutes. Having accepted that the required standard of assessment in a high risk situation such as the recovery room, was every two to three minutes, the court held that the nurses breached their duty of care to Mrs. Laidlaw in this regard and that this failure was the cause of her injury.) In terms of evidence, the court rejected the testimony of Nurse S because of the contradictions in times recorded on the nursing notes. The court accepted the evidence of Dr. C that he received the urgent telephone call at 10:50 a.m. on the day Mrs. Laidlaw was injured.

> " Various times were given both verbally and by way of nurses' charts as to the happening of certain events. I find that times are all approximate times, were not accurate times and cannot be relied upon. " 23

For example, in the reconstruction of events the courts noted that an injection was recorded as having been administered to Mrs. Laidlaw at the same time as an injection was administered to a second patient. Both entries were recorded for 10:40 a.m. and the recording was entered by Nurse M who was not in the nursing unit at 10:40 a.m. but was away on coffee break. The court concluded:

> " . . . this of course, was not possible and illustrates the unreliability of the time recorded on these charts. " 24

The court determined that since Nurse M was not present at the time, she must have obtained the time from Nurse S. (Nurse M testified that the time recorded on the narcotic record would constitute the exact time the demerol was administered to the patient in question. The court noted that the time on this record was in conflict with the time recorded on the nursing notes.)

To comply with the common law rule of evidence the nurse who has *personal knowledge* of the event must be the one who enters the data on the nursing notes. The judge in *Laidlaw v. Lions Gate Hospital*, as an aside, expressed the policy reasons for rejecting third party recording:

> " I digress here to point out that it seems to be the practice of the nurses, in the P.A.R. room to fill in times on charts for one another. This practice leads to inaccuracies. "[25]

The requirement that the recording be made *by a person having a duty to record* was set out by the Supreme Court of Canada in *Ares v. Venner*. (It is also commonly set out in the business records criteria of various provincial evidence statutes.) The next question must then be to determine when the nurse has a duty to record and whether or not it must be a *statutory duty*. Although regulations to the various provincial hospital acts list the various components to be included in the hospital record, there may not be an express statutory duty to make nursing notation, set out. However, it can be implied if not expressed, that there is a contractual, and professional duty to record nursing data. (In practice, a well-organized nursing department will always set a written policy for the direction of members of the nursing department concerning minimum recording requirements.) There is a well-recognized professional obligation on the part of the registered nurse to maintain nursing records, a requirement that has been clearly set out in standards of care published by the various nursing associations in Canada. The professional standards call for documentation of the nursing assessments, the proposed care plan, its implementation and evaluation of the patient's response, in accordance with the policies and in the designated format established by the nursing department of the institution. These statements of standards published by the profession may also call for recording of a nursing history, assessments, diagnosed nursing problems,

nursing care proposals, care actually received by the patient as well as documentation of health teaching.[26] The Canadian Council on Hospital Accreditation also requires accredited hospitals to provide for prompt and accurate record-keeping. The trial court in *Kolesar v. Jeffries et al* referred favourably to the Council's requirements with respect to medical records:

> " ... Council evaluates a medical record on the basis of whether or not it contains sufficient recorded information to justify diagnoses, warrant good treatment and explain the reasons for the end results. In agreement with this principle, the accreditation program has established Standards for record keeping which are regarded as being essential for the assurance of good patient care in the hospital. "[27]

3. The Evidentiary Implications of Absence of Nursing Recordings:

Haines J, in *Kolesar v. Jeffries et al* expressed an important concept with respect to the absence of nursing notations on the Kolesar record. The concept was not rejected by the Supreme Court of Canada and it has taken on the character of a principle of some significance from the perspective of evidence. The reader will recall that there had been no nursing recording made on Mr. Kolesar's chart for the final eight hours of his life despite the fact that the patient was in the immediate post-operative period following a spinal fusion. The trial judge reviewed the purpose of recording on nursing notes at regular intervals prior to expressing the evidentiary principle which is underlined below:

> " On a ward with a great many patients the medical record becomes the common source of information and direction for patient care. If kept properly it indicates on a regular basis the changes in the patient's condition and alerts staff to developing dangers. And it is perhaps trite to say that if the hospital enforced regular entries during each nursing shift, a nurse could not make the entry until she had first performed the service required of her. *In Kolesar's case the absence of entries permits of the inference that nothing was charted because nothing was done.* "

This Kolesar principle was reinterpreted in the 1983 Ontario case *Ferguson v. Hamilton Civic Hospital et al.*[28] This case, which is discussed in chapter three in the matter of informed consent, involved a plaintiff who had experienced difficulty with his vision and underwent a bilateral carotid arteriograph. Following the procedure the plaintiff was quadraplegic. The plaintiff alleged, in addition to lack of informed consent, lack of reasonable nursing care by the nurses in the recovery room, evidenced by the absence of entries in the nursing records from 1:30 p.m. to 3:30 p.m. on June 27, 1973. The court dealt with the issue as follows:

" ... While on the subject of nursing care, this is an appropriate place to say that, although invited so to find, I reject the submission that the absence of any nurse's entry in the nurses' record forming part of the hospital chart between 1:30 p.m. and 3:30 p.m. on June 27, 1973, is an indication of a failure in care on the part of the attending nurses. *I infer that there was no observable change during that period that justified being recorded.* With relation to the nurses' notes *this case is distinguishable from Kolesar v. Jeffies* (1974), 9 O.R. (2d) 41 at pp. 47-48, 59 D.L.R. (3d) 367 367 at pp. 373-4, in which Haines J held that *where there is a positive duty* on the part of a nurse *to perform a physical act, the absence in the nurses' record of any reference to the performance of the act justifies the inference that the act was not performed.* In the absence of any evidence that good nursing practice requires the making of a note every time a nurse attends to observe a patient, even when there is no observable change in the patient's condition, it would be extending that principle too far to apply it to routine inspections of the patient by the nurses. "

Omissions from the nursing notes may be interpreted against the defendant nurse in the absence of other credible evidence which can demonstrate that the nursing care was given in spite of the fact there was no written record of the fact. This burden will most likely be insurmountable. (The Supreme Court of Canada in *Kolesar v. Jeffries* noted, for instance, that Nurse M gave evidence in very considerable detail but the evidence "certainly was not confirmed by any notation in the hospital record ...". The reader

will also recall the evidence given by the nursing assistant without the support of nursing notes. The trial court discounted her evidence in its entirety:

" She impressed me as coming to court prepared to swear positively to one thing from a foggy memory confused by imagination. "

In 1979 the Ontario High Court, in *Traynor v. Vancott*[29] made a finding of nursing negligence in a situation where the patient's chart had a twelve hour gap in which no nursing observations were recorded during the post-operative period. The plaintiff suffered a "wrist-drop" following surgery. Evidence indicated that the injury was caused by continuous pressure on the radial nerve which likely occurred from lying on the arm while in a semiconscious condition. The court concluded that the drowsy post-operative patient had been left unattended for twelve hours and that such constituted nursing negligence. The plaintiff suffered partial loss of the use of her arm and damages of $10,000.00 were awarded.

In institutions which have introduced the use of problem-oriented records, the flow chart meets part of the requirement for regular nursing entries. A sample of the latter is set out later in the chapter.

4. Alterations and Additions:

Obviously, there will be occasions when there is an honest failure on the part of the nurse to record a nursing observation or a particular nursing intervention which actually has been carried out, and nursing record policies do provide for a procedure to correct such omissions. (Later in the chapter, there are suggested options for ensuring that nursing notations are accurately recorded in a chronological manner and for corrections of honest errors in recording.) However, it is at least unethical and certainly contrary to safe recording practice to make alterations and additions to a record following a patient injury and for the express purpose of having the notation appear to have been made prior to the critical incident. The impact of such alterations and additions on the value of the evidence and the credibility of the recorder can be significant. *Meyer v. Gordon et al*[30] points out such evidentiary difficulties. (The reader will recall that this case was analyzed in some detail in Chapter Four, "The Tort of Negligence and the Nursing Process".) This medical and nursing negligence action was heard by the British Columbia Supreme Court in 1981. The parents of the brain-damaged, newborn infant claimed for punitive and exemplary damages in addition to general damages. They alleged that the hospital staff did not act ethically, did not make proper disclosures to the plaintiffs of what had occurred, and that they had altered the hospital records. The courts, after hearing all of the evidence and argu-ments, proceeded to examine the standard of care provided by the hospital before examing the allegations against the defen-dant physicians:

" My criticism of the defendant hospital is not confined to the lack of care of its nurs-ing staff. The hospital chart contains altera-tions and additions which compel me to view with suspicion the accuracy of many of the observations which are recorded. "[31]

" The chart also contains at least one entry which was discovered during this trial ... to have been made after the fact. That also casts suspicion on the reliability of those who made the entries and undermines the accuracy of medical opinions based upon those entries and observations "[32]

Following is a reconstruction of page 6 of the nursing notes which recording casts doubt on the accuracy of the observations and on the reliability of the recorders:[33]

DATE & HOUR	MEDICATION	REMARKS	
21/3/77		Admitted to 303B. Appears to be in good labour	A.W.
11:30		Emesis of undigested food.	A.W.
		Sm. amt. blood tinged liquor on pad.	
12:05	Demerol 50 mgm.		I.M. A.W.
	Gravol 50 mgm.		L.M. A.W.
12.32		Called by husband to help wife.	
		Found baby's head already delivered with very large amount meconium. Delivered body and baby taken to c.r. for resuscita-tion.	L.E.T./McA

On the other side of the record was the record of examinations during labour for March 21, 1977:

Date & hr.	B.P.	F.H.	Contractions Freq Character	Position	Rect Vag	Dil Cervix	Level	Signature
21/3/77								
11:30	118/80	132	Q2 Strong	N.H.	Vag	3. c.m.	Mid	A.W.
11:50		132	Q2 60 sec.					McA
12:00		132	Q2 60 sec.					McA

The court concluded that Nurse W's entry: "Sm. amt. blood tinged liquor on pad" was inserted on the chart after the fact, i.e. after the infant had been delivered and transferred from the defendant hospital to the Vancouver General Hospital. This became evident when a photostatic copy of the chart that had accompanied the infant to the Vancouver General Hospital was introduced and shown to be missing the entry that appeared on the original of the same chart. The copy did not contain the "interlineation" (the insertion between the lines). The copy did not contain the signatures of Nurse T or Head Nurse McA opposite the entry at 12:32.

During examination for discovery, prior to trial, Nurse W stated that the unsigned interlineation was made by her at the same time she charted the injections. However, at trial, the court concluded:

" after nurse W subsequently became aware that the child was in trouble and after the child had been taken to Vancouver General Hospital, Nurse M (head nurse) noted the inadequacy of Nurse W's charting. She communicated her concern of this inadequacy to Nurse W and Nurse W made the interlineated entry. It was not until she was faced with proof at the trial that the interlineated entry was made after the copy of the chart had gone to Vancouver General Hospital that she changed her evidence. "

" A serious question arises concerning the 11:50 and 12 noon entries made on the chart by Nurse McA. Counsel for the plaintiffs and for Dr. G submit that I should find that these examinations did not take place. I have been troubled by that submission because the evidence of Nurse McA concerning the making of those and other entries on the chart was not satisfactory "[34]

Counsel for the Plaintiff in the case called a handwriting expert to the stand who testified that black ink was used on the chart to overwrite a "1" on the "0" in the first line of the chart changing Nurse W's entry of 10:30 to 11:30 and black ink was used to change Nurse McA's first blue ink entry from 11:30 to 11:50 by adding a tail to the figure 3 in the 11:30 figures. The head nurse, under cross-examination, was unable

to explain it but agreed with the plaintiff's counsel that at some point after the first part of the 11:50 and 12 noon entries were made she went back and filled in the contractions and her initials. With respect to the head nurse as a witness her general demeanour and answers persuaded the court that although her recording was not reliable, she had not gone to the extent of making entries of examinations which she had never conducted. The court accepted as fact that the head nurse carried out two examinations but that she did not record them at the time she made them and did not complete her recording of them when she first attempted to do so. More significantly the court noted that the full extent of the unreliable nursing entries unfolded at the trial when a number of medical witnesses gave evidence relying on the entries on the original of the chart. The court stated that the expert opinion and the weight to be attached to it depended in large measure on the accuracy of the nursing observations and the nurse's charting, and since such were unreliable the court rejected the opinion of the expert witness for the defence.

In the 1983 Ontario case, *Hajgato v. The University Hospital*[35] the plaintiff was unsuccessful when she sued in negligence alleging that she had been partially disabled due to defective post-operative care following hip surgery and cast application. Specifically, she alleged that early infection had not been detected and failure to detect the problem resulted in hip complications. Following the injury, the patient's solicitor obtained a photostatic copy of the hospital record in order to obtain the necessary detail to commence a legal action. Many months later, during the pre-trial examination for discovery of the defence witnesses, counsel noted an entry on the original of the hospital record that did not appear on the photostatic copy obtained earlier. On the original of the medical progress notes there was an entry "wound o.k.". At trial, the plaintiff's counsel suggested to the court that the additions to the record were made long after the fact, when litigation was imminent, to suggest that the hip wound was healing well one week following surgery. The court rejected the suggestion.

Alterations and additions to the record after the fact weaken or even destroy the value of the record as evidence.

5. Accurate Recording of Nursing Observations:

One of the more challenging problems both from an evidentiary and a safe nursing care perspective, is to chart nursing data in an accurate and, where possible, quantitative manner. (After all the nautical term "to chart" means to map the course and infers precision in measurement.) It is not only important that recordings be made regularly and honestly but that every effort be taken to accurately perceive the data and to record the findings precisely and objecively, using terminology that most effectively reduces possible misinterpretation. *Meyer v. Gordon*[36] is again referred to in terms of the problems posed by inaccurate recording of data. (The reader is referred to the chart excerpt set out earlier in this chapter.) The plaintiff was in active labour on admission to the labour room of the defendant hospital at 11:30 a.m. on March 21, 1977. At 11:30 a.m. Nurse W recorded the patient "appears to be in good labour". She charted that the contractions were every two minutes and were "strong", that the cervix was dilated 3 centimeters and that the fetus was at "mid" station. However the nurse failed to record the duration of the contractions. An expert nursing witness gave her opinion that in a multiparous patient the cervix might dilate from one to two centimeters during contraction while with the cervix at rest, the dilatation could appear to be much less. The obstetrician who testified stated that he would expect a nursing report to indicate that the cervix was 3 centimeters dilated but expanding to 4 centimeters during contractions. Two of the nursing experts criticized the use of the term "mid" station. One stated that the term was not specific enough in evaluating the progress of labour and the other expert stated that "mid" had no real meaning. In her testimony Nurse W admitted that whether or not contractions were increasing, the size of the cervical dila-

tion and the effacement of the cervix were all important indicators of the progress of the labour and should have been accurately recorded. The court referred to her "inexact approach" and found that her evidence was inprecise and her appreciation of the patient's progress of labour was inaccurate. The infant was delivered thirty-two minutes following admission and was subsequently diagnosed as having cerebral palsy and mental retardation which the court determined was due to the "manifest negligence" of the nurses. A much lesser degree of liability was attached to the attending physician.

In summary, effective recording tends toward quantitative expressions. Use of terms such as "good labour", "strong labour", "slept well", "ate well" are at least useless terms but sometimes may be highly misleading and dangerous terminology. (The reader is referred to the summary of twenty-one suggested recording practices which addresses the problem of quantifying and specifying the nursing data required. The summary is set out at the end of the chapter.)

Set out below is a brief outline of the problem-oriented recording system. Its use is gaining acceptance in hospitals as one method of improving the communication potential in recording and reporting the nursing process.

VII. Problem Oriented Recording:[37]

This is a method of organizing the hospital record as an ongoing audit of the management of the patient's problems which focuses in on those problems that require immediate attention. At its best the system encourages an interdisciplinary approach to the plan of care to cope with the identified problems in their order of urgency. During the 1960's Dr. Lawrence Weed originated a problem-oriented medical record system (POMR) in the United States which more effectively prevented problems and complications than the traditional record method, because it provided a more systematic and logical analysis of problems. The traditional hospital record system consists of a series of reports and diaries kept by the various professionals having input into the care of the particular patient. These reports and diaries were not consistently related to each other and had some overlap of data recorded. This system contained, for instance, separate medical history, nursing history and social history; separate medical orders and nursing orders, separate nursing notes and medical progress notes. It resulted in much duplication of effort and did not guarantee that certain urgent problems were being addressed. In contrast the original *POMR* system (problem oriented medical record) contained four records: a data base, a problem list, progress notes and a care plan. The original system has been modified in its use in some Canadian hospitals and usually calls for two additional records: *a flow chart* and a *discharge plan*. There has been some apprehension for possible legal implications of the newer approach. However since the objective of the system is to keep the patient's health problems in focus for intervention on a timely basis and in priority of their urgency, it is, potentially, a safer system than the traditional approach. The latter tended to focus on routines rather than problems, and with the various professionals recording in separate parts of the chart, the record tended to fragment rather than to "chart" a safe course for the patient.

The Tools of POMR:

1. The Data Base:

This contains information from a variety of sources. It is initiated on the admission of the patient. It includes general background, medical and nursing history data, results of physical assessments done by the attending physicians and nurses, and laboratory workups. The purpose of the data base is to allow for *identification* of *actual problems* being experienced by the patient as well as the *probable problems* to be anticipated by virtue of his condition and or the therapies being administered. The data base would form part of the permanent hospital record on discharge of the patient.

2. Problem List:

The active problems identified in the data base are described in the problem list for the purpose of continuous monitoring and intervention. The problems can be of several kinds:
— they may be psycho-social in nature such as anxiety, depression, grief or hostility
— the problem may be the disease complex such as arthritis, coronary and pulmonary diseases, metabolic disorders, orthopedic diseases or accidents
— the problems may consist of symptom and complication complexes such as pain, infection, inflammation, elevated temperature, limited movement, insomnia, bleeding, fluid and electrolyte disturbance, loss of appetite, nausea, vomiting, constipation, diarrhea, malnutrition, obesity, urinary retention, abdominal distention, dyspnea, disturbances in levels of consciousness, visual, auditory or other sensory imbalance or disturbance, and allergic responses to internal and external matter.

The problem list is commonly documented in pencil by the nurse, signatured by the recorder of the problem and the urgency or priority is scored numerically. Marriner at page 48 of her text *The Nursing Process: A Scientific Approach to Nursing Care* suggests that the problem list summarizes all the known problems of the patient and serves as an index for the patient's chart. For this reason the problem list is the first document in the chart. Marriner proposes that the problems on the list should be dated and numbered according to the order in which they emerge, and include a system for noting when the problems are resolved.

3. Nursing Care Plan:

The identified active problems are transferred to a record designed by the nursing members of the health team. The plan is initiated on admission of the patient and is updated on a regular basis. The plan incorporates the specific medical orders and nursing orders for the management of the identified problems. Managers of the institution should strike a policy as to whether the nursing care plan is to be incorporated as part of the permanent record on discharge of the patient from the institution. The nursing care plan (the nursing order sheet) is an important document. It may be as important, from an evidentiary standpoint as the medical order sheet. The latter forms part of the permanent record of the institution.

4. Flow Charts:

One of the concerns of nurses in the use of problem oriented records is whether to chart all routine care and if so where to record. This concern relates in part to the relatively new common law principle that "absence of charting infers absence of care". The flow charts partially meet this concern and as well meet the concern for contemporaneous recording. The flow chart is a work sheet which is kept at the patient's bedside. The intent is that the nurse record all routine care *at the time of the event* and by a check mark rather than the traditional essay type recording on the nursing notes. The flow chart contains a listing for checking of vital signs, skin care, diet, intake and output records, girth measurements, weight, post-operative dressing changes, bowel and bladder treatments, diabetic routines, etc. The flow chart eliminates time consuming recording of "routine care" which, in absence of a flow chart, would have to be described on the nursing notes. The graphed data allows one to see at a glance the progress of the patient. The flow chart should form part of the permanent record of the institution.

5. Progress Notes:

In the POMR, these replace both nursing notes and the medical progress notes. Depending on the policy of the institution, all of the health care professionals assigned to the patient may make entries of their observations. It may or may not contain notations shift by shift or even day by day depending on whether or not there has been a positive or negative change in the patient's status and response to nursing intervention. Progress notes are recorded in ink and should form part of the permanent record.

6. Discharge Plan:

Prior to the patient's discharge, a duplicate record is prepared outlining the patient's current problems requiring ongoing monitoring and management. This plan is for the information of the patient, and for the direction of any community resource agencies to whom the patient has been referred. It outlines the ongoing plan of care needs. This is an important tool for continuity of care and patient safety and education. The original of the record forms part of the permanent record and the copy is forwarded with or on behalf of the patient.

Following is a summary of proposed nursing recording practices which are applicable whether the record system is a traditional one or the more current problem oriented record. Following this summary is a brief outline of an incident-reporting system to deal with the reality that despite the best care, accidents and injuries can occur. It is important that such be appropriately documented and reported.

VIII. Reasonable and Prudent Nursing Recording Policies, Practices and Systems:

1. The classes of patients expected to require nursing recording, and the detail and frequency of the recording is dictated by the complexity of the health problems, the level of risk posed by the patient himself, his condition, or by the medical, nursing and other therapies. A statement of nursing policy should be expressed in writing and published for the direction of nurses in care and control of patient care.

2. The higher the risk to which the particular patient is exposed, the more comprehensive, indepth and frequent should be the nursing recordings. Patients receiving care in post-operative recovery rooms, coronary care units, intensive care units and patients in active delivery and immediate post partum are potentially high risk patients. It is reasonable to expect that the registered nurse will, in addition, to any policy statement, exercise sound profes-

sional judgment in any one case, and build in the recording demanded by the situation.

3. Effective recording is *chronological* i.e. arranged in the order of time. The chronological flow is maintained by recording on each and every line. Absence of vacant lines prevents the conclusion that the chronological order was tampered with after the fact.

4. Effective recording avoids *interlineations* i.e. writing between the lines and avoids *erasures*. If charting was omitted through error, enter the time of the entry and document the time the actual observation was made or care given. If and when an erroneous note has been recorded, a line is drawn through the error, *"error"* is noted and the author signatures the error, follows it with the correct entry and signatures and enters the time of the corrected notation.

5. Effective recording is clearly *signatured* to prove the author of the recording. The signature includes as well the status of the recorder (registered nurse, registered nursing assistant, nursing student) with the appropriate initial, to facilitate identification and avoid proof problems for trial purposes.

6. Effective recording is made on hospital records, containing the hospital letterhead, clear identification of the patient concerned, the proper date per sheet and the precise time immediately accompanying each separate nursing notation.

7. Effective recording is *contemporaneous* i.e. data is recorded *at the time* of the event or as close as is prudently possible after the event (and never in anticipation of the event). It is not reasonable and prudent practice to delay critical notations to the end of shift. Delay in recording creates distortion because of memory lapse. Delayed recording is fraught with potential for omission, error and inaccuracy. The higher the risk situation, the greater should be one's effort to record within proximity to the event.

8. Effective recording is *authored* by the nurse having the *personal knowledge* of the matters being recorded. In emergency and resusitation events the accepted practice is to have one nurse assigned to record the events carried out by other players but the recording nurse is involved in the process and thereby has "personal knowledge". Within the limits of such modifications, the prudent nurse avoids having absent third parties record her nursing assessment data and nursing interventions. To fall into recording for each other is unreasonable and not prudent since it promotes distortion, omission and error, and may ultimately prevent the admissibility of the documents pursuant to the *Ares v. Venner* principle cited earlier.

9. Effective recording is *factual*. It is important that the nurse record honestly, and that the recording be based on accurately perceived data. (Data determined directly from *visual cues* such as patient's skin tones, presence of diaphoresis, unequal pupillary dilatation, slow, shuffling gate; from *verbal cues* such as the variety of patient's responses to questions of sleep patterns, dietary habits, etc, through touch (*palpation*). (In the previously cited Kolesar case, palpation would have detected the dangerous problem of full bladder and distention. Olefactory cues such as the acetone breath led to diagnosis of diabetes mellitus in *Yepremium v. Scarborough General Hospital*.

10. Effective recording is absent of *bias*. Any tendency to pre-judge or to label patients is a dangerous and detrimental practice. The labelling by its nature throws up a smokescreen which can mask the real and possibly urgent, life-threatening problems. The nurses who perceived a teenage girl (who had been in hospital for ten days with undiagnosed chest pain) as attention-seeking and spoiled, missed the cues of the real problem, (pulmonary embolism). The latter failed to be diagnosed until autopsy. (This case was not litigated.)

11. Effective recording tends toward *quantitative* expression: For the patient with a probable or actual sleeping problem

avoid general expressions such as "good night", "fair night", "usual night", "poor night". Such not only have no meaning but occupy and waste charting space and nursing time, and may distort or even mask a serious sleeping problem needing urgent medical and or nursing intervention. Do chart: "slept from 0200 hours to 0400 hours and patient states she slept soundly and feels rested".

For the patient with potential, probable or actual fluid intake and output problems, avoid charting "fluids taken q.s." or "voided q.s." Such terms not only have no meaning, and occupy and waste charting space and nursing time, but may distort or even mask a serious fluid balance and or urinary condition requiring urgent medical and or nursing intervention. Do chart: September 12, 1983 0400 hours: Voided 100 c.c.s. cloudy urine. Do check visual cues. Do record results of palpation over the bladder area. Do record patient's descriptions. Do record and report any abnormal findings. For the patient with a potential, probable or actual bowel disturbance, note distention and or tenderness; do not chart "moderate distention"; do chart actual measurement of the girth and note any increase from previous record of measurement. For the patient with a potential, probable or actual nutrition problem avoid "ate well" as such not only has no meaning but can mask severe nutritional problems.

12. Effective recording has *continuity*: i.e. the record clearly identifies the problems as they appear, the resolutions used to address the problems and the change in status of the problem.

13. Effective recording notes the date and time of all physician-patient visits of which the nurse has notice, and the date and time of all nurse-physician consultations, both face to face and by telephone. Details showing timely reporting of those nursing assessments containing particular abnormal findings together with the facts given and the directions received and the subsequent nursing actions taken, should be recorded.

14. Effective recording documents all nurse-physician consultations regarding any questionable medical orders, together with notations of directions received confirming, cancelling or modifying medical orders, and the nursing responses taken as a consequence. (Failure to evidence the questioning of unreasonable or unsafe medical orders could draw the imprudent nurse into the liability net in the event the patient is injured.)

15. Effective recording documents current nursing assessments carried out prior to the administration of all medical orders involving use of drugs and therapeutic agents, and — documents timely assessments of the patient's responses to the therapy.

16. All "routine care" documentation may be provided through the use of flow records. This is a record on which repetitive nursing observations and procedures are documented and is a shorter charting route than was historically included by way of the traditional nursing notes. The flow chart is commonly kept at the patient's unit with the expectation that when the routine activity is carried out, it is charted contemporaneously with the event. This flow chart, on discharge of the patient, becomes part of the hospital's permanent record.

17. Reasonable and prudent nursing recordings are *problem*-oriented. The purpose of such recording is to identify and describe the patient's problems, in a clear and timely manner, and to record the therapy used to resolve the problems, as well as to show the patient's responses to the therapy.

18. Effective recording includes a *nursing history* which record should be retained and should form part of the permanent record on discharge of the patient.

19. Effective records include a written *nursing care plan* which sets out, in ink, the nursing problems, and nursing orders,

FLOW CHART — BASIC PATIENT NEEDS

DATE

TIME

OXYGENATION	NO PROBLEMS	
	COMMENTS	
H		

	BATH	C Century
		P Puli
		B Bed
HYGIENE		S Shower
		SZ Sitz
		ASSISTED
		MOUTH CARE
		A M CARE A B C
		H S CARE A B C

SKIN	INTACT
INTEGRITY	COMMENTS
	TURN & RUB q h

ACTIVITY	BED REST
(N/A M I)	DANGLE
	CHAIR
	BRP
	UP WALKING
	REST PERIOD
	ASSISTED
	COMMENTS

ACTIVITY AIDS	
	ASSISTED
	COMMENTS

NUTRITION	EATING WELL
	EATING POORLY
	FASTING
	WITH ASSISTANCE
	TOTAL FEED
OTHER	

STOOL	NORMAL

ELIMINATION	BRP
(N A T U P R.)	VOIDED
	CATHETER
	INCONTINENT
URINE	CLEAR
	COMMENTS

PSYCHOLOGICAL ASSESSMENT	ADJUSTING
	VERBALIZING
(N/A PSYCH)	COMMENTS

NIGHT SLEEP	WELL
	PERIODS
	COMMENTS

SAFETY	RESTRAINT
	L Limb
	J Jacket
	B Belt
	M Mitts
	SIDE RAILS

OTHER NURSING PROCEDURES	ISOLATION MAINTAINED
OTHER	

ANALGESIC EFFECTIVE   YES   NO

TEACHING COMPLETE   DATE   SIGNATURE

SIGNATURE

DISCHARGE ASSESSMENT

MODE OF DISCHARGE

ACCOMPANIED BY

DATE _____ TIME_____ SIGNATURE _____

See endnote 38

i.e. nursing actions to help the patient in resolving or controlling the problem. The nursing care plan forms part of the permanent record on discharge of the patient.

20. Effective recordings include narrative recording of *progress notes* directed to the problems identified in the nursing care plan.

21. Effective records include a *discharge plan* containing instructions for the patient and for the follow-up community service. This record is made in duplicate, with the patient or guardian obtaining the copy and the original is attached to the permanent record.

22. Reasonable and prudent nursing records document all critical incidents involving the patient and of which the nurse has personal knowledge. Such recording is in addition to that which is placed on a *critical incident record*. This latter document does not form part of the patient's chart. Recordings of accidents or injuries to the patient should include facts about the time and circumstances of the event, and the actions taken to safeguard the patient in order to demonstrate that the care was reasonable and prudent in the circumstances. Failure to record on the nurses notes by the person having care of the patient at the time may well reflect on the credibility of the nurse concerned.

IX. Use of Incident Reporting Systems:

From time to time unplanned incidents occur in the hospital which place people at potential or actual risk. The complexity of the hospital environment, its programs and equipment, together with the large variety and numbers of health care workers, patients and visitors circulating within the environment on a daily basis, create these potential and actual hazards. It is expected that hospital management will have a system in place to accurately document, report, monitor and appropriately intervene in hazardous situations. The following paragraphs define a critical incident report, its purposes, the policy considerations and suggested content and evidentiary use of a critical incident reporting system.

An incident may be defined as any happening which is not in accord with the routine operation of the institution or the routine care of a particular patient. It may involve a patient, visitor, staff member or all three and could involve as well, supplies, equipment, procedures or particular services or programs. A critical incident report, as a management tool, is a document prepared by an authorized reporter, in accordance with the policy and procedure, and is directed to an authorized management person for further action.

1. Purposes:

There are at least five reasons for maintaining a critical incident reporting system:

— to monitor the type and frequency of risks relative to certain approved programs and hospital activities. (The process stimulates regular review of the methodology of such programs, so that a concerted effort can be made to reduce risks to a minimum without jeopardizing the desired goals of the enterprise.)

— to provide data prior to taking action to eliminate the causes of untoward incidents. For example, if an incident is due to the lack of knowledge and skill on the part of a particular worker appropriate action may call for retraining of the person in knowledge and skills, increased supervision and increased performance evaluations of the worker concerned. If the incident is due to a worker's carelessness and indifference to patient safety, the required remedial action will likely differ. Appropriate action may call for termination of the person's employment.

— to collect information necessary for preparing a defence to civil and criminal proceedings, public inquiries or grievance arbitrations.

— to provide confidential communication to the hospital's legal counsel for ongoing legal advice or for preparation for trial of a particular dispute.

— to constitute evidence that management practice in the particular agency was reasonable and prudent in the prevention of or reduction of foreseeable risks.

2. Policy Considerations:

Written policies governing the monitoring of critical incidents should clearly state when such reports are to be completed, by whom they are to be completed and with whom they are to be filed. Such reports should be completed *at the time* the incident occurs, and should be *objective* and *factual* and use a *critical incident method* of documenting the data. The report, to be useful, must identify the parties and witnesses in the incident, the date, time, place and patient involved and particulars of the event. (The patient's name should be codified for confidentiality since critical incident reports are sometimes used for research and statistics.)

Critical incident reports and their statistics have been used at trial. (It may well be that the defendant hospital would not wish the data to be used for trial purposes and may attempt to claim privilege which is discussed later in the chapter.) In *Meyer v. Gordon* the court considered the critical incident reports completed by the three nurses who were on duty on March 21, 1977 when the Meyer infant was severely injured during labour and delivery. Two reports were completed a day after the incident. Nurse W's critical incident report was not completed until two days after the event. The court had the following to say:

> " Indeed all three incident reports are rather bland statements. If they were meant to guide those responsible for the policies of the defendant hospital to prevent reoccurrence of the tragic event which happened they were obviously woefully inadequate. "[39]

The court compared the content of the report completed by Nurse W with her nursing notes. The nursing notation contained an interlineation (words written between the lines) of "blood-tinged liquor". The addition did not refer to any meconium. In the report which she completed two days after the event, Nurse W stated "there was no meconium in evidence". The court concluded that the nursing notes had been altered after the fact and that at the time of the delivery Nurse W was unaware of the urgent significance of meconium presenting at delivery. (The infant was delivered with large quantity of meconium covering its face, nose and mouth.) The court discounted the oral evidence of Nurse W.

Incident reports should be marked confidential and directed to the administrative person designated. (If it is a nursing incident, the report is directed to the director of nursing.) Critical incident reports should not be circulated, and unless required by legislation (as in Quebec) the report should not be placed on the patient's chart. However the incident itself, a burn, fall, or assault for example should be noted chronologically in the nursing notes.

3. Suggested Content of Critical Incident Record:[40]

The hospital should have a pre-printed critical incident form to ensure that the critical elements of the event are recorded accurately and comprehensively. Such a record would contain such minimum data as:

— the name, address, and status of the patient involved
— dates of admission, date and time of incident and date and time report was completed
— patient's condition prior to event (i.e. well oriented, senile, sedated)
— if surgical patient, the number of days post-op
— ambulatory state of patient prior to event
— if patient is a minor, or is not well-oriented, confirm directions from physician concerning notification of next of kin
— safety measures in effect prior to incident (side rails, signal lights, high-low beds and position of)
— location of incident
— type of incident: burns, falls, bumped, struck

— contributing factors: limited vision, seizure, intoxicated
— degree of injury
— persons notified and date and time of notification
— persons who examined the patient following the incident, the date and time of the examination
— wishes of patient concerning notification of next of kin
— brief account of incident
— statement of patient if feasible
— if incident was witnessed, a list of witnesses and statements by them
— reporter's suggestions for prevention of similar incidents in future
— date and time the report was filed with administration and further action to be taken.

4. Critical Incident Reports as Evidence: Confidentiality and Privilege

The critical incident report is primarily a management tool in place for the ongoing improvement of safety of the institution, its equipment, programs and practices. To this end it is important to maintain its confidentiality.

As a general principle, documents prepared in the course of patient care, are admissible at trial for specific purposes and as determined by compliance with rules of evidence. However, records which can be brought within the ambit of privilege may be exempt. *Wigmore on Evidence*[41] states that in order for a communication to be privileged and thereby free from exposure in open court it must meet four conditions:

— the communications must originate in a confidence that they will not be disclosed
— the confidentiality must be essential to the full and satisfactory maintenance of the relation between the parties
— the relation must be one which in the opinion of the community ought to be sedulously fostered
— the injury that would inure to the relation by disclosure must be greater than the benefit thereby gained for the correct disposal of litigation.

Critical incident reports prepared by hospital management for the hospital solicitor for the purpose of instructing counsel about potential or actual litigation will be "privileged":

" ... when something goes wrong ... which reasonably gives rise to anticipation of litigation, any statement which is then made by persons concerned with the patient in anticipation ... is quite clearly privileged. "[42]

However if such a report is made for the purpose of internal discipline the report is not privileged and would, therefore, be admissible at trial if the document otherwise complies with the evidentiary rules for admissability.

X. Hospital Records: Confidentiality and Access to Health Information:

" Knowledge is power. Knowledge about another person, knowledge, that is, that the person does not have, is surely, power over that person ... "[43]

The patient has not always been well served by either the law or institutional practice in terms of control of the information within hospital records. The patient has had virtually no power to enforce confidentiality of the very personal information recorded about him in the records, and little power to obtain information from his record should the authority decide that he cannot have it:

" ... we are an information society and health information is potentially the most sensitive information that can be collected in connection with an individual ... the evidence disclosed during the Commission hearings that the very same health information concealed from the patient, has been revealed to third parties — sometimes quite justifiably — but often times indiscriminately, with the result that, to a substantial extent, many third parties know what the health care professionals think about the patient but the patient does not ".[44]

1. Ownership

Both case law and statutes confirm that the hospital corporation has ownership of the physical property of the hospital records. Ownership implies an exclusive right to control, use, enjoy and dispose of one's property as one sees fit. For example, the following section of Ontario's *Public Hospitals Act* is fairly typical:

" The medical record compiled in the hospital for a patient or an outpatient is the property of the hospital and shall be kept in the custody of the administrator ".[45]

Ownership of the property does not, however, extend necessarily to the information contained in the record. Neither the common law nor statute have yet clarified who owns the information. In the 1980 Ontario case, *Re. Mitchell and St. Michael's Hospital*,[46] the court suggested that the patient or his personal representative "has something akin to a proprietary (property) interest in the contents of the records". Yet the court refused access to the information by the father of a deceased patient because of the power given by statute to the hospital authority pursuant to Ontario's *Public Hospitals Act*.

Although ownership of information is not clear, for all practical purposes the authority in possession of the record controls use and dispersal of the information therein. The burden is on the person who is not in possession of the record to find a legal route should he wish to ensure that its information about him is kept confidential, or should he wish to obtain the information concerned. The person wanting the confidentiality preserved, or wanting access to the information could be the patient himself, or such third parties as spouses, parents, children, or relatives of the patient, or insurance investigators, parties to a legal dispute, the accused and crown in a criminal matter, or tribunals holding investigations or hearings into disputes.

The person wishing access to or preservation of the confidentiality of a particular record can only bring it about if there is a legal duty on the part of the authority having custody of the record, which duty can

be enforced by the applicant for his benefit. In theory, there are five sources of duty to maintain confidentiality and to provide access to information. Following is a brief examination of the status of these duties:

2. Sources of Legal Duty to Maintain Confidentiality:

The sources of the duty include professional, contractual, common law and statutory sources, and court orders.

Professional employees are privy to very personal and delicate information. There are definite ethical obligations imposed on professional persons not to disclose such information to third parties except where there is a legal duty to do so, or a moral duty to do so because the public interest is honestly perceived to out-weigh the private interests of the patient. This professional responsibility is set out in the code of nursing ethics adopted by the provincial nursing association in the province where the nurse is currently practicing. The physician is guided by the code of medical ethics published by the Canadian Medical Association.

It has been argued that the corporate authority itself owes a duty to the patient being serviced, to protect the confidential nature of the hospital record being compiled about him. This duty is based in contract, and would be an implied term of the contract.

In the event that information is published about the patient that is untrue, the patient may choose to commence an action for defamation. A defamatory statement is an oral or written statement which is derogatory and tends to lower the person concerned in the estimation of other members of the community, and causing hatred, contempt or ridicule. Actionable defamation includes the torts of slander and libel with the distinction between the two being based on the mode of publication — the former is spoken defamation, the latter, written. The law of defamation is directed to the protection of the individual's reputation. The offending statement must be "published", i.e. communicated to third parties. Once published, (and assuming a legal action is taken by the offended patient), the burden is on the defendant nurse, or physician to prove one of the defences recognized at common law, that the statement was either a true statement, or was one made in circumstances of qualified privilege.

If the statement were true, this will constitute an absolute defence and the plaintiff is without a remedy. However, if the statement is not true, the defendant may still escape liability by establishing that the statement was fairly and honestly made upon a privileged occasion. Privilege refers to a particular and peculiar benefit or advantage enjoyed by a person or class beyond the common advantage of other citizens. In a defamation suit, the defendant, pursuant to this defence, is contending that by virtue of the nature of the event or occasion the statement was privileged. Absolute privilege operates in Parliament, in the provincial legislatures and in the courts. A qualified privilege will excuse the defendant if he had a private or public duty to speak the words and he spoke them honestly, fairly and without malice. In *C v. D*[47], (1924), a decision of the Ontario High Court, the defendant physician succeeded in this defence when he was sued by the patient subsequent to telling the plaintiff's parents and employer that the plaintiff had a venereal disease. In a leading case on the subject, *Arnott v. The College of Physicians and Surgeons of Saskatchewan* the plaintiff, a licensed physician, allegedly developed the "Koch treatment" as a cancer treatment. The defendant college in its professional journal stated that the treatment was quackery. The college did not attempt to determine the truth of its statement. On appeal to the Supreme Court of Canada the plaintiff's case was dismissed on the basis that:

> " the report was published on an occasion of qualified privilege and the words used did not go beyond what was reasonably germane to the performance of the duty giving rise to the privilege. "[48]

Any statement to the effect that the patient is insane, has a venereal illness or is unfit to occupy a certain profession or occupation is potentially defamatory. However statements made in the nursing process to a physician or other colleague in relation to the therapeutic aspects of the case, will likely be covered, in the absence of malice, by qualified privilege.

There are only four provinces which provide a statutory right of action to persons whose privacy has been invaded. Quebec's *Charter of Human Rights and Freedoms*, and the *Privacy Acts* of British Columbia, Manitoba and Saskatchewan[49] provide such rights of action to protect the individual's right to withhold himself from public scrutiny. Persons in the remaining provinces have no real personal remedy in the absence of defamation. (In a 1981 unreported Quebec case, a woman sued a Montreal hospital for breach of privacy. She alleged that she had been filmed while giving birth to her baby at the defendant hospital.) Where statutory rights to privacy are recognized, the patient's right to consent and withdraw consent to privacy is valued and enforceable. In contrast, where patients have to rely on the limited duties expressed in the public hospitals acts of the various provinces there is no recourse for the patient himself. The statute commonly provides that the corporation has a duty to keep records confidential. The act provides for release of information to named persons or authorities, and for imposition of a fine against persons convicted of breaching the act. The statutes do not, however, provide a right in the patient to enforce the authority to comply with the obligation to keep information confidential nor do they give the patient a right to sue for damages.

Ontario's *Krever Royal Commission of Inquiry into the Confidentiality of Health Records in Ontario* published its findings and recommendations in 1980 after two years of intensive investigation and hearings. Its findings are of interest to persons who wish to design reasonable policies on the management of hospital records. The Krever Commission reported several hundred instances in which people and agencies obtained confidential information from hospital records by illegal means. The persons involved included detectives, insurers, police, lawyers, physicians and nurses. Included in the recommendations made by the Commission to correct the problems were:

— that procedures should be established by health care institutions to protect patient confidentiality including staff education, and patient consent forms for disclosure

— that any patient whose health information has been disclosed without consent, should have the statutory right to sue for a minimum of $10,000.00. The actions could be against the person who discloses the information and as well the person who induces the disclosure.

A duty to maintain confidentiality of records is mandated by the Canadian Council on Hospital Accreditation. The Council requires that policies and procedures in hospitals conform to the Canada Health Records Association Guidelines to the Code of Practice. The Council stipulates in the new standards published in January 1983, (standard V), that:

> " There shall be current written policies and procedures to provide clinical record staff with clear direction of the scope and limitations of their functions and responsibilities and to ensure that patients' clinical records shall be confidential, current, complete, accurate, legible and suitably available. "[50]

The Council, in its interpretation of the foregoing standard (standard V) confirms that the clinical record is the property of the facility and is maintained for the benefit of the patient, the medical staff and the facility. It goes on to say that the facility has the responsibility to safeguard the information in the record against loss, or use by unauthorized persons.

3. Exceptions to the Duty to Maintain Confidentiality:

There are four categories of exceptions, the presence of any one of which authorizes the release of information:

(a) Patient's Consent:

The Canadian Council for Hospital Accreditation requires that written consent of the patient be obtained for the release of information to third parties (other than those persons specifically listed for access pursuant to the hospital's act.)

(b) Statutory Duty:

There are a number of statutes which make it mandatory for designated health care personnel to report certain illnesses, (such as venereal and other contageous diseases), and most jurisdictions have amended their child welfare legislation to compel health care workers who have notice of child abuse to report such incidents to a designated social services authority. (For clarity the hospital should provide a written reporting guideline for the direction of medical records personnel, nursing office personnel, personnel in emergency and outpatient departments and nursing staff in other units.) Hospitals tend to require that only the medical records supervisor shall be authorized to release information from the clinical record and to require that the would-be recipient be identified and legally authorized. Otherwise, information is released only on court order.

(c) Court Order:

Commonly, for trial purposes, a subpoena is directed to a named person within the hospital employ ordering the person to attend at trial to give evidence. The subpoena directs that certain clinical records be brought to court. In such an instance the medical records department should arrange for photostating of the documents before releasing the originals for court purposes. In most jurisdictions now there is also available a pre-trial discovery process. The solicitor on behalf of the party (the plaintiff or defendant) obtains a court order directing certain witnesses to appear for questioning by counsel of the opposing party. The purpose of productions of records and witnesses pre-trial is to avoid surprise and delay and to encourage the parties to settle the dispute short of trial.

4. Right of Access to Information:

In order for a person to obtain access to clinical information contained in the hospital records, he would need authority by way of agreement or contract, statutory authorization or a court order. Historically, access by patients and their agents to hospital records has been a contentious issue and health care personnel have hesitated to release information to the patient or his authorized agent, in the belief that access was not in the patient's best interests.

The various provincial hospital acts provide for limited access to hospital records by patients. For example, Ontario's *Public Hospitals Act* provides for access at the discretion of the hospital board. In *Re. Mitchell and St. Michael's Hospital*, mentioned earlier in this section, the father of the deceased child requested the child's hospital record. The hospital refused. The court reviewed the refusal and concluded that the Act gave the board the discretion to refuse access. At that stage, the father was not interested in commencing a legal action, but rather, wanted to satisfy himself about the care his child had received. (In Ontario one can get access after a legal action is commenced, through the discovery process mentioned earlier.) As the court said in *Re. Mitchell and St. Michael's Hospital*:

> " there is something illogical in saying that first someone must start an action against a hospital making whatever allegations may be made against it, and only then be entitled to get production of the hospital records pertaining to the person in question. It seems to me that that is a rather backward way of going about it. "[51]

Alberta's Mental Health Act, which was interpreted in 1981 in *Lindsay v. D.M.*, shows a more realistic balance in favour of the patient than is available through most of the public hospital legislation in Canada. The Alberta Mental Health Act provides that a person may apply to the courts if the request for access to information is denied and the courts might order the hospital authority to release the information. This happened in *Lindsay v. D.M.* (in which a former psychiatric patient applied to see his hospital record.) The court, in ordering the release, stated:

> " In my view, its first purpose was to protect the privacy of the patient. Therefore, the court should be vigilant, and demand compelling grounds before permitting access to medical records. There is, obviously, one special case: the patient himself. Access by him to the records in no way interfers with his right of privacy. "[52]

In addition to any permissive rights available pursuant to public hospital legislation, there may be access pursuant to Freedom of Information Statutes. Such legislation has been introduced in New Brunswick, Nova Scotia and Newfoundland.[53] Newfoundland's *Freedom of Information Act* expressly states that hospitals are included in the schedule of bodies coming within the ambit of the legislation. (Alberta, British Columbia, Saskatchewan, and North West Territories do not have such legislation.) The intent of freedom of information legislation is to create a right in citizens to information in records held by government. The act lists information that would be available to the public, declaring such information accessible (unless brought within the expressed exceptions.) It is too soon to determine how such legislation will be reconciled with the confidentiality requirements of the public hospitals legislation in the event that freedom of information legislation is applicable to hospitals in the particular province. Such legislation, if applicable, will not give an applicant access to the clinical record of other patients or former patients. However, the legislation will enlarge the applicant's right to obtain access to his own record. It could also provide possible access to internal administrative reports which heretofore were limited to a few persons within the management and corporate board levels.

5. Storage and Disposal of Hospital Records:

The various purposes of the hospital record were set out at the beginning of this chapter. Such purposes include planning for safe health care, educational and research purposes, and finally, the use of the hospital record as an evidentiary tool. The health care agency is expected to have a written policy governing retention and disposal of its clinical records. Such a policy would need to consider the purposes of the record in the particular institution; the content of the statute of limitations and the evidence act in the particular province; the effect of the age of majority act; and any statutory requirements for storage and disposal of records set out in the provincial hospital's act. For example, Sec. 14 (1) of the Operation of Approved Hospitals Regulations Alta. Reg. 146/71 pursuant to *Alberta Hospitals Act* R.S.A. 1980 chapter 11 states:

" Diagnostic and Treatment Service Records shall be retained by the hospital for

(a) a period of ten years from date of discharge from hospital, and in addition;

(b) in the case of the patient being a minor, for a period of at least two years following the date on which the patient reaches the age of eighteen years. "

Most of the provinces provide by way of regulations pursuant to the hospitals act for storage of the original of the hospital record. New Brunswick, Ontario, Prince Edward Island and Saskatchewan also provide for photographing, or electronic reproduction or microfilming of original hospital records. (All of the provincial evidence acts provide for admissibility of microfilm copies of records.) Following reproduction, the original of the record is retained for a minimum number of years and the reproduced copy is stored for a further period of time. For example, in Ontario and Prince Edward Island, if the records are not reproduced they are retained for a minimum of twenty years following discharge of the patient, or five years following the patient's death. If the record is photographed, the original is retained for two years from the date of the patient's discharge and the photographed record is retained for fifty years from the date when it was made. Records of minors, if not photographed, are retained for twenty years following the eighteenth birthday (or in the event the minor patient died, for five years after the patient, would have become eighteen years of age if he had lived.) New Brunswick legislation provides for retention of *unreproduced records* of adult patients for ten years following discharge of the patient or the date of the last visit of the outpatient, or six years following the death of the patient. If the patient is a minor, *unreproduced records* are retained for ten years following discharge or two years following

the nineteenth birthday of the patient, whichever is the longer. *Reproduced records* are retained for a minimum period of twenty-one years. British Columbia, by way of regulations under the Hospitals Act, provides for different retention periods for hospital records, depending on whether the document is "primary", "secondary" or "transitory". The regulations define primary documents to include case histories, consultation reports, discharge summaries and other documents prepared by attending and consulting physicians. Secondary documents include diagnostic reports and nursing notes among other documents. In British Columbia, primary records are retained for a period not less than ten years from date of discharge and secondary documents are retained for a minimum period of six years. The transitory records which include graphs and check lists may be destroyed following discharge of the patient and completion of the record by the attending physician for purposes of storage. Manitoba provides for retention and disposal policies by way of guidelines rather than regulations. Their system categorized records into primary and secondary documents. Primary documents are retained for a minimum of twenty years following the last date of service and secondary records are retained for a period of two years. However, the primary records of minors (persons under eighteen years) are held for twenty years after the person reaches eighteen years and secondary records are held for two years following the age of majority of the patient.

Some of the provinces make particular provision for storage and disposal of x-ray film — New Brunswick, Prince Edward Island, and Ontario. Ontario also provides for storage of slides for microscopic examination for a period of five years where the slide has shown some abnormality or where the hospital administrator has received notice that a court action has been commenced. Where the slide was reported as not showing any significant abnormality, the slide is stored for two years after the date when it was made.

Ontario's regulations provide for destruction of the records following the expiry

of the retention period, at the discretion of
the chief executive officer and in accordance
with a procedure approved by the board of
directors of the corporation or some other
authorizing body expressly provided for by
statute.[54]

In summary, the hospital record serves
not only as a basis for planning care but as
an important means of communication
among the various members of the health
team delivering care to the patient. As such
it can profoundly influence the quality of
care received by the patient and will stand
as an enduring record of the quality of
patient care in the institution concerned. It
is, finally, documentary evidence of the
course of the patient's illness, treatment
and care and the patient's response to the
treatment and care. Its examination may
reveal compliance or non-compliance with
the required standard of care.

XI. Endnotes:

1. Ares v. Venner [1970] S.C.R. 608, 14, D.L.R. (3d) 4 (S.C.C.)
2. Dowey v. Rothwell [1974] 5 W.W.R. 311 (Alta S.C.)
3. Supra n. 2
4. Sopinka J. Lederman S.N. *The Law of Evidence in Civil Cases*, (Toronto Butterworths 1974) p. 66
5. Supra n. 1
6. Supra n. 1 at 40 W.W.R. 96 at 105
7. Supra n. 1, (1970) 14 D.L.R. (3d) at 16
8. Supra n. 4
9. Supra n. 4 at 78
10. Supra n. 4 at 79
11. MacDonald v. York County Hospital et al [1976] 2 S.C.R. 825 (S.C.C.)
12. Supra n. 11: Excerpt of nursing notes from the case report
13. Duff et al v. Brocklehurst (1978) 20 N & P.E.I.R. 256
14. Re. Griffin's Estate (1979) 21 N & P.E.I.R. 21
15. Aynsley v. Toronto Gen. Hospital [1968] 1 O.R. 425 affirmed: [1969] 2 O.R. 829; affirmed [1972] S.C.R. 435 (S.C.C.)
16. Adderly v. Bremner [1968] 1 O.R. 621
17. Supra n. 16
18. Kolesar v. Jeffries et al (1974) 9 O.R. (2d) 41, varied 12 O.R. (2d) 142, affirmed 77 D.L.R. (3d) 161 (S.C.C.)
19. Supra n. 18
20. Good S.R., Kerr J.C. *Contemporary Issues in Canadian Law for Nurses* (Toronto, Holt, Rinehart, and Winston of Canada Ltd. 1973) p. 129 by Grady, P.E.
21. Supra n. 18
22. Supra n. 18
23. *Laidlaw v. Lions Gate Hospital* (1969) 70 W.W.R. 272, 72 W.W.R. 730
24. Supra n. 23 730 at 734
25. Supra n. 23
26. See *Quality of Nursing Care Standards* by the Association of Registered Nurses of Newfoundland
27. Supra n. 18 at 47.
28. Supra n. 18 at 47-48
29. *Traynor v. Vancott* (1979) 3 L. Med. Q. 69
30. *Meyer v. Gordon* 17 C.C.L.T. 1
31. Supra n. 30 at 15
32. Supra n. 30 at 15
33. Supra n. 30 at 15-16
34. Supra n. 30 at 18
35. *Hajgato v. The University Hospital* (1983) 36 O.R. (2d) 669
36. Supra n. 30 t 7, 11, 12 and 53
37. See Miller B.F., Keane C.B., *Encyclopedia and Dictionary of Medicine, Nursing and Allied Health* W.B. Saunders Co. Philadelphia, 1983, p. 822, and also Marriner A. (Ed) *The Nursing Process: A Scientific Approach to Nursing Care* C.V. Mosby Company St. Louis 1983
38. See *Can. Nurse* Dec. 1981 p. 41
39. Supra n. 30 at p. 53
40. The reader is referred to the publication of the Ontario Hospital Association: a model critical incident form.
41. *Wigmore on Evidence*, Little, Brown & Co., 1961, Vol. 8 at page 527
42. *Patch v. United Bristol Hospital's Board* [1958] 1 W.L.R. 955
43. Lindsay v. D.M. [1981] 3 W.W.R. 703 at p. 710
44. *Health Law in Canada*, (Spring 1981): "Experience with the Royal Commission of Inquiry Into Confidentiality of Health Records in Ontario. Strosberg p. 6
45. Public Hospitals Act R.S.O. 1980 c. 410 (The equivalent sections of the hospital legislation in Alberta and Newfoundland refer to "Every Record..." instead of the medical record which suggests confirmation of ownership of a wider variety of records than the record of the particular patient.)
46. Re: Mitchell and St. Michael's Hospital (1980) 29 O.R. (2d) 185
47. *C v. D* (1924) 56 O.L.R. 209

48. *Arnott v. The College of Physicians and Surgeons of Sask.* [1954] S.C.R. 538

49. Charter of Human Rights and Freedoms 1975 (Que.) c. 6; Privacy Act S.B.C. 1968 c. 39; Privacy Act S.M. 1970 c. 74; Privacy Act S.S. 1974 c. 80

50. *Canadian Council on Hospital Accreditation*: Standards For Accreditation of Canadian Health Care Facilities, January 1983, Ottawa, Ontario at p. 83

51. Supra n. 46 at p. 189

52. *Lindsay v. D.M.* [1981] 3 W.W.R. 703

53. Right to Information Act S.N.B. 1978 c. R 10.3; Freedom of Information Act S.N.S. 1977 c. 10; Freedom of Information Act. S.N. 1981 c. 5

54. See: Hospitals Act R.S.A. 1980 ch. 11
Hospitals Act R.S.B.C. 1979 c. 176
Hospitals Act R.S.M. 1970 ch. 20
Hospitals Act S.N. 1971 #81
Public Hospitals Act R.S.N.B. 1973 c. P-23
Hospitals Act R.S.N.S. 1967 c. 249
Public Hospitals Act R.S.O. 1980 c. 410
Hospitals Act R.S.P.E.I. 1974 c. 11
Health Services and Social Services Act R.S.Q. c S-5
Hospitalization Act R.S.S. 1978 c. S-23

Chapter Six:

Regulation of Nursing Practice in Canada:

I. Concept Objectives:

This final chapter will focus on nursing as a self-governing profession. Specifically, it will briefly review regulatory aspects of the nursing profession, its legislated goals and the regulatory and disciplinary process by which the profession carries out its statutory mandate. The regulatory mandate of each provincial and territorial nursing authority is to protect the public by publishing and consistently and fairly enforcing those standards of nursing practice to be met by its registered members. This chapter will:

— examine the statutory authority, legal structures, powers and duties of the provincial body which regulates nursing practice
— identify the duties, rights, remedies and professional accountability of the individual member of the profession
— describe the nursing behaviors which are subject to discipline by the regulatory authority and the sanctions which may be imposed by law
— describe the disciplinary process and the rules governing fair hearings in disciplinary matters
— examine the roles of codes of nursing ethics and standards of nursing practice in the protection of the public from unsafe, incompetent or unethical nursing practice.

II. Introduction:

     " Any misuse or abuse by any member of a profession is an indictment against the whole because the definition of a profession implies the concept of joint responsibility. **"** [1]

A profession exists to provide to the public the needed quality of service in a particular field. As a profession evolves historically, it may become a legislatively constituted organization empowered to establish its own rules and standards of practice. If and when a government legislates a profession into legal existence, it usually does so to protect the public and not for the purpose of giving the particular profession a monopoly on the service free from economic competition. Government's intent is to protect the public from unsafe, incompetent and unethical practices through legislative safeguards. In return for a certain autonomy and freedom, the particular legislated profession is expected to accept a mandate to police the practice of its members. Such a mandate may involve the profession in approval of the required educational base of professional practice, setting of criteria for initial admission into the profession, and mechanisms for monitoring and enforcing of standards of practice required of its members on an ongoing basis. In principle, the law regulating a profession exists to prevent harm to the public through maintenance and enforcement of approved standards on a consistent basis and in a reasonable manner. In practice, however, the ability of a profession to prevent unsatisfactory practice hinges in part on the members' commitment to quality of service to the public, in part on the will of the profession to enforce standards, and in part on the strength of the legislative tools for enforcement given to the profession in its statute and regulations.

The Canadian Nurses Association is the national federation of provincial and territorial nursing associations. The object of this national body is to improve and maintain the ethical and professional standards of nursing education and nursing service. However, the immediate regulation of nursing practice of the individual registered nurse is a provincial matter. Each province and one of the territories has, by legislation, an independent, incorporated body which exists for the purpose of carrying the intent of the nursing act into effect. Statutory authority for the regulation of nursing has been delegated to the nursing profession in the following Acts:

— Alberta   Nursing Profession Act S.A. 1984 cN-14.5 (proclaimed January 15, 1984)

— British Columbia   Nurses (Registered) Act R.S.B.C. 1979 c. 302
                           Nurses (Psychiatric) Act R.S.B.C. 1979 c. 301

— Manitoba	Registered Nurses Act S.M. 1980 c. 45
— New Brunswick	The Nurses Act S.N. 1984 c. 71 (Royal Assent June 20, 1984)
— Newfoundland	Newfoundland Registered Nurses Act R.S.N. 1970 c. 268
— Nova Scotia	Registered Nurses Association Act R.S.N.S. 1967 c. 264 (Proposed legislation being reviewed by government in 1984)
— Ontario	Health Disciplines Act R.S.O. 1980 c. 196
— Prince Edward Island	Nurses Act R.S.P.E.I. 1974 c. N-3
— Quebec	Professional Code S.Q. 1973 c. 43 Nurses Act S.Q. 1973 c. 48
— Saskatchewan	Saskatchewan Registered Nurses Association Act R.S.S. 1978 Supp. c
Territories:	
— Northwest Territories	Nursing Profession Ordinance R.O.N.W.T. 1975 c. 6
— Yukon	—

Each of the foregoing statutes delegates power to the nursing association concerned (and in Ontario, to the College of Nurses of Ontario) to create rules, regulations and standards governing nursing practice. The rules provide for setting of admission criteria, the management of the disciplinary process and the invocation of sanctions or penalties for breach of the statute by a member of the profession.

There are individual differences in nursing legislation across Canada. The newer acts are more comprehensive in their code of procedures than are the older statutes, and more importantly, the newer legislation provides for definition of nursing practice. Without the professional field being clearly defined it is difficult to regulate the practice effectively.

III. Mandatory and Permissive Legislation:

The profession's regulatory body ensures through registration that only those persons considered qualified will be admitted to the profession and registered with it. The statute usually provides that the regulatory body keep a register on which is entered the names of the members of the association. The register is evidence that the persons whose names are entered on it are members of good standing. Absence of the name is evidence that the person is not a member of the association concerned. However, the mere fact of registering a person is not of itself a guarantee that a certain standard of education and practice has been met.

A strong profession requires strong and effective legislation, that is, legislation which is *mandatory* rather than *permissive* with the field of practice well defined. The basic object of mandatory legislation is to control who shall be permitted to practice in the field. A regulatory statute that is mandatory in nature usually calls for a *licensing* and *registration* system. A licence effectively confers a permission from a competent authority to do an act which, without such permission, would be unlawful. In theory, it confers a right or power which does not otherwise exist. (For example, on obtaining a driver's licence the candidate has permission to operate a motor vehicle, an activity which, without a licence, would be unlawful.)

The practice of medicine is governed by mandatory legislation and physicians are required to hold a current medical licence as determined by medical legislation. The intent of the statute is to limit medical practice and restrict use of the title to persons licensed and registered in accordance with the particular statute. Legislation has defined the practice of medicine to include medicine, surgery, midwifery, cardiology, dermatology, geriatrics, gynecology, neurology, obstetrics, opthalmology, orthopedics, pathology, pediatrics, psychiatry and radiology.[2] Historically, the practice of medicine has incorporated acts of diagnosing, prescribing and treating of accidents and diseases. The particular medical practice statute commonly provides that violation of the act could constitute a criminal offence and there have been instances where non-physicians have been prosecuted for alleged practice of medicine. However, the courts have tended, in such instances, to interpret the legislation narrowly. For example, in the 1981 Ontario case *R. v. Gauline*[3] the Crown appealed an acquittal of a defendant acupuncturist charged with engaging in the practice of medicine without a licence contrary to the province's *Health Disciplines Act,* and with using the title "doctor" contrary to the legislation. The appeal was dismissed when the court determined that the particular statute favoured a restricted definition of the term "medicine" and concluded as well that the use of the title "doctor" was forbidden only when it led the public to believe that the user was licensed under the Act. The court concluded that the acupuncturist's methods of diagnosis and treatment differed radically from those of licensed physicians and did not come within the restricted meaning of the term "medicine". The court also concluded that the accused's use of the title "doctor" was not prohibited as he represented himself to be a practitioner of Chinese medicine and did not claim to be a licensed physician.

Regulatory statutes which are permissive in nature usually provide for *certification* and *registration*. Historically, nursing legislation has been permissive and did not prohibit non-registered persons from practicing nursing. (One of the meanings of "permissive" is failure to prevent.) Nursing legislation tends to protect only the title of registered nurse. For example, Ontario's *Health Disciplines Act* regulates the practice of five health disciplines in the province including medicine and nursing. The legislation provides for issuance of licences to physicians and certificates to nurses. The nursing certificate certifies that the named person has qualified for initial registration with the College of Nurses of Ontario and is authorized to use the title "registered nurse". Section 76(2) of the Act provides that:

" No person shall use the title "registered nurse" or the designation "Reg. N." or "R.N." or other designations representing the title unless such person is the holder of a certificate as a registered nurse under this Part "[4]

An important tool in the control of quality of practice within a particular field is a clear definition of the body of knowledge and area of practice exclusively contained within the profession's legislated mandate. The defining exercise is not a simple matter. Manitoba's *Registered Nurses Act* defined the practice of nursing within its statute as:

" . . . representing oneself as a registered nurse while carrying out the practice of those functions which, directly or indirectly in collaboration with a client and with other health workers have as their objective promotion of health, prevention of illness, alleviation of suffering, restoration of health and maximum development of health potential and without restricting the generality of the foregoing includes:

i.   collecting data relating to the health status of an individual or group of individuals

ii. interpreting data and identifying health problems

iii. setting care goals

iv. determining nursing approaches

v.   implementing care, supportive or restorative of life and well being

vi. implementing care relevant to medical treatment

vii. assessing outcomes and

viii. revising plans "[5]

Quebec's Nurses Act defines nursing as:

" Every act the object of which is to identify the health needs of persons, contribute to methods of diagnosis, provide and control the nursing care required for the promotion of health, prevention of illness, treatment and rehabilitation, and to provide care according to a medical prescription constitutes the profession of nursing. "[6]

Section 37 of the Act also provides that a nurse may in the practice of nursing inform the population concerning health problems.

A particular profession seeking legislative recognition and power to control practice and enforce such rights in the court if necessary, must clearly describe their field of practice. If the field is not clearly defined there can be both intentional and unintentional overlap of functions by non-members of the particular profession. Nurses have voiced concerns about the legal implications of potential overlap between medical practice and nursing practice. Although the Canadian courts have not been inundated with prosecutions of nurses for illegal practice of medicine there is some room for concern and vigilance.

There is a close relationship between the practice of medicine and the practice of nursing particularly in the dependent nursing functions and interdependent nursing functions described in Chapter One of this text. For example, three functions have been traditionally recognized within medical practice — those of diagnosing disease, of prescribing medication and treatments, and of performing medical and surgical treatments. In the event that a nurse makes a medical diagnosis (as distinguished from a nursing diagnosis) such could be perceived as the practice of medicine. If a nurse gives a medication without a physician's order, or substitutes one drug for another, or determines the drug dosage when the medical order is unclear, such could be interpreted as "prescribing" within the practice of medicine. (The more probable risk of such questionable practice is not criminal prosecution however but a potential negligence suit in the event of a patient injury. The fact of practising beyond one's field could serve as evidence of substandard conduct.)

The roles of medicine and nursing are evolving and changing with nursing moving to more independent practice and to incorporation of functions which previously belonged in the field of medicine. This incorporation or transfer is effected through a transfer of function mechanism as described in Chapter One of this text. Role evolution, if uncontrolled tends to blur some of the demarcation lines between medicine and nursing and cause role confusion for the individual practitioner. The

process presents a challenge to the two professions to ensure that the function approved for transfer is appropriate and performed by persons having the requisite knowledge and skill to do the task.

IV. Conduct Subject to Discipline:

In addition to other activities the monitoring and enforcement of standards involve careful attention, on a case by case basis, to complaints of unsafe or unethical conduct within the meaning of the particular nursing statute or ordinance. Once the individual nurse is registered and licensed or certified to practice, the regulatory nursing authority has the power to monitor performance and to discipline within the limits of the legislation.

The various statutes differ in their description of nursing behaviors which are subject to discipline but essentially the behaviors come within three categories:
— professional misconduct
— incompetence
— incapacity

1. Professional Misconduct:

A number of the statutes group misconduct with "conduct unbecoming a nurse". See, for example, the Manitoba and Newfoundland legislation. Professional misconduct usually involves breach of the statute or regulations. For example, section 84(3) of Ontario's Health Disciplines Act provides that a nurse may be found guilty of professional misconduct if he or she has been found guilty of an offence relevant to his suitability to practice, upon proof of such conviction. The Manitoba statute provides for discipline in the event of conviction for an indictable offence, the British Columbia Act may discipline for fraud, Nova Scotia for wilful fraud, and Saskatchewan for a criminal offence which make the person unfit to practice. The British Columbia and Newfoundland statutes may also discipline for dishonesty. In addition, Ontario's *Health Disciplines Act* provides for a codification of professional misconduct by way of regulations which set out sample behaviors of professional misconduct such as:

— abusing a patient verbally or physically while employed as a registered nurse or registered nursing assistant
— misappropriating a patient's personal property
— having a conflict of interest
— directly influencing a patient to change his will
— abandoning a patient
— misappropriating drugs or other property belonging to a member's employer
— participating in advertising or endorsing a product
— failure to inform the member's employer of the member's inability to accept specific responsibility in areas where special training is required or where the member does not feel competent to function without supervision
— failure to report the incompetence of colleagues whose actions endanger the safety of a patient
— failure to exercise discretion in respect of the disclosure of confidential information about a patient
— falsifying a record in respect of the observation or treatment of a patient; and
— conduct or an act relevant to the performance of nursing services that, having regard to all the circumstances, would reasonably be regarded by members as disgraceful, dishonourable or unprofessional.[7]

Some of the foregoing prohibited behaviors are self-explanatory. Others however require interpretation in light of the facts of the particular complaint of professional misconduct. For example, *Abandonment*: Once the nurse-patient relationship is initiated the nurse owes a duty of care to the patient not to jeopardize his welfare by termination of the relationship without notice. There are occasions when a withdrawal from the relationship is warranted. For example, if the nurse becomes ill, or if an irreconcilable conflict arises, or when a nurse proceeds to exercise a legal right to strike. In all of the foregoing the nurse has a duty to give reasonable notice before taking leave of the patient during a tour of duty. Before terminating the relationship, she is

expected to report to her immediate supervisor and pass over care and control to a duly qualified registered nurse. *Participation in Advertising*: The intent of such a prohibition is to prevent the nurse lending her professional status to a product or service as a means of influencing the buying public unduly and to the public's possible disadvantage. *Disclosure of Confidential Information*: The Ontario regulations provide for discipline for failure to exercise discretion in respect of disclosure of confidential information. The particular wording appears to provide for a balancing of the public interest with the private interest of the patient. (This is discussed in chapter five under the concept of confidentiality of and access to information.) In the absence of an overriding public interest, the nurse is expected to keep patient information confidential. As mentioned earlier, the *Krever Commission on the Confidentiality of Health Records* documented instances of breach of confidentiality by physicians and nurses. A nurse whose name was published in the Krever Report as having revealed confidential information from a patient's chart to her husband for use in his business, was terminated from her employment and disciplined by the College of Nurses of Ontario.

Conduct unbecoming to a nurse is not a closed category since what would amount to such professional misconduct would change over time as customs and mores change. It usually concerns conduct that is considered to reflect on the honor and integrity of the profession and is not necessarily directly related to nursing practice. (However, the Ontario regulations suggest that the conduct is tied to the performance of nursing services and is conduct which would reasonably be regarded by the profession as disgraceful, dishonourable or unprofessional.) The statute or the regulations usually provide for the publication of a Code of Nursing Ethics. The code is perceived as binding on the profession and breaches of it would likely be dealt with under the category of professional misconduct. However there are limits to the behaviors that can be brought under this category. For example, in 1954, an American court overruled the decision of a board of nurse examiners revoking a nurse's licence for "gross incompetency, unprofessional conduct and certain habits rendering the nurse unsafe to care for the sick" within the meaning of the particular nursing legislation. One of the incidents giving rise to the charges against the accused nurse was her alleged use of profane language. The court determined that:

> " ... if it was held to be the rule that profanity is a ground for revoking a licence then there could be a serious depletion in the ranks of all professions. " [8]

2. Incompetence:

This term has been defined by the Oxford dictionary to mean not qualified to do or not able to do an act. British Columbia's nursing legislation permits discipline for "incompetence" as does the Newfoundland Registered Nurses Act, whereas the Nova Scotia legislation permits discipline for "gross incompetence" and the Saskatchewan statute provides for discipline for "malpractice" and "negligence". To determine what particular behaviors would constitute "incompetence", the wording of the particular act must be carefully examined in light of the facts involved in the particular complaint. If the act itself does not define incompetence (within the statute itself or in its regulations or by-laws) the courts will give it the meaning generally accepted by society. Ontario's *Health Disciplines Act* defines the term in section 84(4) of the Act:

> " ... in the opinion of the committee member has displayed in his professional care of a patient, a lack of knowledge, skill or judgement or disregard for the welfare of the patient of a nature or to an extent that demonstrates he is unfit to continue in practice. " [9]

The foregoing statutory definition provides clearer direction to a disciplinary committee in invoking appropriate penalties for nurses found to be incompetent. If the nurse lacks appropriate knowledge, the penalty may call for further study, while if the problem is lack of manual skill, the appropriate recourse may be a supervised experience and retesting. A nurse may be well prepared academically to give safe care but be unable to translate the knowledge into the safe manipulation of equipment and supplies, i.e., the nurse may know how to prepare a safe injection but be unable to manipulate the syringe safely. Or the nurse may have safe knowledge and skills but on any one day be careless thereby demonstrating disregard for the patient's welfare. The appropriate corrective measure for carelessness would not necessarily involve study of theory or repractice of manipulative skills.

Another jurisdiction provided by guidelines for the definition of "incompetence" to include but not necessarily be limited to the following behaviors:

— an act or omission, or series of acts or omissions, demonstrating a lack of reasonable knowledge, skill, judgment and/or lack of concern for the patient's welfare to the extent that the patient's safety was placed in jeopardy.

— failure to carry out a patient assessment such that the patient's safety was placed in jeopardy

— failure to develop and implement a reasonable plan of care such that the patient's safety was placed in jeopardy

— failure to carry out the nursing portion of the prescribed medical regime

— failure to use judgment in relation to individual competence when accepting and delegating and/or carrying out duties. [10]

In the 1979 case, *Mason v. Registered Nurses' Association of British Columbia* [11] a nurse appealed a finding by the disciplinary tribunal of incompetence. The court upheld the finding of the tribunal. The complaints laid before the nursing disciplinary body included the following alleged incidents, that the nurse:

— administered penicillin to a patient whom she should have known was allergic to penicillin. (When asked why she administered the penicillin, if she knew the patient was allergic, the accused allegedly answered that "a lot of people think they are allergic to penicillin when they are not".)

— administered tetracycline intravenously instead of into at least 500 ml of intravenous solution

— recorded an error in a blood transfusion number

— failed to perform a nursing assessment of a maternity patient with a history of miscarriages, over a period of two hours and failed to record during this period

— administered the wrong preparation for a diagnostic test causing a delay in the performance of the test

— recorded that a patient had had a fat free diet three quarters of an hour before the tray was delivered to the unit.

The particular legislation did not contain a definition of incompetence and the review court therefore accepted a definition of the term set out in the American case, *Crotwell v. Cowan*, which common law definition appears to equate incompetence with carelessness:

" . . . while a nurse may be fully qualified and able, if her conduct demonstrates a pattern of carelessness and she is of a disposition or temperament whereby she fails to respond to advice as to her shortcomings, she may be found guilty of incompetence. "[12]

(The court suggested that negligence and incompetence are not interchangeable terms; that a competent person may sometimes be negligent without necessarily being incompetent but habitual negligence may amount to incompetence.)

The courts have placed limitations on the kind of omissions and commissions that may constitute "incompetence". As mentioned earlier, the express terminology of the legislation will determine the extent of the power to discipline. For example, in the 1977 case *Crandell v. The Manitoba Association of Registered Nurses*[13], a nurse was held to be incompetent by the disciplinary tribunal which decision she appealed to the Queen's Bench Division of the Manitoba Court. The charge arose when four institutions in which the nurse had been employed complained tht she was unable to get along with other members of the staff and as a result could not render efficient service. The court in its review was satisfied that the nurse in

question had difficulty getting along with other staff members but concluded that one of the reasons was due to her absolute frankness. The court noted that if, in her judgment, she felt something was not being done in accordance with her interpretation of the requirements, she would not hesitate to change it even though such change entailed discarding well-established practices in the institution.

The court went on to say that:

" I can appreciate how important it is for members of a nursing team to cooperate, but I would not want to think that blind acceptance of established practices is preferable to cooperation which is given after questioning and scrutinizing. "[14]

Neither the Manitoba Nurses Act or by-laws in effect at the time, defined incompetence and the court therefore gave it the meaning generally accepted by society and concluded:

" . . . I do not think the appellant has to show she is possessed of exceptional qualifications to practice the nursing profession. As long as she has the qualifications to meet the minimum requirements of the association, she should have a certificate entitling her to practice the nursing profession. Whether or not she has the temperament or emotional stability to qualify as a member of an operating room team does not matter. "[15]

The court quashed the suspension order of the nursing association.

In *Brown and the College of Nurses of Ontario*[16], (1979) the meaning of the statutory definition of incompetence as defined in the *Health Disciplines Act* 84(4) was reviewed by the court. A complaint of incompetence had been registered against a director of nursing for alleged failure to ensure the safe care of patients. (The specific complaint stated that the member of the College of Nurses, in her employment position, had expanded the role of the registered nursing assistant beyond her preparation and capability). The reviewing court overturned the finding of the disciplinary tribunal and specifically excluded administrative functions from the ambit of incompetence. The decision effectively narrowed the applicability of incompetence to those omissions or commissions in direct nursing care which demonstrate lack of knowledge, skill, judgment, disregard for a patient's welfare.

3. Incapacity:

The intent of this particular legislative category is to deal with physical and mental health problems and abuse of alcohol and drug problems on the part of its nurse members. Such health problems on the part of a working member of the profession can place the public at risk.

The British Columbia nursing legislation empowers its disciplinary committee to determine whether a member is incapable of nursing because of a physical or mental condition, or a habit or condition resulting from abuse of drugs or alcohol, of such a nature and extent that practice should be prohibited in the interests of the public and the nurse. The Manitoba legislation refers to an "ailment which might, if she continues to practice, constitute a danger to the public" and the Nova Scotia Act refers to "a habit rendering a nurse unsafe to be entrusted with or unfit for the care of the sick". The various acts couch the language and duty in terms of a function of the disciplinary tribunal. However the Ontario legislation excludes "Incapacity" from the disciplinary umbrella and assigns it, after appropriate investigation, to a registration committee. The Ontario Act defines an "incapacitated member" as one who:

> **"** is suffering from a physical or mental condition or disorder of a nature and extent making it desirable in the interests of the public or the member that he no longer be permitted to practice or that his practice be restricted. **"** [17]

This is an appropriate approach since it is not reasonable to discipline for a health problem. The object is to properly monitor mental and physical illness including alcohol and drug abuse and to assist the nurse to obtain treatment. In the interim, the professional authority is obliged to ensure, that while the nurse is so disabled she not be placed in a position where she can cause harm to patients.

V. The Disciplinary Process and the Rules of Natural Justice:

Whereas the term "judicial" refers to formal legal procedures and judgments, the term "quasi-judicial" relates to court-like proceedings and decisions of public and private regulatory bodies. These latter authorities may be entrusted with duties to ascertain facts, draw inferences from the facts, exercise discretion and make decisions. Nursing regulatory bodies and their disciplinary committees engage in such quasi-judicial functions in the course of their decision making, as for example, each time a nursing licence or certificate is suspended or revoked. Such quasi-judicial functions must be exercised within certain limits defined by the *rules of natural justice*, statute and the Charter of Human Rights and Freedoms.

1. Limits set by the Rules of Natural Justice:

In exercising their judge-like functions, nursing tribunals have a duty to act fairly because their exercise of a disciplinary function culminates in a binding decision which could result in depriving a particular registered nurse of the means of earning her livelihood. The possible harsh consequences of the tribunal's decisions require that it not only stay within its statutory powers but to exercise those powers in a way that will not breach the rules of natural justice. There are two such rules: the *Audi Alteram Partem rule*: "no man shall be condemned unheard", and the *Nemo Judex in Causa Sua* rule: "no man can be a judge in his own cause". The duty to act fairly does not necessarily mean, however, that the nursing disciplinary tribunal must observe each and every procedural rule of the formal courts of civil and criminal jurisdiction, but only that, as a minimum, an accused nurse shall have a right to a *hearing* and a right to a *fair* hearing.

a. Audi Alteram Partem Rule:

The rule that "no man shall be condemned unheard" applies to disciplinary hearings held by provincial and territorial nursing associations. Even if there is no express statutory requirement for the nursing discipline committee to hold a hearing, the courts will likely determine, (on application by an aggrieved nurse), that a hearing should have been provided. If the statute itself fails to set out a complete code of what constitutes "a hearing", the courts may impose additional requirements. For example, in *Rex v. the Chancellor et al of Cambridge University*[18] (1723) a superior court nullified the decision of the university where it had deprived a Dr. Bentley of his university degree without first giving him an opportunity to appear and state his case. (The governing body of the university, composed of faculty and students, attempted to deny Dr. Bently his degree because of an alleged debt of five pounds owed to a member of the university.) The British House of Lords in *Ridge v. Baldwin*[19] (1963) considered a situation in which the plaintiff police chief, having been acquitted of conspiracy to corrupt the course of justice, was later terminated from his post. The position was terminated by a committee that had a statutory power to dismiss anyone whom the committee thought "negligent in the discharge of his duty". The police officer was neither present at the meeting when the decision was made, nor given notice of the committee's intention to dismiss him, nor of the specific grounds on which the decision was made. He had not been given an opportunity to put his case before the committee. The court held that when exercising a discretion set out in the statute, the committee was bound by the rules of natural justice and that failure to abide by them in this instance, had caused the committee's decision to be contrary to law. In *Walls v. Commissioners of St. John G. Hospital*[20] (1973) the New Brunswick Supreme Court considered the application of a former nursing student for review of her dismissal from a school of nursing. The court determined that the faculty had failed to adhere to the principles of natural justice and, in particular, failed to give the student an opportunity for a fair hearing. (This case is discussed further later in the chapter relative to remedies available to a person aggrieved by a decision of a disciplinary committee.)

The content of the *audi alteram partem* rule varies depending on the kind of function being exercised by the particular tribunal. It would appear that if the body is exercising a discretion given it by statute, as, for example, with respect to licensing of persons for membership in a profession, an applicant for membership should not be refused unheard. Again, where the function is a disciplinary function involving accusations of misconduct, a hearing should also be held. In effect, a disciplinary process takes on some of the shape of a prosecution of the accused with the latter being a "defendant" at the hearing. There is a duty to ensure that the accused is not condemned unheard. This duty imposes on a statutory body certain obligations with respect to notice, access to legal counsel, and freedom to cross-examine one's accusers.

b. Nemo Judex in Causa Sua Rule:

This second rule of natural justice, that "no man can be a judge in his own cause" prohibits a person who has an interest in the dispute, from being a judge at the hearing into the dispute. Such a person as a "judge", would be in an actual or a perceived conflict of interest that would create unacceptable *bias* in the exercise of quasi-judicial functions. Justice must not only be done but be perceived as being done.

There are a variety of relationships and involvements of a member of a tribunal both before and during the actual hearing that could constitute bias. (The test applied by courts in reviewing the disciplinary process being complained about, is not the presence of actual bias, but whether a "real likelihood" or a "reasonable apprehension" of bias exists. For example, if the complainant (the person who registers the complaint against the accused) later sits on the disciplinary tribunal and hears the complaint and the evidence and enters into the decision to suspend or revoke the nurse's licence or certificate to practice, the decision can be challenged and will be overturned on the basis that there was a real likelihood of bias in the tribunal. Bias can also arise because of previous association with the issues before the tribunal. Persons perceived as having a direct interest in the hearing who participate in the adjudication of the conflict, will, if challenged, lead the review court to determine that the tribunal was improperly constituted. If during the adjudication of the complaint one or more members of the tribunal take on the role of prosecutors such could void their subsequent decision. For example, in *Re Golomb and the College of Physicians and Surgeons of Ontario*[21] (1976) the physician, charged with professional misconduct, called a minister as a character witness on his behalf. One of the members of the disciplinary tribunal attacked the veracity of the witness's testimony on the ground that the minister's character evidence in general was worthless. The Ontario High Court of Justice overturned the tribunal's finding of professional misconduct. The court did so because the attack on the witness and the influence that this must have had on the other members of the tribunal raised a reasonable apprehension of bias. The same member of the tribunal took part in the questioning of witnesses to such an extent that he gave "the appearance of descending into the arena and taking part in the prosecution". It was apparent from the nature of the questioning that the committee presumed the physician to be guilty of the charge. The court ruled that since the physician had not been given a fair and impartial hearing the decision of the disciplinary committee must be set aside.

Particular care should also be observed after the hearing is completed when the tribunal withdraws to deliberate and render a decision. For example, in *Fooks and Johnstone v. the Alberta Association of Architects*[22] (1982), the court overturned the decision of the disciplinary tribunal. One of its grounds for doing so was that the solicitor, the registrar and a committee chairman remained with the tribunal during the latter's deliberations. Because of the presence of these non-tribunal members, a real apprehension of bias was held to have been created.

Care should also be taken to keep the investigating committee membership quite separate from the membership making up the disciplinary tribunal. Ontario's *Health Disciplines Act* and Manitoba's *Registered Nurses Act*, for example, prohibit members of disci-

plinary tribunals from engaging in the preliminary investigation into complaints of incompetence or professional misconduct etc. Even if the act is silent on the matter however it is a better approach to keep membership of investigating committees and disciplinary committees from overlapping to prevent the possibility of unacceptable bias.

2. Limits set by Statute and by the Charter of Human Rights and Freedoms:

The particular nursing statute and its regulations define the limits of the profession's authority to regulate and police its own membership's activities. Commonly such statutory instruments give the professional association corporate status, empower boards of directors to manage the affairs of the corporation and delegate power to the authority to create the by-laws required to attain the various objects set out in the particular regulatory statute. The statute usually sets out the academic criteria for admission to practice, and provides for the functioning of particular committees assigned to monitor and enforce the required standards of practice, (through education and discipline). In exercising its statutory powers and duties the designated committees must not exceed the boundaries of the statute in applying and enforcing its own rules. The creation of by-laws, for the internal government of the association, must be done in accordance with the legal protocol set out in the applicable legislation. Otherwise such internal rules may be challenged and struck down at a later date.

How Canada's new Charter of Human Rights and Freedoms will check and balance the exercise of disciplinary powers is yet to be finally determined by the Supreme Court of Canada. Section 11 of the Charter, concerning proceedings in "criminal and penal" matters stipulates that any person charged with an offence has the right to be informed without delay of charges, to be tried within a reasonable time, and to be presumed innocent until proven guilty according to law in a fair and public hearing by an impartial tribunal. This section has been interpreted by the Manitoba courts in relation to disciplinary hearings. For example, in *Law Society of Manitoba v. Savino*[23] the Manitoba Court of Appeal ruled that section 11 of the Charter applied to criminal proceedings, not disciplinary hearings. (The appellant had been disciplined by the Society for breach of the latter's rules against advertising.) The Court held that even if the Charter did apply to such hearings, the provisions of the Law Society Act constituted reasonable limits on the right to a fair and public hearing by an impartial tribunal. In *Rosenbaum v. The Law Society of Manitoba*[24] (1983) the applicant was found guilty of professional misconduct relative to his conviction of a criminal offence. The court held that although the alleged misconduct constituted a criminal offence in another context and had potentially serious professional consequences, the misconduct did not convert the proceedings into "penal proceedings" so as to render applicable s. 11 of the Charter.

VI. Disciplinary Proceedings:

Usually the disciplinary process is activated when the association receives notice that a member has been convicted of a criminal offence; or when a complaint, from a member of the public or from another member of the profession, has been registered with the professional body. However, whether or not a criminal conviction should and will give rise to a disciplinary hearing is sometimes difficult to determine. A conviction for capital murder, procuring of illegal abortions, theft, possession of narcotics for the purpose of trafficking will likely activate the process (but a conviction for possession of marijuana may not likely do so). Serious complaints of non-criminal professional misconduct or incompetence within the meaning of the particular act will likely result in an investigation and hearing.

The procedural detail in the matter of the laying of the complaint, the giving of proper notice to the accused, the right to legal counsel and the right to cross-examine one's accusers are all determined, in part by the content of the particular statute, and in part by the rules of natural justice.

1. *Laying of the Complaint:*

Usually the statute calls for the complaint to be made *in writing* before a tribunal has jurisdiction to hold a disciplinary hearing. Whether or not the statute demands that the complaint be put in writing, fair practice should require it. (In some jurisdictions the complaint must not only be in writing but must be supported by an oath or solemn affirmation of the truth of the statement.) The complainant may be an employer, colleague, patient, member of the patient's family or a member of the public. Unless the statute expressly requires, the complaint need not be based on the direct knowledge of the complainant but would become a matter of evidence of the observers of the event at the subsequent disciplinary hearing. For example, complaints may be laid by a director of nursing following termination of the person concerned from employment. The director may not have directly observed the various omissions cited in the written complaint but would have made the statement to the "best of her knowledge and belief".

2. *Right to Notice:*

To constitute a real notice the written complaint must have sufficient detail of the nature of the offence, its time, place and circumstances. The intent of the written complaint is to provide the accused with sufficient particulars to know precisely the allegations he faces. Notice is the very essence of justice and the want of notice has been held to invalidate all subsequent proceedings and to require that the accused party be restored to his previous status no matter how flagrant the accused's conduct had been. Natural justice requirements for adequate notice demand that the person accused should be provided with sufficient information concerning the nature and intent of the proceedings and the consequences of a finding against the accused:

> " Not only must the charge be correct in form and sufficient to inform the person charged, in general terms, of the charge against him but must contain sufficient particulars to enable him to properly prepare his

defence. If the charge lacks those particulars essential to a fair hearing such particulars must be furnished before the person charged can be called upon to answer the charge. "[25]

The particular regulatory statute usually sets out the required notice period and manner of service on the accused. Notice would reasonably require that the specific charge be set out in sufficient detail together with the time and place where the charge is to be heard. In Quebec, the accused nurse has a statutory right to a notice of not less than three days. In Newfoundland, a notice of not less than seven days is required, and in British Columbia and Nova Scotia, a thirty-day notice is required. Any statutory requirements should be treated as mandatory by the tribunal, since failure to comply with statutory notice requirements may result in lack of jurisdiction to hear the complaint.

Ontario's *Health Disciplines Act* provides for two notices, one by the complaints committee (which investigates the complaint) and further notice in the event a disciplinary hearing is to take place. The accused nurse is notified of the written complaint by the complaints committee and has at least two weeks to submit any explanation, or have representation made by or on behalf of the accused to that particular committee. *Re Baldry and the College of Nurses of Ontario*[26] (1980) stated that the committee could begin its investigation before a complaint in writing was received by the committee. It also stated that the committee in its investigation is not restricted to the initial complaints. This particular committee has a discretion to refer or not to refer the matter to the disciplinary committee following its investigation. A nurse who receives notice from the complaints committee would need to seek legal advice as to the advantages and risks of intervening at the complaints stage. (If the complaints committee refers the matter to the disciplinary committee, it is this latter body which holds the hearing and makes the determination of the presence or absence of incompetence or professional misconduct with which the particular nurse has been charged.)

3. Right to Legal Counsel:

The particular nursing act may or may not provide a statutory right to legal counsel. If the nursing act is silent on the question, the rules of natural justice may conclude that denial of legal counsel at a particular disciplinary hearing resulted, in the instance, in an inadequate opportunity to be heard. Nursing legislation in Alberta, British Columbia, Manitoba, Newfoundland, Nova Scotia and Quebec permits counsel for the accused at a disciplinary hearing.

VII. Procedure at a Disciplinary Hearing:

The particular procedural content of a disciplinary hearing will be determined by the requirements set out in the nursing act itself and, where the act is silent, procedure will be determined in accordance with the basic rules for a fair hearing. Procedural content concerns itself with the recording of evidence, subpoenaing of and swearing of witnesses, serving of proper notice, taking of evidence (oral, documentary, as well as admissions of the accused, use of judicial notice, use of nursing texts as evidence), establishing the required standard of nursing practice against which to compare the alleged incidents of incompetence or professional misconduct, the matter of reaching a decision or judgment about the presence or absence of incompetence or professional misconduct etc, and the process of invoking appropriate penalties in the presence of misconduct.

1. Preliminary Matters:

Commonly, a disciplinary hearing follows a trial-like process, beginning with the swearing in of a reporter to record the proceedings, confirmation that proper service of the notice of hearing on the accused was made, and confirmation that the accused nurse is a member of the particular professional association thereby giving the association the jurisdiction to hold a hearing. If there is no statutory provision for summoning witnesses and administering an oath (which power may be contained in the nursing legislation or the evidence act), such a lack may present problems in holding an adequate hearing. If there is no statutory provision for abridgment of proof, the length of the hearing could be unduly extended. Many of the nursing acts, for example, provide for abridgment of proof of registration of the accused including, the Acts of Alberta, Manitoba, Newfoundland, Ontario, Prince Edward Island and Quebec. Section 12 of Manioba's *Registered Nurses Act*, for example, provides that:

> " A statement certified under the hand of an officer of the association respecting the registration of a person is admissible in evidence as prima facie proof that the person therein specified is registered under this Act and is prima facie proof of any conditions or limitations set out in the statement as applicable to that person. "[27]

This prima facie evidence stands as true if no other cogent evidence is raised by the accused to the contrary. Even if the particular statute provides for admission of the registration evidence without calling oral evidence from the registrar, the accused nurse can object to its admission and request to cross-examine the registrar if such is in her best interest. In the absence of statutory abridgment of proof (or consent of opposing counsel), it would be necessary to call the registrar to the stand to prove that the person charged by the association is, in fact, registered. The notice, setting out the specific complaints, is then read into the record and the accused nurse, if present, is requested to enter a plea to the complaints. Should the accused nurse choose not to appear at the hearings she cannot complain if the tribunal proceeds in her absence unless she failed to receive the proper notice of the hearing.

2. *Presentation of Evidence*

Following the foregoing preliminaries, the tribunal will call for evidence from the witnesses for the complainants. Whether the particular tribunal is bound wholly or in part by strict rules of evidence will depend upon whether the particular provincial evidence act applies to disciplinary hearings in

that jurisdiction. The Evidence Acts of Alberta, British Columbia, Manitoba, New Brunswick, Nova Scotia, Prince Edward Island and Saskatchewan appear to apply to such hearings. The strictness of evidentiary rules is also determined by specific provisions in the nursing legislation concerned. Where there are no statutory limitations, the common law will fill the gap. Ontario's *Health Disciplines Act*, for example, provides that nothing is admissible that would be inadmissible in a court in a civil case and requires that the tribunal's decision be based exclusively on evidence before it. The Quebec Code allows the tribunal to have recourse to all legal means to ascertain the facts alleged in the complaint. If there are no minimum requirements set down by statute, the tribunal will be relatively free from the strict evidentiary rules applicable in civil and criminal trials. Where there is no statutory prohibition, for example, the common law will likely allow hearsay evidence (reported evidence by a person who is before the tribunal but not the actual witness to the event being reported). Even though hearsay evidence may be admissible, however, the tribunal is not permitted to rely solely on hearsay evidence in reaching a decision affecting the accused. To do so would result in the failure of the tribunal to meet the standard of proof required, the onus of which proof remains with the tribunal and not with the accused nurse. This was pointed out in *Crandell v. the Manitoba Association of Registered Nurses*[28] (1977). The accused, who had graduated twenty-five years prior to the disciplinary hearing, appealed the suspension of her registration by the board of directors of the nursing association. The tribunal had failed to call the complainants, and instead, made its decision on the sole evidence of the registrar's report of complaints obtained from the various institutions where the accused had been employed. The court held that where there is no procedure provided either by nursing statute or by-law, a hearing to consider the suspension of a member's licence or certificate and registration should require that the complainant testify orally in the presence of the person to be affected by the evidence. The court stated that it could not be justified under any circumstances for a tribunal to proceed with the hearing and to actually suspend registration on hearsay evidence.

After the complainant's witnesses have been examined and cross-examined, the accused member is commonly given an opportunity to present evidence subject to cross-examination by opposing counsel. If the accused chooses not to call evidence on her own behalf, the tribunal may make its decision on the basis of the evidence already before it. It may well be in the interest of the accused nurse to challenge the evidence through her own testimony, or through use of expert witnesses and use of character evidence. For example, in *Re. Cunningham v. the College of Nurses of Ontario*[29] (1975), the disciplined nurse applied to the court for a judicial review of the association's 1973 suspension of her registration. (The applicant had been terminated by an employer for incompetence and notice of the termination had been reported to the College of Nurses of Ontario, the certifying and registering body.) The court in its review determined that the disciplinary committee was entitled to infer from the specific complaints of incompetence that the applicant was incompetent, especially in view of the lack of sufficient general evidence that the applicant was competent.

Admissions by the accused to the tribunal will become evidence for consideration by them. Such admissions may also be admissible before subsequent court hearings (such as public inquiries, criminal trial, or civil actions in negligence arising from the same incidents), unless the accused is able to and does take advantage of statutory protection from self-incrimination. The Quebec Code expressly protects an accused in evidence given before a disciplinary tribunal from use in subsequent proceedings.

The tribunal is free to consult nursing texts and draw inferences from them and is also permitted to take "judicial notice" of certain facts and principles concerning nursing matters of which it has personal knowledge. For example, in *Re. Reddall and the College of Nurses of Ontario*[30] (1981), the court

examined the make-up of the tribunal and noted that the panel consisted of one registered nurse, two nursing assistants and one lay person. The court noted that there was no expert evidence contained in the record of the disciplinary hearing supporting the committee's finding of incompetence against the accused nurse. The review court upheld the finding of the tribunal on the basis that disciplinary tribunals are courts of one's own professional peers sitting in judgment of the accused. The tribunal therefore, is not necessarily required to use nursing experts as witnesses to set out the required standard of nursing practice to which nurses are expected to comply. The tribunal may, instead, rely on its own expertise where the committee, taken as a whole, may be accepted as expert. This principle was upheld on further appeal. But the appeal court went on to state that because there was no evidence on the record to support a finding as to the seriousness of the errors the penalty of revocation must be set aside.

3. Arriving at a Decision:

On completion of evidence, counsel are invited to make submissions on the evidence and law, after which the tribunal withdraws to deliberate and render a decision or judgment. When the tribunal retires to consider its decision, it again must be guided by the requirements set out in nursing legislation and in the rules of natural justice. For example, the Manitoba, Ontario and Quebec Acts all require that only those members of the tribunal who have heard all the evidence and arguments may participate in the actual decision or judgment. Even if the statute is silent on the point, the rules of natural justice would prohibit a member of the tribunal who had not heard all the evidence and arguments from joining in the decision. Ontario's *Health Disciplines Act*[31] mandates the Discipline Committee to:

a. consider the allegations, hear the evidence and ascertain the facts of the case
b. determine whether upon the evidence and the facts so ascertained the allegations have been proved

c. determine whether in respect of the allegations so proved the member is guilty of professional misconduct or incompetence

d. determine the penalty to be imposed as hereinafter provided in cases in which it finds the member guilty of professional misconduct or of incompetence.

Disciplinary hearings are not criminal proceedings and as such do not require the criminal burden of proof "beyond a reasonable doubt". However, proof must be clear, convincing and based on cogent evidence, and the burden remains with the tribunal to show, on a balance of probabilities, that the accused committed the alleged acts within the meaning of the nursing statute. The evidence admitted into the record must be sufficient to prove the allegations and, if they are not, the accused must be exonerated.

There are four cases in which the College of Nurses of Ontario through its Discipline Committee, made a finding of incompetence against the nurse concerned. On review, the courts upheld the Committee's finding in two cases and overturned the decision in the other two. A review of the cases concerned points out the burden on the tribunal to determine whether, in respect of the allegations proven against the member, such constitutes incompetence within the meaning of section 84(4) of the *Health Disciplines Act*. The section states:

> " The Discipline Committee may find a member to be incompetent if in its opinion he has displayed in his professional care of a patient a lack of knowledge, skill or judgment or disregard for the welfare of the patient of a nature or to an extent that demonstrates he is unfit to continue in practice. " [32]

In *Pettit v. The College of Nurses of Ontario* [33] (1978) the court upheld the decision of the disciplinary tribunal that the member was incompetent within the meaning ˌ ˎie *Health Disciplines Act*. The tribunal reac¹ ˌ its decision after consideration of evidence that the nurse concerned had administered a unit of blood to the wrong patient and had administered 1000 ml. of intravenous solution at an improper rate to an elderly patient suffering from congestive heart failure. (The nurse allegedly had permitted the fluid to infuse within a period of forty-five minutes when the medical order called for it to be infused at a rate of 100 ml. per hour.)

In *Re. Matheson v. The College of Nurses of Ontario* [34] (1979) the court overturned the decision of the Disciplinary Committee. This case is important because it clarifies and narrows the tribunal's power to find incompetence to incidents arising in "hands on" nursing care and excludes administrative acts. The accused was a sixty-year old nurse who had been registered to practice for approximately thirty-five years and had been employed as a public health nurse for sixteen years. In 1978, the nurse concerned had been dismissed from employment because of alleged incompetence. Notice of the termination was subsequently forwarded to the College of Nurses. Approximately fifty-four incidents of alleged incompetence were reviewed by the Complaints Committee of the College of which twelve were considered by the Discipline Committee in a hearing. The Discipline Committee made a finding of incompetence relative to the Standards of Nursing Practice. (These standards entitled "Minimum Standards and Criteria for the Assessment of the Practice of the Registered Nurse and Registered Nursing Assistant" [35] were published by the College of Nurses in 1976.) There are four such standards:

Standard I: The Registered Nurse effectively uses the nursing process

Standard II: The Registered Nurse participates as a member of the health team

Standard III: The Registered Nurse fulfills his/her responsibilities as a member of the nursing discipline

Standard IV: The Registered Nurse maintains nursing records for persons for whom nursing care is provided.

The court in *Re. Matheson*, referred to the above standards, in general terms only and within the context of the alleged incidents of incompetence and section 84(4) of the Act. The court separated the specific incidents (seven administrative acts) from the five incidents related to actual delivery of nursing care. The court recognized the importance of the standards and lauded the College of Nurses of Ontario for its promotion of them. The Court then went on to say that failure to comply with the standards may not, by itself, be sufficient to support a finding of incompetence within the meaning of section 84(4) of the Act. The court interpreted from the section that the Ontario Legislature intended the Discipline Committee to exercise its power to find incompetence in clear cases where nurses cannot be entrusted any longer to administer health care to patients. The particular section permits a finding of incompetence when the member "displays in his professional care of a patient a lack of knowledge, skill or judgment or a disregard of the patient's welfare of a nature or to an extent that demonstrates he is unfit to continue in practice". The court concluded that there was no evidence that the five incidents related to the professional care of the patient by the accused had harmed the patient or placed the patient at risk and overruled the finding of incompetence by the Discipline Committee. (However, the Standards of Nursing Practice can be relevant to the issue of incompetence arising during the nursing process in the furnishing of health services directly to the patient.) Re. Matheson refers to Re. Brown v. the College of Nurses of Ontario[36] (1979), where the courts separated out administrative acts from the meaning of incompetence as defined in section 84(4). In Re. Brown a director of nursing was disciplined for extending the role of the registered nursing assistant at her place of employment. The court overruled the finding of the Disciplinary Committee and confirmed that section 84(4) of the Act:

" requires that the acts of incompetence must be in relation to the furnishing of health services directly to patients. It is not enough to fall within this section for a nurse to make mistakes in relation to administrative duties or the other responsibilities which do not relate directly to the administration of health care to a patient for whom the nurse is responsible. It may well be that inability in other spheres such as administrative ones, would lead to a nurse being discharged from the particular employment, or being demoted to a job which does not require administrative skill. But it is quite another matter to deny to a nurse altogether the privilege of continuing as a member of the profession in good standing. The Legislature has meant to remove that privilege only from those nurses who have demonstrated that they are unfit to furnish medical care to patients. " [37]

In Re. Reddall and the College of Nurses of Ontario[38] (1981), the High Court of Justice was requested to review the Disciplinary Committee's decision that the member was incompetent and to review as well the penalty that had been imposed (revocation of the certificate to practice nursing). The nurse in question had practised nursing from 1970. In 1977 when she applied for and obtained a transfer to the intensive care unit of a hospital, she experienced difficulty almost immediately. She was not successful in her application for a transfer from the unit and felt at the time that she could not afford to resign or take a leave of absence. She was subsequently terminated from employment for alleged incompetency and notice of the termination was reported to the College of Nurses of Ontario. The Discipline Committee held a hearing into nineteen incidents of alleged incompetence concerning medication errors, errors and omissions in patient care and in reporting and recording. The Disciplinary Committee made a finding of incompetence pursuant to section 84(4) of the Act. The written decision stated she displayed in her professional care of patients, a lack of knowledge, skill and judgment and disregard for the welfare of the patients of a nature and to an extent that demonstrated she was unfit to continue in practice. The written decision of the Committee referred to the Standards of Nursing Practice and stated that the member had committed serious errors which had endangered the lives of the patients to whom she had been assigned. The court stated that it was the seriousness of the alleged errors that was central to the issue of the appropriateness of the Committee's decision on incompetence and penalty. The court stated that it was not bound to accept without question the opinion of the Committee on such a matter as the seriousness of the errors. It did accept the Committee's opinion, in this instance, because the question had not been challenged at the hearing and there was nothing in the record that would support a challenge. The court stated that:

> " it does not follow necessarily that an error, or errors, committed in one area of nursing imply incompetence in others. They may or may not. It depends upon the nature and gravity of the errors. The seriousness of the errors is, again, the test of the appropriateness of the Committee's decision. " [39]

The court related the question of general competency and fitness to continue practice to the nature and gravity of the alleged failures.

Once the tribunal has completed its deliberations and arrived at a decision, it is usual to commit the decision to writing. If there is a finding that the Act has been breached (a finding of incompetence for example), counsel will then have an opportunity to address the matter of penalty. Such provision may or may not be provided for in the statute or in its regulations. For example, Quebec's *Professional Code*,[40], section 146, provides that following a conviction, the parties may be heard with respect to penalty. It requires the committee to impose the penalty within thirty days after conviction.

The content of the written decision varies and is determined first by the legislative requirements. Manitoba's *Registered Nurses Act*[41] requires that the decision and the reasons for the decision be embodied in a formal order of the tribunal. Quebec's *Professional Code*,[42] section 50, requires that the decision of the committee be in writing, signed by the members, and that it contain, in addition to the committee's decision or conclusions, the reasons for the decision or conclusions.

4. *Invoking a Penalty:*[43]

Disciplinary tribunals are empowered to invoke penalties, not as a means of punishing a member of the profession (a function reserved for criminal law), but for the purpose of protecting the public from unsafe or unethical conduct. The particular wording of the nursing legislation determines the nature and extent of the penalizing powers of the disciplinary tribunal. Some of the nursing regulatory bodies are limited to suspending or revoking of certificates to practice and to striking the member's name from the register or roster of the particular professional body. Other jurisdictions, however, also give the professional body the power to *fine*. (Ontario may apply a maximum fine of five thousand dollars, and Quebec's *Professional Code* provides for a minimum fine of two hundred dollars for each offence.) British Columbia, Ontario, Quebec and Saskatchewan may *reprimand*.

This may or may not be in public. British Columbia and Prince Edward Island are also empowered to *censure*. Manitoba, Ontario and Quebec may *impose conditions* or limitations on the nursing practice of the disciplined nurse, which, in light of the reality of present complex health care situations, may be the most appropriate and positive remedy. Alberta, the Northwest Territories and Prince Edward Island are empowered to expel, and all of the professions may suspend or revoke the certificate or licence to practice. The term "to suspend" means to keep inoperative for a period of time, or, temporarily. Suspension is usually set for a definite period of time. The *Health Disciplines Act* of Ontario, for example, is empowered in section 84(5)(b) to "suspend the certificate of the member for a stated period". However, even if the act does not specify that suspension must be for a time definite case law suggests that it must. In *Mason v. the Registered Nurses Association of British Columbia*[44] (1979), the disciplinary tribunal had ordered that registration be suspended until the nurse provided the committee with evidence that she had satisfactorily completed an approved educational program. The suspension was for an indefinite period and the court, on appeal, ruled that such a penalty "was vague, and indefinite as to time and in those respects was improper". The most severe penalty is that of *revocation*. To revoke means to repeal, annul or withdraw. The penalty is frequently accompanied by a striking or removing of the member's name from the association's register so that, for example, a nurse is no longer a "registered nurse". Linden J, in the previously mentioned *Re. Matheson v. The College of Nurses of Ontario* (1979) referred to revocation as "a sentence of professional death". Reid J. in *Re. Reddall v. The College of Nurses of Ontario*[45] (1981) suggested that Linden J's "aphoristic description of revocation" was unjustified because, in Ontario, the nurse is permitted, by statute, to reapply for certification and registration one year following revocation. In fact, there is no automatic reinstatement at the end of that one year period. In the previously mentioned *Re. Pettit and the College of Nurses of Ontario*[46] (1978) the High Court of Justice, reviewed the charges against the nurse, and the penalty imposed (revocation). The Disciplinary Committee had been satisfied that the person concerned had administered a wrong unit of blood to a patient, and had permitted intravenous fluid to infuse in forty-five minutes when the medical order called for it to be infused over a ten hour period. The tribunal had considered the fact there was no evidence that the accused, since her dismissal for incompetence, had made an effort to update her knowledge or skill in the areas concerned. The appeal court reviewed the powers of the Disciplinary Committee to penalize and concluded that, in the circumstances of the particular offences and the finding of incompetence, the Committee had a choice between suspension or revocation. The court then suggested that the difficulty with suspension was lack of assurance that the errors committed would not be repeated upon the expiry of the suspension period. The Committee found that the serious errors were ones involving basic nursing principles in hospital procedure. The Court upheld the decision of the Disciplinary Committee to revoke the certificate:

" It is therefore our view that the Committee was right in revoking the certificate. We take some comfort from the fact that this revocation of licence is not permanent. Under ... the Act ... she may apply any time after one year from the date of cancellation for the issuance of a certificate to her. We do not, of course, in any way, wish to direct the Committee as to how they should react to such an application if it should be made but we note that in her conduct there appears to have been nothing deliberate, callous and it would be our hope that the committee would give her application favourable consideration if she can establish to their satisfaction that similar errors are not likely to occur. "[47]

The intent of Ontario's *Health Disciplines Act* is to empower the Disciplinary Committee to deal with incompetence (or professional misconduct) of varying degrees of severity, with penalties of varying degrees of severity and a tribunal is given, by the statute, a wide variety of penalizing powers to correct the incompetency or misconduct problem complained about. The legislation permits the Committee to make an order to revoke, suspend, or impose restrictions on one's certificate, or any combination of these penalties and other penalties (reprimand or fine) as listed in the Act. The Committee can set certain conditions to be met by the nurse concerned prior to reapplication for admission, and, or, may set certain limitations on any certificate to practice issued following revocation. If at the time of a disciplinary hearing, the tribunal determined that the conduct was so inappropriate and unsafe or unethical as to warrant revocation, and if no evidence is presented at the time of reapplication, showing the situation has been corrected, the application for reinstatement may be rejected. Certainly the nurse applicant has a right to reapply each year and the committee's rejection may be reviewed by a higher court at the instance of the nurse. Ordinarily however, the matter of penalty imposed by a disciplinary tribunal is not overturned by a superior court except as to whether the penalty is authorized by the act or is so harsh as to amount to an error in principle.

The decision of the tribunal and the penalty imposed may be published in accordance with the power to do so under the legislation. For example, Ontario's *Health Disciplines Act* through its regulations, provides that the College of Nurses shall publish the findings of incompetence or professional misconduct in its annual report. The regulations also give the College a discretion whether or not to publish the name, registration number, conviction and penalty through other avenues. In practice, the College does publish such data in its newsletters circulated to all its members. Its purpose is to place members on notice of possible job applications by nurses whose certificate has been suspended or revoked. (Section 44 of Manitoba's Registered Nurses Act also provides that the Board of the Association may publish notices of suspension, revocation and reinstatement. Such notices may or may not contain the reasons. The board has an absolute discretion in this matter.)[48]

VIII. Remedies:

The courts do not lightly interfere with decisions of professional disciplinary tribunals. Such tribunals deal with standards of conduct on a regular basis and are considered by the courts (and legislators) to be in the best position to assess the presence of incompetence, or professional misconduct, and to be the most appropriate bodies to impose an appropriate penalty for such behavior.

If a nurse is dissatisfied with the decision of a disciplinary tribunal she may, depending on the rights set out in the nursing legislation of the particular jurisdiction, apply successfully or otherwise, for a review of the disciplinary process and decision. She may proceed by way of an appeal, or, where an appeal is not available, by application for an appropriate prerogative writ.

1. *Appeals:*

Right of appeal is a statutory remedy, i.e., is available only if the nursing act, or some other applicable legislation, provides such a right. An appeal involves a written application to a superior court, in which application the aggrieved person complains that an error was committed by the disciplinary tribunal. The applicant requests the superior court to correct the decision of the tribunal or to modify or reverse it. The Nursing Act of Alberta, British Columbia, New Brunswick, Newfoundland, the Northwest Territories, Ontario and Saskatchewan all provide for a right of appeal. However the aggrieved nurse must not sit on her rights should she wish to challenge an adverse decision of the tribunal. Legal counsel will consult the legislation to determine the nature and scope of review available by way of appeal and the limited time period available to file a notice of appeal. For example, Ontario's *Health Disciplines Act*[49] confers wide powers of review by way of appeal to the superior court. The court may review questions of law and questions of fact. It may affirm or rescind the decision of the disciplinary tribunal. It may order the tribunal to take certain actions, or the court may substitute its opinion for that of the disciplinary committee or refer the matter back to the tribunal for a rehearing in whole, or in part. The Act states that the aggrieved nurse may succeed on appeal if the tribunal's decision resulted from proceedings that were not fair and impartial, or if the findings of fact were not supported by the evidence before the tribunal, or if the decision was not justified by the particular finding of fact. The aggrieved nurse may also succeed if the penalty was unduly severe in light of penalties imposed in similar cases, or if the decision was based on an erroneous admission or exclusion of evidence. In Ontario the applicant must appeal within thirty days after the date of the refusal or order of the tribunal. (Manitoba's *Registered Nurse Act* (section 42(1)) provides for an appeal to a Court of Queen's Bench. The appeal must be launched within thirty days of the date of the order or decision. The legislation provides for an appeal by members of the association who have had their certificates revoked, suspended or limited. It also provides a right to appeal to persons who apply to the association for admission if the admission is denied unlawfully. The Manitoba Act provides that in the absence of recorded evidence an appeal will be by trial *de novo*. This is a retrial in an appellate court in which the entire case is proceeded with as if there had been no hearing before the disciplinary tribunal.) For review purposes, the Quebec legislation provides that minutes of the disciplinary tribunal constitute prima facie proof of their contents. Ontario's *Health Disciplines Act* requires that once a notice of appeal is filed with the court and served on the College of Nurses, the board of directors is required, on request, to provide to the nurse concerned a certified copy of all records on which the disciplinary tribunal acted. If there is no transcript, and or where the court considers its necessity in the interests of justice, a new hearing can be held at the appeal level.

2. *Application for Issuance of a Prerogative Writ:*

If there is no statutory right of appeal the aggrieved nurse is limited to the availability of an appropriate prerogative writ. Depending on the particular facts of the case, the aggrieved nurse may need to apply for a writ of prohibition, writ of certiorari, a writ of mandamus, declaratory judgment, or an injunction, or some combination of the foregoing remedies. (The nurse may, in very limited circumstances, also successfully apply for damages.)

a. Writ of Prohibition:

Is an ancient common law means of bringing a matter before a superior court for the purpose of preventing a tribunal from acting unlawfully. The circumstances giving rise to a need for such a writ are similar to the circumstances giving rise to a need for a writ of certiorari. Whereas the writ of prohibition is intended to prevent the tribunal from acting or from continuing in excess of its jurisdiction, certiorari is used to quash the decision of the tribunal once it has been made. For example, the accused physician, in *Sen. v. the Discipline Committee of the College of Physicians and Surgeons of Saskatchewan*[50] (1969) was successful in his application for a writ of prohibition. He had been charged with unprofessional conduct in allegedly providing unnecessary professional services. However the tribunal had no particulars of the allegations. The lack of specific patients' names and type of services being complained about placed the accused in an unfair position of having to defend himself against charges that were general in nature. In the opinion of the court this amounted to a denial of natural justice and the court ordered that a writ should issue to prohibit the tribunal from holding such a hearing.

b. Writ of Certiorari:

Proceeding by way of certiorari is a common method of questioning decisions of administrative tribunals. Its purpose is to annul or void the tribunal's decision causing it to cease to exist on the ground that it was made erroneously because of (1) a jurisdictional error or (2) an error on the face of the record. For example an application is made for such a remedy in circumstances where there has been an alleged failure to provide a notice, or because inadequate notice was provided; failure to provide a hearing at all or failure to provide a fair hearing; error in the admission of certain evidence, or refusal to admit admissible evidence; or failure to abide by rules that had been set out for the compulsory direction of the tribunal. In their review for possible jurisdictional error the superior court will examine the transcript of evidence from the disciplinary hearing. However if the allegation is that there is an error on the face of the record the superior court is limited to examining the record itself (i.e. the complaint, the notice, the record of the decision), and is preventing from reviewing the transcript of the evidence heard at the disciplinary hearing. For example, the applicant in *Johnston v. the Association of Professional Engineers of Saskatchewan*[51] (1969) was successful in his application for certiorari to quash the disciplinary decision of the association. He alleged error on the face of the record. He had been served a notice that an inquiry was to be held into certain complaints set out in the notice. At the hearing evidence was led of other acts of which the applicant had no prior notice. A finding of guilt was made regarding the complaints of which he had notice and, those of which he had not received notice. The superior court held that there was clearly an error on the face of the record and therefore the tribunal's decision must be quashed.

c. Writ of Mandamus:

This is an order which issues, at the discretion of the superior court, commanding a public person or authority to perform a duty which has been imposed by statute or at common-law. The purpose of this remedy is to correct an arbitrary exercise of power in the performance of mandatory duties. If the tribunal has a discretion concerning the matter being complained about the court will not order the tribunal to exercise its discretion in the direction of performing the duty. However if the duty is absolute (mandatory) the order will issue. For example if a particular nursing act sets out the comprehensive list of requirements or qualifications for admission to the profession and states that the association shall grant a licence to practice to those meeting the requirements, the body cannot then arbitrarily refuse to issue a licence to an applicant who meets those requirements.

d. Declaratory Judgment:

This remedy is merely an order of a superior court declaring what the legal rights of the parties to the dispute are in the circumstances. The judicial order has no coercive force. For example in the previously mentioned case *Walls v. the Commissioners of St. John's*[52] (1973) the New Brunswick Supreme Court issued a declaratory order to the nursing school in which the applicant had been a student. (The applicant had applied for a declaratory judgment, an order that she be reinstated and damages and costs.) The student alleged that the school of nursing authority had wrongfully dismissed her in that she was denied natural justice because:

— the faculty had failed to give her notice that they were about to consider her dismissal from the school
— the faculty had denied the student an opportunity for a fair hearing
— there was bias on the part of one or more faculty members
— the faculty meetings concerning the dismissal were not conducted in compliance with the rules of natural justice.

In their own defence the school faculty contended that the applicant had been negligent and incompetent, lacked responsibility and judgment and was frequently absent without justification.

The court concluded that there were no valid rules or regulations in legal force to give the faculty arbitrary powers to expel; that in the absence of such arbitrary powers, and in the exercise of the particular disciplinary decision the authority was in fact exercising a quasi-judicial function. In exercising such a function certain requirements should have been met that were not in fact met. The faculty had failed to adhere to the principles of natural justice, failed to give the student notice of their intention to consider her dismissal, failed to give notice of the grounds they would be considering and they failed to provide her with an opportunity for a fair hearing. The court incorporated the foregoing in a declaratory judgment. However it refused to order that the applicant be reinstated because "to make an order would require a determination that the faculty had reached the wrong decision". Damages were also refused. The court did suggest in closing, that it hoped the nursing association of the province would assist the applicant to be accepted at some other school of nursing.

e. Injunction:

In appropriate circumstances the superior court has a discretion to order a party concerned to refrain from doing a particular act which the court considers unlawful. Injunctions have been obtained against administrative tribunals in Canada when they exceeded their jurisdiction.

f. Damages:

This remedy will not be easily available to a nurse offended by the decision of a disciplinary tribunal even if the tribunal failed to comply with the duties imposed on it. The general rule appears to be that such a tribunal, in exercising its quasi-judicial powers will not be held liable in damages in the absence of fraud, collusion, or malice, should it make a wrong decision. The onus is on the plaintiff to show that the tribunal not only acted without authority but fraudulently or maliciously. Also certain nursing statutes expressly provide for statutory immunity of its tribunal from civil suits. Manitoba, for example provides such immunity from damages suffered by any person as a result of anything done by the association, in good faith in the administration of the Act. The Ordinance for the Northwest Territories also provides such a save harmless clause for its board of directors, discipline committee, employees and agents for acts done in good faith.

IX. Ethical Standards: The Professional Code of Ethics:

A code of ethics is a written and published statement of minimum standards of ethical conduct adopted by the membership of the particular professional group for the guidance and self-discipline of its individual members.

Regulatory legislation governing the particular profession may expressly empower the corporation to pass by-laws concerning a code of ethics. For example, Quebec's Professional Code which regulates all of the health professions in that province, empowers its Board to ensure that each professional corporation adopts a code of ethics in accordance with section 85 of the Code. This particular section requires that the code of ethics be made by regulation and contain provisions identifying acts which are considered derogatory to the dignity of the particular profession, provisions which define the duties incompatible with the dignity or practice of the profession and provisions concerning the confidentiality of information.

Once a code of ethics is adopted by the membership and published, each member is on notice of the tenets in the code, is expected to regulate his or her practice accordingly and can be held accountable through the disciplinary arm of the profession for infractions of the adopted code of ethics. In this sense the code is a legal tool.

X. Endnotes:

1. Globe and Mail, May 15, 1971 paraphrasing from speech of: The Honourable B. Lawrence, the then Minister of Health of Ontario.
2. The Medical Act, 1974, S.N. 1974 No. 119 sec. 2(i) defining the Practice of Medicine.
3. R. v. Gauline (1981) 35 O.R. (2d) 195
4. The Health Disciplines Act S.O. 1980. c. 196, Part IV, sec. 84
5. The Registered Nurses Act R.S.M. 1980 c. 40 sec. 1
6. The Nurses Act S.Q. 1973 c. 48 sec. 36
7. Supra n. 4 and O. Reg 598/75 sec. 21. See also West and the College of Nurses of Ontario 32 O.R. (2d) 85
8. Cited in Mason v. The Registered Nurses Association of British Columbia [1979] 5 W.W.R. 509
9. Supra n. 4 sec. 83(5)
10. Defined by the Association of Registered Nurses of Newfoundland
11. Supra n. 8
12. Supra n. 8 citing Crotwell v. Cowan (1938), 236 Ata. 578, 184 So. 199
13. Crandell v. The Manitoba Association of Registered Nurses [1977] 1 W.W.R. 468, 72 D.L.R. (3d) 602
14. Supra n. 13, 72 D.L.R. 602 at p. 604
15. Supra n. 13 602 at p. 606
16. Re. Brown and the College of Nurses of Ontario (1979) (unreported) but referred to in Matheson case at n.34
17. Supra n. 4
18. Rex v. the Chancellor et al University of Cambridge, 93 E.R. 698
19. Ridge v. Baldwin [1963] All E.R. 66
20. Walls v. Commissioners of St. John G. Hospital (1973) 9 N.B.R. (2d) 106
21. Golomb and the College of Physicians and Surgeons of Ontario (1976), 12 O.R. (2d) 73 (Ont. H.C.)
22. Fooks and Johnston v. Alberta Association of Architects (1982) 139 D.L.R. (3d) 455
23. Law Society of Manitoba v. Savino [1983] 6 W.W.R. 538
24. Rosenbaum v. the Law Society of Manitoba [1983] 5 W.W.R. 752
25. Sen v. the College of Physicians and Surgeons [1969] 69 W.W.R. 201, 6 D.L.R. (3d) 520
26. Re. Baldry and the College of Nurses of Ontario 30 O.R. (2d) 311 at 313
27. Supra n. 5 sec. 12
28. Supra n. 13

29. Re. Cunningham and the College of Nurses of Ontario 8 O.R. (2d) 60 at 62

30. Reddall and the College of Nurses of Ontario, 123 D.L.R. (3d) 678, 33 O.R. (2d) 129, 42 O.R. (2d) 412 (Appeal allowed in part)

31. Supra n. 4 sec. 83(2)

32. Supra n. 4

33. Pettit and the College of Nurses of Ontario L.M.Q. 21 (1978) 137

34. Matheson v. the College of Nurses of Ontario 27 O.R. (2d) 632, 107 D.L.R. (3d) 430 (affd. 28 O.R. (2d) 611, 111 D.L.R. (3d) 179

35. College of Nurses of Ontario, Minimum Standards and Criteria for the Assessment of the Practice of the Registered Nurse and Registered Nursing Assistant, publ. 1976, revised July 1982

36. Supra n. 34 (27 O.R. (2d) 632 at 634)

37. Supra n. 34 (27 O.R. (2d) 632 at 634)

38. Supra n. 30

39. Supra n. 30 (123 D.L.R. (3d) 678 at 686)

40. The Professional Code S.Q. 1973 c. 43. sec. 146

41. Supra n. 5

42. Supra n. 40

43. Reader is referred to the particular provincial or territorial act and regulations as amended. Note also Alberta's Health Occupation Act R.S.A. 1980 c. H.5.1 as amended.

44. Supra n. 8 (at 102 D.L.R. (3d) at 240) (See also Re. Singh & College of Nurses of Ont. 33 O.R. (2d) 92)

45. Supra n. 30 (123 D.L.R. (3d) at 688)

46. Supra n. 33

47. Supra n. 33

48. See Supra n. 4 and n. 5

49. Supra n. 4

50. Supra n. 25

51. Johnston v. the Association of Professional Engineers of Saskatchewan [1970], 75 W.W.R. 740, affirming 70 W.W.R. 600 (Sask C.A.)

52. Supra n. 20

Appendix 1
Codes of Ethics Governing Nursing Practice

In 1973 the International Council of Nurses, the organized professional body at the international level, brought into effect a statement of its code of ethics. This code was subsequently adopted by the Canadian Nurses Associations and its provincial counterparts and is as follows:

I.C.N. Code for Nurses—Ethical Concepts Applied to Nursing

The fundamental responsibility of the nurse is fourfold: to promote health, to prevent illness, to restore health and to alleviate suffering.

The need for nursing is universal. Inherent in nursing is respect for life, dignity and rights of man. It is unrestricted by considerations of nationality, race, creed, colour, age, sex, politics or social status.

Nurses render health services to the individual, the family and the community and coordinate their services with those of related groups.

Nurses and People

The nurse's primary responsibility is to those people who require nursing care. The nurse, in providing care, promotes an environment in which the values, customs and spiritual beliefs of the individual are respected.

The nurse holds in confidence personal information and uses judgment in sharing this information.

Nurses and Practice

The nurse carries personal responsibility for nursing practice and for maintaining competence by continual learning.

The nurse maintains the highest standards of nursing care possible within the reality of a specific situation. The nurse uses judgment in relation to individual competence when accepting the delegated responsibilities.

The nurse when acting in a professional capacity should at all times maintain standards of personal conduct which reflect credit upon the profession.

Nurses and Society

The nurse shares with other citizens the responsibility for initiating and supporting action to meet the health and social needs of the public.

Nurses and Co-Workers

The nurse sustains a cooperative relationship with co-workers in nursing and other fields. The nurse takes appropriate action to safeguard the individual when his care is endangered by a co-worker or any other person.

Nurses and the Profession

The nurse plays the major role in determining and implementing desirable standards of nursing practice and nursing education.

The nurse is active in developing a core of professional knowledge.

The nurse, acting throughout the professional organization, participates in establishing and maintaining equitable social and economic working conditions in nursing.

The Canadian Nurses Association: A Statement on an Ethical Basis for Nursing in Canada:

In 1978 the Canadian Nurses Association, at its annual meeting, passed a resolution to develop a Canadian code of nursing ethics. By 1980 a person oriented care ethic, applicable to nursing education, service, research and administration, was approved by the Board of Directors of the Association. The statement was then published and circulated to members of the profession for possible approval at the 1980 annual meeting of the Association. During debate at the annual meeting concerns were raised relative to part III of the statement "Caring and the Healing Community" and possible conflict of certain of the ethical standards with the mandate of nursing unions in Canada. ***Part III of the statement was suspended and the statement is currently under review by a C.N.A. Committee.** In November 1983 the Canadian Nurses Association published another draft document of a Code of Ethics. The document was included in the February 1984 edition of the Canadian Nurse, Volume 80, #2. The nursing membership were invited to respond to the document by May 1, 1984. Following is a reproduction of the 1980 Statement:

I. Introduction

Nursing is a person-oriented health service. It is a service called forth by the experience of human pain and suffering, and directed to the promotion of health, the prevention and alleviation of suffering, and the provision of a caring presence for those for whom cure is not possible. The ethical norms that guide this service evolve from a belief system that perceives the human person to be of incalculable worth, and human life to have a sacred, precious and even mysterious character. Nursing is practiced in the context of human relationships, the dominant ethical determinant of which is the principle of respect for persons.

The concept which constitutes the unifying and ethical focus for nursing practice, education, administration, and research is the concept caring. Caring, as a characteris-

tic descriptive of all authentic human action is expressed within the discipline of nursing through the following attributes.

1. *Compassion* — the human response through which nurses participate in the pain and brokenness of humanity, by entering into the experience of another's suffering, misfortune, or need in such a manner that the needs of that person are the primary basis for the use of the nurse's personal and professional skills.
2. *Competence* — the state of having the knowledge, skills, energy, and experience adequate to provide the required service.
3. *Conscience* — the sense of what is right or wrong in one's conduct, and the awareness of, and the will to apply relevant ethical principles.
4. *Confidence* — the quality which fosters the development and maintenance of trusting relationships.
5. *Commitment* — a pledge, based on free choice, to devote oneself to meeting one's professional obligations.

In nursing, the human capacity to care is developed and professionalized through the acquisition of those intellectual, affective and technical skills required to carry out the responsibilities of specific nursing roles. The ethical obligations arising from caring as required by these roles are met at different levels of practice and within varying contexts. This statement considers three categories of obligation, namely, caring and the profession, caring and the healing community, and caring and the individual nurse.

II. Caring and the Profession

The nursing profession as a whole has ethical obligations to society as well as to its own membership. The profession has an obligation to examine its own goals and the service it offers in the light of existing health problems, and to design its programs in collaboration with other professionals which also provide health services within the society. Nursing, in keeping with its mandate as a service profession, is bound to see itself, not as an end to be promoted and served by society, but as a professional body, constituted and legitimized by society's approval, to offer a prescribed service required for the improvement of the health status of people.

In meeting its obligations to society, nursing has responsibility for monitoring the quantity and quality of persons entering the profession, and for identifying and implementing standards that promote the type and quality of nursing service dictated by society's needs. Nursing has a related responsibility to work for those conditions which will enable its members to provide the quantity and quality of service deemed necessary and desirable.

The nursing profession also has responsibilities to the international community. Since health is a basic condition for human development, and as no one nation or country can develop its potential in isolation, the interests of the profession transcend national boundaries. In fact, our credibility as a profession is called into question if we do not collaborate on an international level to promote the health of all peoples, and to work toward the relief of human suffering wherever it is experienced.

These broad obligations constitute the grounds for the ethical responsibilities of nursing's organized professional body, and include the following commitments:

1. In the context of existing health needs and problems, to identify Canada's need for nursing activities and services.
2. To establish relevant and realistic goals for the profession of nursing within Canadian society.
3. To foster collaboration with other health professions, political bodies, and other agencies in responding to the health needs of Canadians.
4. To collaborate with professional groups, institutions and agencies in promoting the welfare of peoples in other countries of the world.
5. To provide measures which will ensure that only those with the potential, motivation, and discipline required to function as caring persons are accepted into, and endorsed by the nursing profession.
6. To work for the realization of working conditions which enable nurses to function as caring persons with the required degree of autonomy.
7. To promote conditions for nurses which provide for legitimate personal, professional, and economic rewards.
8. To demonstrate, in its own transactions, accountability for the use of internal and external resources.

III. Caring and the Healing Community
***This part has been suspended.

IV. Caring and the Individual Nurse

The final test of the credibility of ethical standards in nursing lies in the behavior of the individual nurse—educator, practitioner, administrator, and researcher. Many of the responsibilities arising out of obligations of the profession as a whole, and the ethical demands of the caring community itself, are fulfilled only in the actions of the individual nurse. While the profession has the obligation to identify, promote, and monitor ethical standards, the execution of such standards is a personal responsibility, the final guarantee of which is in the conscience and commitment of the individual nurse.

V. Guidelines

The following guidelines include general principles, with statements of ethical responsibility which flow from these principles. They are intended to provide a guide for the reflection and for the articulation of more specific ethical rules and standards applicable to concrete experiences. With the increasing complexity of ethical conflicts in nursing, and the potential for greater ethical concerns in the future, ethical discernment in nursing is an exciting challenge, requiring knowledge, skill, and great moral sensitivity. We have the capacity to meet this challenge—one which could be the greatest in the history of our profession.

A. General Principles
1. The human person, regardless of race, creed, color, social class or health status, is of incalcuable worth, and commands reverence and respect.
2. Human life has a sacred and even mysterious character, and its worth is determined not merely by utilitarian concerns.
3. Caring, the central and fundamental focus of nursing, is the basis for nursing ethics. It is expressed in compassion,

competence, conscience, confidence, and commitment. It qualifies all the relationships in nursing practice, education, administration, and research including those between nurse-client; nurse-nurse; nurse-other helping professionals; educator-colleague; faculty-student; researcher-subject.

B. **Statements of Ethical Responsibility**

1. Caring demands the provision of helping services that are appropriate to the needs of the client and significant others.
2. Caring recognizes the client's membership in a family and a community, and provides for the participation of significant others in his or her care.
3. Caring acknowledges the reality of death in the life of every person, and demands that appropriate support be provided for the dying person and family to enable them to prepare for, and to cope with death when it is inevitable.
4. Caring acknowledges that the human person has the capacity to face up to health needs and problems in his or her own unique way, and directs nursing action in a manner that will assist the client to develop, maintain or gain personal autonomy, self-respect, and self-determination.
5. Caring, as a response to a health need, requires the consent and the participation of the person who is experiencing that need.
6. Caring dictates that the client and significant others have the knowledge and information adequate for free and informed decisions concerning care requirements, alternatives, and preferences.
7. Caring demands that the needs of the client supersede those of the nurse, and that the nurse must not compromise the integrity of the client by personal behavior that is self-serving.
8. Caring acknowledges the vulnerability of a client in certain situations, and dictates restraint in actions which might compromise the client's rights and privileges.
9. Caring, involving a relationship which is, in itself, therapeutic, demands

mutual respect and trust.

10. Caring acknowledges that information obtained in the course of the nursing relationship is privileged, and that it requires the full protection of confidentiality unless such information provides evidence of serious impending harm to the client or to a third party, or is legally required by the courts.
11. Caring requires that the nurse represent the needs of the client, and that the nurse take appropriate measures when the fulfillment of these needs is jeopardized by the actions of other persons.
12. Caring acknowledges the dignity of all persons in the practice or educational setting.
13. Caring acknowledges, respects, and draws upon the competencies of others.
14. Caring establishes the conditions for the harmonization of efforts of different helping professionals in providing required services to clients.
15. Caring seeks to establish and maintain a climate of respect for the honest dialogue needed for effective collaboration.
16. Caring establishes the legitimacy of respectful challenge and/or confrontation when the service required by the client is compromised in incompetency, incapacity, or negligence, or when the competencies of the nurse are not acknowledged or appropriately utilized.
17. Caring demands the provision of working conditions which enable nurses to carry out their legitimate responsibilities.
18. Caring demands resourcefulness and restraint — accountability for the use of time, resources, equipment, and funds, and requires accountability to appropriate individuals and/or bodies.
19. Caring requires that the nurse bring to the work situation in education, practice, administration, or research, the knowledge, affective and technical skills required, and that competency in these areas be maintained and up-dated.
20. Caring commands fidelity to oneself, and guards the right and privilege of the nurse to act in keeping with an informed moral conscience.

Appendix II

Nursing Practice Standards and The Nursing Process: References

I. Federal and Provincial Nursing Practice Standards:

— Canadian Nurses Association: *A Definition of Nursing Practice for Nursing Practice*, June 1980
— Alberta Association of Registered Nurses: *Nursing Practice Standards*, 1980
— Registered Nurses Association of British Columbia: *Quality Assurance Program-Demonstration Project*, March 1, 1981 to July 1, 1982
— Manitoba Association of Registered Nurses: *Standards of Nursing Care*, 2nd. ed. June 1981
— Association of Registered Nurses of Newfoundland: *Quality of Nursing Care Standards* (1984)
— Registered Nurses' Association of Nova Scotia: *A Framework for the Practice of Nursing in Nova Scotia: Guidelines and Standards*, Oct. 3, 1975
— College of Nurses of Ontario: *Minimum Standards and Criteria for the Assessment of the Practice of the Registered Nurse and the Registered Nursing Assistant* revised July 1982

II. Texts:

— Bower, Fay Louise: *The Process of Planning Nursing Care: A Model for Practice*, 2nd ed. St. Louis. C.V. Mosby Co. 1977
— Kron, Thora: *The Management of Patient Care: Putting Leadership Skills to Work*, 5th ed. Toronto. W.B. Saunders Pub. Co. 1981
— Marriner Ann: *The Nursing Process: A Scientific Approach to Nursing Care*, St. Louis. C.V. Mosby Co. 1975

III. Reports and Articles:

— Hospital Systems Study Group: *Nursing Information System Saskatchewan (NISS)*, Saskatoon, Saskatchewan, 1983
— Canadian Council on Hospital Accreditation: *Guide to Accreditation of Long Term Care Centres*, June 1978
— Canadian Council on Hospital Accreditation: *Standards for Accreditation of Canadian Health Care Facilities*, Jan. 1983
— Gordon M.: Nursing Diagnosis and the Diagnostic Process. *American Journal of Nursing*, 76:1298, August 1976
— Mundinger M.O., and Jauron G.D.: Developing a Nursing Diagnosis. *Nursing Outlook*, 75:94, February 1975
— Allison S., and Kinloch K.: Four Steps to Quality Assurance. *Canadian Nurse* 77:36, November 1977

Appendix III
Table of Health Care and Law Terminology

1. Accountability:

Answerability to an authority for one's conduct or performance.

2. Accreditation:

A process by which a recognized authority evaluates certain programs, or agency and grants official recognition of those which comply with the standards of the authority.

3. Accused:

A person charged with a criminal offence; charged with a fault.

4. Act:

A written law (statute) passed by Federal Parliament or a provincial legislature pursuant to powers delegated to the particular legislative authority by the British North America Act. Acts may be private, relating to a particular group in a community, or public legislation governing the relationship of the individual and the community. (See also regulation and by-law.)

5. Action:

A proceeding in court initiated for the purpose of enforcing a private legal right or preventing a wrong (civil action) or for the purpose of prosecuting a public offence (a criminal action.)

6. Acquittal:

A formal judgment of a court of criminal jurisdiction declaring that the accused is not guilty of the crime with which he has been charged.

7. Administrative Law:

A branch of public law which concerns the powers and duties of certain regulatory bodies created by Federal Parliament or a provincial legislature for the purpose of carrying out specific functions. (For example, the regulation and discipline of a particular profession such as medicine, nursing, pharmacy etc.)

8. Adversarial Process:

A court or court-like proceeding in which there are opposing parties to a dispute.

9. Advocate:

From advocate: to summon to one's assistance; a person who assists and pleads the cause of another. In some jurisdictions a lawyer is known as an advocate. (See Patient Advocate)

10. Agent:

A person authorized by another (a principal) to act for him in the transaction of some business with power delegated to him to carry out certain functions in the name of the principal. An agent may, through his action, create a contractual relationship between his principal and a third party.

11. Agreement:

A mutual understanding and purpose of two or more parties intended to change or affect the individual rights and obligations of each party to the agreement. The agreement may be expressed in writing or inferred from the behavior of the parties. (See contract)

12. Allegation:

A statement made by a party to an action which that party will attempt to prove at a trial or hearing of the particular dispute.

13. Appeal:

A proceeding to a higher court for the purpose of reviewing, reversing or correcting an alleged erroneous decision of a lower court or administrative tribunal. Each province has a court of appeal whose appeal decisions may, in certain instances, be further appealed to the Supreme Court of Canada.

14. Appellant:

A party to an action, either plaintiff or defendant, who disagrees with the decision of the lower court and applies to a court of appeal for a review and possible revision of the decision. The opposing party is known as the respondent.

15. Assault (and Battery):

A threat to do physical harm to another in circumstances coupled with an apparent ability to carry out the threat. Battery is the actual touching of a person without his consent and in the absence of privilege. Civil assault gives rise to a possible remedy in damages, and criminal assault, recognized in the Criminal Code of Canada, gives rise to a possible fine and, or imprisonment.

16. Assessment:

In the context of health care it is a systematic collection of information; analysis, and interpretation of the information gathered about the patient for the purpose of reaching a conclusion about the appropriate plan of care to be implemented. In certain circumstances the physician has a legal duty to carry out a medical assessment and the registered nurse has a legal duty to carry out a nursing assessment. (See diagnosis and history.)

17. Authority:

A delegated right to act and make decisions on behalf or in place of the authority who delegated the power.

18. Bargaining Agent:

A union granted the exclusive right to represent the employees and to bargain with the employer for the purpose of reaching a collective agreement.

19. Bargaining Unit:

A defined group of employees approved by a labour relations tribunal for representation by a particular union. A unit may be a homogenous group such as registered nurses or may be a heterogenous grouping of health disciplines and other workers.

20. Battery: (See Assault)

21. By-Law:

A rule made by a body to whom by-law making power has been delegated by legislation, for the purpose of day to day management of the group's activities. By-laws are subordinate to the particular governing statute and regulations. In hospitals by-laws identify the authority and structure of the board of governors and board committees, and the authority of the chief executive officer, and the authority of the medical staff through medical staff by-laws.

22. Certificate:

A written and signed statement by an authorized official certifying that some act has been done or some requirement has been met by the person named in the certificate.

23. Certification:

The confirming of peer recognition for individual achievement and superior clinical practice; approval by a labour relations tribunal of a particular union as the exclusive bargaining agent for the employees in a particular bargaining unit.

24. Certified Nursing Assistant:

An assistant to the registered nurse who has met the requirements for certification by an approved certifying body; such an assistant provides selective and basic nursing care as delegated by the registered nurse and is accountable to the registered nurse for the performance of the delegated nursing functions. (In some provinces the title is registered nursing assistant.)

25. Charge Nurse:

A registered nurse who has been assigned to the care and control of a patient care unit on a particular shift.

26. Clinical Nursing Coordinator:

A clinical specialist recognized in the health care field and delegated responsibility to coordinate and direct nursing activity on a particular clinical unit. A nursing specialist with experience and a minimum academic preparation of a master's degree in the appropriate field.

27. Collective Bargaining:

A process of negotiation between an employer representative and an employee group representative (commonly a union) for the purpose of reaching a collective agreement defining the terms of the employment relationship.

28. Common Law:

As distinguished from statute law (law enacted by Federal Parliament or a provincial legislature) comprises a body of written and unwritten principles and rules which derives its authority from the judgment of the court.

29. Competence:

The state of being fit or capable. Ability to demonstrate knowledge, skills, and judgment in the performance of a particular function.

30. Complex:

Means involved or intricate and requiring a variety of skills, knowledge, and judgment to identify and resolve.

31. Compulsory Arbitration:

In the collective bargaining process, if negotiation breaks down between the employer representative and the union, the dispute may be referred to an arbitration board or a single arbitrator for a binding decision. Compulsory arbitration is used in some jurisdictions in place of the right to strike.

32. Coordinate:

To bring into order as parts or units of the whole.

33. Consent:

An act of reason, a voluntary yielding of one's will to the proposal of another; the making of an informed choice.

34. Constitution:

The fundamental and overruling law of a nation, state, institution or association setting out the basic principles governing the exercise of power and regulation of the community concerned.

35. Contempt of Court

A willful disobedience of a court order causing obstruction in the administration of justice. Criminal contempt is an offence which can give rise to a fine or imprisonment for the purpose of punishment.

36. Contract:

A set of promises between two or more parties to perform certain activities or to refrain from performing certain activities, which promises are recognized by the courts as legally binding on the parties. A contract is a set of promises or agreements which the court will enforce. Not all promises or agreements are contractual. (See also employee and independent contractor.)

37. Contributory Negligence: (See Negligence)

38. Convict:

To find a person guilty of the criminal offence with which he has been charged.

39. Coroner:

An officer of the court having judicial and administrative duties to inquire into the causes and circumstances of deaths which occur under suspicious circumstances. The hearing involved in the examination of the circumstances is for the purpose of declaring the cause of death is known as a coroner's inquest. (See also forensic.)

40. Corroborative Evidence: (See Evidence)

41. Costs:

Fees and charges awarded by a court to the successful party to an action recoverable from the unsuccessful party. (See Damages.)

42. Criminal Law:

A branch of public law which concerns prosecution of disputes between an accused and the state, i.e. the prosecution of criminal offences.

43. Criterion:

A test or measurement against which behaviour can be compared and assessed. (See Performance Evaluation.)

44. Crown:

Monarch or sovereign power. In the context of criminal law offences against the public peace are prosecuted in the name of the Crown: R. v. Doe, R. v. Smith

45. Custom:

A long and unvarying habit or practice which, over time, acquires the force of law.

46. Damages:

Compensation in money awarded by the court to a party for injuries and losses.

47. Defamation:

The making of a false oral or written statement which injures the reputation or community standing of the defamed person, and which statement is unjustified in law. (See Fair Comment.)

48. Defence:

Facts which when proven to a court frees the defendant from liability or reduces the damages to be paid by the defendant to the plaintiff.

49. Defendant:

The party to an action opposing the claim of the plaintiff. (See Plaintiff)

50. Dependent Nursing Function:

Those nursing functions which flow directly from the presence of a legitimate medical order, or from a reasonable institutional policy. (See also Independent and Interdependent Nursing Functions.)

51. Diagnosis:
— Medical:

A determination of the nature of a disease or injury according to cause and manifestations. A medical diagnosis is performed by a physician and is based on data obtained from the patient's history, a physical examination and the findings from appropriate clinical testing.
— Nursing:

A determination of the relevant nursing problems; a concise description of a health problem that may be actual or potential, covert or overt. When a basic need continues unmet (need for oxygen, nutrition, rest, activity, etc) it presents a problem with which nursing is concerned. Nursing diagnosis excludes those problems that are treated by physician intervention by surgical and medical means including the prescription of drug therapy.

52. Dicta:

(Obiter dictum) is a remark made by the court concerning some legal principle which remark is not essential to the determination of the case before the bar and therefore is not binding on subsequent cases heard by the same or lower courts in the hierarchy.

53. Employee:

A person who is hired to perform services for another who has the right to control and direct the worker as to the outcome to be accomplished and the means by which the job is to be accomplished. The employer-employee relationship is contractual in nature. (Originally the relationship was referred to as the master-servant relationship.) (See also Independent Contractor.)

54. Equity:

Means fairness, and justice; a system of remedial justice exercised by the courts separate from the common law, to provide relief where relief before the courts is not otherwise available.

55. Ethics:

Is concerned with principles of moral right and wrong. Professions concern themselves with professional ethics, standards of conduct by which the individual member is expected to govern his professional practice.

56. Evidence:

Oral and documentary information and physical objects produced at trial for the purpose of proving or disproving the truth of the facts alleged in the dispute. The law of evidence concerns rules and principles which determine the admissibility, relevancy and weight of evidence introduced at trial or in other legal proceedings.

— Circumstantial evidence:

The proof of certain minor facts or circumstances related to the principle fact in issue in the dispute. From proof of the minor fact some other fact in issue or relevant to the fact in issue may be inferred.

— Corroborative evidence:

Evidence which supplements and tends to strengthen the accuracy of evidence already given in the hearing.

— Hearsay evidence:

Evidence which does not proceed from the personal knowledge of the witness giving oral evidence at trial. The witness is repeating information from a third party. Hearsay evidence is not admissible at trial unless it comes within the exceptions to hearsay as determined by the common law and statute law governing evidence.

57. Examination for Discovery:

A pre-trial process provided for by legislation and intended to permit parties to a legal action to examine under oath, witnesses of the opposing party. Such examination may concern any matter that is not privileged and is for the purpose of giving each party access to the other's case, in order to aid settlement, or to shorten the trial process.

58. Fair Comment:

A statement on matters that are in the public interest and which may constitute a complete defence to the defendant in an action brought against him in defamation.

59. False Imprisonment:

The confinement of a person without legal justification.

60. Felony:

A historical term to describe crimes of a serious nature and consequences (such as murder). Originally felonies resulted in the death penalty and in forefeiture of the convict's property to the state. The term is no longer used in Canada's Criminal Code.

61. Forensic Medicine:

A term which is also known as medical jurisprudence, is a mixed science which uses the principles and practices of medicine, chemistry, biology, and physics to identify the causes of unexpected or suspicious deaths and injury for trial and proof purposes.

62. Foreseeability:

This is a legal principle which states that if a person knew or should have known that his actions would injure his neighbour he should have taken care to prevent such an injury. The foreseeability test is used by the courts in determining whether negligent behaviour should result in liability of the defendant.

63. Governor in Council:

Is the executive arm of government, and consists of the federal cabinet (the prime minister and his ministers). The executive committee is empowered to make law in the form of orders in council and regulations, for the purpose of carrying out the intent of a particular statute. (In each province there is also an equivalent executive arm of government.)

64. Grievance:

A complaint that an injury or injustice was caused by the fault of another. The term is commonly used in the employer-employee relationship governed by a collective agreement. The system usually provides that either party may complain that the other has breached a term of the collective agreement. (A difference arising out of the interpretation, application, administration or alleged violation of the agreement). This is a rights dispute and may go to arbitration for resolution.

65. Health Care:

Refers to the various services provided by health disciplines and institutions in combination. It includes not only medical services such as diagnosis, prescription and treatment but also health education, maintenance of health programs for prevention of illness and disability.

66. Health Team:

Representatives of such health professions as medicine, nursing, dietetics, pharmacy, physiotherapy, occupational therapy, chaplain services, social services in communication for the resolution of health problems.

67. Home Care Service:

Health service brought to the client in his home.

68. Homicide:

Is the killing of a human being by any means and may or may not be a criminal offence. Culpable homicide is a criminal offence and death is culpable if caused by an unlawful act or by criminal negligence. There are three categories of culpable homicide identified in the Criminal Code of Canada: murder, manslaughter and infanticide.

69. In Camera:

Is a term which refers to a hearing or trial held in private, i.e. the public is excluded from the court room by order of the court.

70. Independent Contractor:

In contrast to the legal relationship existing between an employer and employee, an independent contractor contracts to do or perform a particular task but is not subject to the supervision of the person who contracts with him. He is engaged to produce a particular result and the means the contractor uses to produce the result are determined by him. For example when a patient directly engages a surgeon to perform a particular surgical procedure the physician does not become the employee of the patient; rather the physician remains an independent contractor.

71. Independent Nursing Functions:

Those nursing functions which, in contrast with dependent nursing functions, flow directly from the presence of a legitimate nursing order and involve independent decision-making on the part of the members of the nursing team.

72. Indictment:

A written accusation of a crime against one or more accused persons which has been laid by the Crown setting forth the offence with which the accused is charged and which document is signed by the attorney-general or his agent. Indicted means to be charged in an indictment with a criminal offence.

73. Indemnity:

A legal right arising usually by agreement to require another person to pay a debt or damages for which one is liable.

74. Information:

A written complaint upon oath by a person (the complainant) stating that he has either personal knowledge or reasonable cause to believe that a named or unknown person has committed an indictable offence.

75. Intervening Act:

A separate event which serves to break the negligence chain of causation and thereby, in law, relieves one or more of the persons involved in the chain of events from liability in a negligence action.

76. Judgment:

A formal and binding decision of the court upon the respective rights and liabilities of parties to a court action or proceeding.

77. Judicial:

Pertains to the administration of justice and concerns the exercise of judgment in a binding determination of legal rights and duties.

78. *Labour Relations:*

Refers to the institutionalized management of conflict in the workplace and involves the use of union organization, management organization, and collective rather than individual employment agreements, and use of mediation and arbitration of labour disputes in accordance with labour legislation.

79. *Licence:*

Permission by some competent authority to do some act which, without such permission, would be illegal. To confer a right or power which does not otherwise exist.

80. *Limitation Period:*

Those time limits defined by statute at the expiry of which limits the plaintiff is prevented from maintaining an action in court. Limitation periods vary depending on whether the cause of action is in contract, or negligence or in some other tort, and may also be determined by whether the expected defendant is a member of the public or a member of a special group such as hospitals or particular professions protected by special limitation statutes.

81. *Litigation:*

To engage in a law suit for the purpose of enforcing a right. (Civil litigation.)

82. *Lockout:*

Refers to the closing of the place of work, or suspension of work by the employer as a means of compelling employees to agree to the terms of employment in the process of negotiations of collective agreements.

83. *Manslaughter:*

Is unlawful homicide; the unlawful killing of a human being without malice.

84. *Murder:*

Is unlawful homicide and is the unlawful killing of a human being with malice. (See also Homicide.)

85. *Negligence:*

— **Civil Negligence:**
The failure to do something which a reasonable man, guided by those considera-

tions which ordinarily regulate human affairs, would do, or the doing of something which a reasonable and prudent man would not thereby causing injury. One may be personally negligent for his own omissions or commissions, or in certain situations, vicariously negligent for the acts of his "servant". If it can be proven at trial that the injured plaintiff was himself negligent, i.e. contributorily negligent, such negligence will decrease or eliminate an award of damages.

— **Criminal Negligence:**
Is defined in the Criminal Code of Canada to mean that a person is criminally negligent if in doing anything or in omitting to do anything that is his duty to do shows wanton or reckless disregard for the lives or safety of another person.

86. *Nursing Assessment:*

The initial and ongoing step in the nursing process characterized by a methodical approach to collecting patient data, and grouping the findings for the purpose of reaching accurate nursing diagnosis.

87. *Nursing Audit:*

A method of evaluating nursing activities in relation to their effectiveness; the process includes an appraisal of a particular nursing process recorded in the hospital records of discharged patients. The appraisal of the nursing care outcome is intended to disclose any deviations from the required standard of care set by the institution for the purpose of correcting the problems in future care planning.

88. *Nursing Care Plan:*

A written plan of care based on patient needs as determined through the patient's history, and nursing assessment. The plan defines the expected outcomes of the intervention and the methodology to be used to achieve the outcomes.

89. *Nursing History:*

A record in writing completed on admission of the patient for the purpose of providing data for assessing the care needs of the patient.

90. Nursing Process:

Is a method of nursing operation which commonly involves a number of sequential steps and is intended to bring about a particular change in the patient's level of comfort, wellness and, or ability to cope. The steps or phases involve assessment, planning, intervention and evaluation.

91. Nursing Problem:

Any condition or situation in which a patient requires help in order to maintain or regain his physical, emotional and or social equilibrium.

92. Objective Data:

In contrast to subjective data, and relative to the nursing process, refers to the patient data collected by the registered nurse from his or her own observation, physical examination and inspection of clinical laboratory reports.

93. Patient Advocate:

A person within a health care agency who speaks for those clients who are unable to speak for themselves. (In time of actual or potential conflict such clients may be unable to speak for themselves because of illness, aging, lack of physical or mental ability, or lack of will to do so.) The advocacy function may be viewed by the authority as a legitimate function of all the health care workers, or an advocate may be formally appointed by management to intercede in appropriate situations on an ongoing basis.

94. Performance Evaluation:

A process which identifies the required duties and standards of performnce of particular categories of persons who offer service within the service agency (including voluntary trustees, as well as employees.) On a regular basis an individual's performance is assessed against the approved standards for the purpose of improving his performance and remedying sub-standard practice.

95. Perjury:

A willful false oral or written statement made by a witness under oath for use at a judicial proceeding.

96. Plaintiff:

The party who initiates a legal action against an opposing party known as the defendant. These parties are named in the written document initiated by the plaintiff known usually as a writ of summons.

97. Pleadings:

The various formal written statements of the plaintiff and the defendant used in court to set out the various allegations of the parties to the dispute.

98. Policy:

A course of action approved by an authority for the direction, and limitation of persons for whom the policy was written and published. In the hospital hierarchy there are various levels of policies including policies of the governing board, the administration, the medical staff and the nursing department.

99. Prima Facie:

"On the face of it"; a fact presumed to be true unless disproved by evidence to the contrary.

100. Problem Oriented Records:

An integrated approach to patient's records in which the specific health problems of the patient are identified, labelled and priorized in order of urgency for the attention of the various members of the health team called on to intervene in the care.

101. Preliminary Inquiry:

A hearing held before a magistrate of a charge of an indictable offence against an accused for the purpose of determining whether the Crown has sufficient evidence to place the accused on trial.

102. Privilege:

A particular and peculiar benefit or advantage enjoyed by a person, company, or class, beyond the common advantage of citizens. For example the solicitor-client privilege.

103. Procedure:

A step by step description of a medical or nursing treatment which is based on scientific principles and which identifies the approved methodology for performing the activity and identifies the precautions to be taken to prevent foreseeable injury. (Commonly contained in policy and procedure manuals located in the nursing unit.)

104. Procedural Law:

Is a remedial form of law which exists in statute form. Such statutes set out methods and mechanisms for enforcing rights or obtaining a remedy when rights are invaded, through access to the courts. (See Substantive Law.)

105. Prorogue:

To direct the suspension of proceedings of Parliament (or the legislature); to terminate a session.

106. Prosecution:

A criminal action instituted by the Crown to determine the guilt or innocence of a person charged with a criminal offence. (See also Preliminary Inquiry.)

107. Public Health:

A field of health care directed to safeguarding and improving the health of the community as a whole. It requires the coordinated effort of a number of health disciplines, programs and institutions and involves a variety of health care professionals for the care and management in their home and community environments or appropriate substitute environments.

108. Quality Assurance:

The establishment of agency wide goals and the design of programs and mechanisms for the appraisal of clinical, human and material resources, and procedures and policies on an ongoing basis for the purpose of determining their effectiveness in the achievement of the established goals within the constraints of available resources.

109. Quasi-Judicial:

A term evolving from the word "judicial"; it applies to the functions of public bodies empowered to investigate facts, draw conclusions, and to exercise discretion. Decisions of such public bodies can affect members of the community and may have serious consequences. Such bodies are expected to exercise their powers fairly and judicially.

110. Regulation:

A term employed to describe subordinate rules which the Governor in Council has power to create, and which regulation is brought into existence to facilitate the carrying out of the intent of the governing statute. Provincial Hospital Acts have regulations (for example, the Health Disciplines Act of Ontario). (See also Governor in Council.)

111. Remoteness of Damage:

Those damages or losses suffered by the plaintiff and caused by the defendant but which the court rules shall not be compensated by the wrongdoer because there was not a sufficiently close connection between the defendant's wrong and the injury, i.e. the cause was too remote.

112. Respondeat Superior:

A maxim which means a master is liable in certain cases for the wrongful acts of his servant, and a principal for those of his agent, when such a servant or agent acts within the scope of his employment in a negligent manner thereby causing injury to others.

113. Revoke:

To annul or make void by recalling or taking back, cancel, rescind, repeal, reverse. Revocation is the recall of some power, authority, or thing granted, or voiding of some deed that had existence until the act of revocation made it void. Revocation may be by the intention of the party or by law, i.e. produced by a rule of law irrespective of the intention of the parties.

114. Role:

A set of behaviors which society expects one to present in a specific position or situation. Example, roles of a trustee, chief executive officer, chief of medical staff, director of nursing are distinctly different.

115. Search Warrant:

An order of the court empowering a police officer to search the place named in the warrant and for use by the officer for a specified time period.

116. Slander:

Defamation by means of the spoken word or gesture (in contrast to libel which is written and published defamation.)

117. Stare Decisis:

The principle of precedent in common law which states that like cases are decided alike to provide for certain predictability from case to case.

118. Standard:

A model accepted as correct or perfect to which people must conform; that minimal level of behaviour, performance below which, is "sub-standard", unsafe, unacceptable. Standards are stated in operational terms which can be measured or evaluated.

119. Statute (Act):

An act of federal Parliament or the provincial legislature.

120. Statutory Duty:

A duty imposed pursuant to an act of Parliament in contrast to a contractual duty or a common law duty.

121. Strike:

A cessation of work by employees in combination designed to restrict or eliminate output as a means of exerting economic pressure.

122. Subjective Data:

In terms of patient information collected by the physician for the medical history and by the nurse for the nursing history, is that information provided by the patient or his relatives etc. concerning the patient's perception of his illness experience.

123. Subpoena Ad Testificandum:

A document containing an order to a witness to appear and give evidence at a judicial hearing. The subpoena orders him to appear before the court named at a time set out in the order.

124. Subpoena Duces Tecum:

A document containing an order to a witness to bring to court certain documents in his possession or control for the purpose of providing evidence at the hearing for the party named in the subpoena.

125. Substantive Rights:

As distinguished from procedural rights in law, refers to those rights and duties recognized in law as identified in such public law as the Criminal Code of Canada, and in private law such as the law of contracts.

126. Summons:

As distinguished from writ of summons, is a legal document notifying the defendant to appear on a day named to address himself to the complaint set out in the summons. It is also a legal document used in courts of criminal jurisdiction. (See Writ)

127. Suspension:

In terms of professional disciplinary bodies it is a common penalty imposed on a disciplined member relative to his or her licence or certificate. To suspend a licence is to interrupt, or cause to cease or to discontinue temporarily with an expectation of resumption, the practical result of which is to forbid the person from performing his duties or functions for a more or less definite period.

128. Tort:

A civil wrong committed by one person against another arising out of a breach of duty owed to that person recognized in negligence, assault, defamation, false imprisonment, for example.

129. Ultra Vires:

Acts determined by the court to have been beyond the power or authority of the government, corporation, government agency or administrative tribunal and therefore void or of no legal effect.

130. *Union:*

An unincorporated association of persons coming together for a common purpose (as a trade or labour union for example.)

131. *Venue:*

Designates the particular locale within a country in which a court is to hear and determine a case.

132. *Vet:*

To check and correct.

133. *Writ:*

A legal document under seal issued from the court in the name of the Crown directed to a party cited in a legal action, or to an officer of the court authorizing the performance of a particular act. (Writ of Summons which acts to initiate a legal action; Writ of Attachment to enforce compliance with a judgment or order of the court and directed to the sheriff to compel the appearance of a defendant in order to answer for his non-compliance with the judgment or order.)

Subject Index